ISTANBUL

Russell C. Arslan

ISTANBUL

Copyright

Copyright © 2015 by Russell C. Arslan
Edited by Mary Ann Peck
Cover by Mary Ann Peck
ISBN 978-0-9857695-6-7   (Paperback)
ISBN 978-0-9857695-8-1   (eBook)
All rights reserved.
No part of this publication may be reproduced in any form, or by any means, electronic or mechanical, including photocopying, recording, or any information browsing, storage, or retrieval system, without permission in writing from the publisher.

Obtain information or ask questions at:

www.russellcarslan.com

ISTANBUL

Dedication

"ISTANBUL" is dedicated to Coach Ed Goorjian whose life has influenced so many. An old Armenian adage states:

A man's wealth is measured by his family, his friends, his memories and the impact he had upon others.

Edward Goorjian is a man of immense wealth because he made everyone he touched a better and wiser person.

We are a collection of our actions which are influenced by exigent factors. The principles Coach Goorjian lived by are our ever present guidepost. He created a life's template with his philosophies of excellence and goodness residing in all of us who have known him.

Table of Contents

Copyright ....- 2 -

Dedication ....- 2 -

Table of Contents ....- 2 -

Introduction ....- 2 -

Part I -- Istanbul ....- 2 -

    Chapter 1 ....- 2 -

    Chapter 2 ....- 2 -

    Chapter 3 ....- 2 -

    Chapter 4 ....- 2 -

    Chapter 5 ....- 2 -

    Chapter 6 ....- 2 -

    Chapter 7 ....- 2 -

    Chapter 8 ....- 2 -

Part II -- Bordum ....- 2 -

    Chapter 9 ....- 2 -

    Chapter10 ....- 2 -

    Chapter 11 ....- 2 -

    Chapter 12 ....- 2 -

    Chapter 13 ....- 2 -

Part III – Gumusluk ....- 2 -

    Chapter 14 ....- 2 -

    Chapter 15 ....- 2 -

Part – IV Istanbul ....- 2 -

Chapter 16 ....- 2 -

Chapter 17 ....- 2 -

Chapter 18 ....- 2 -

Chapter 19 ....- 2 -

Part V -- Malgan Malgan ....- 2 -

Chapter 20 ....- 2 -

Chapter 21 ....- 2 -

Chapter 22 ....- 2 -

Chapter 23 ....- 2 -

Chapter 24 ....- 2 -

Chapter 25 ....- 2 -

Chapter 26 ....- 2 -

Chapter 27 ....- 2 -

Chapter 28 ....- 2 -

Part VI – Los Angeles ....- 2 -

Chapter 29 ....- 2 -

Chapter 30 ....- 2 -

Chapter 31 ....- 2 -

Chapter 32 ....- 2 -

Chapter 33 ....- 2 -

Chapter 34 ....- 2 -

Chapter 35 ....- 2 -

Chapter 36 ....- 2 -

Chapter 37 ....- 2 -

Chapter 38 ....- 2 -

Part VII -- Steven Malgan ....- 2 -

    Chapter 39 ....- 2 -

    Chapter 40 ....- 2 -

    Chapter 41 ....- 2 -

    Chapter 42 ....- 2 -

    Chapter 43 ....- 2 -

    Chapter 44 ....- 2 -

    Chapter 45 ....- 2 -

    Chapter 46 ....- 2 -

    Chapter 47 ....- 2 -

    Chapter 48 ....- 2 -

    Chapter 49 ....- 2 -

Part VIII -- Lebanon ....- 2 -

    Chapter 50 ....- 2 -

    Chapter 51 ....- 2 -

    Chapter 52 ....- 2 -

Part IX – Home Again ....- 2 -

    Chapter 53 ....- 2 -

    Chapter 54 ....- 2 -

    Chapter 55 ....- 2 -

    Chapter 56 ....- 2 -

    Chapter 57 ....- 2 -

    Chapter 58 ....- 2 -

Part – X Istanbul ....- 2 -

    Chapter 59 ....- 2 -

Chapter 60 .... - 2 -
Chapter 61 .... - 2 -
End Notes... **- 2 -**

ISTANBUL

Introduction

Uncharacteristically, Matt Papaz was sitting in an oversized chair with a glass of wine in his hand when Bi Ba entered their newly reconstructed Bel-Air home. The horrifying bombing and fire that took place 18 months earlier was not physically evident but the emotional trauma of death and mayhem still had to run its course. Matt would usually come home after Bi Ba had arrived as to not be isolated with thoughts of regret and pain caused by the gangland bombing of their mansion a year and a half earlier.

The hillside villa had been brought back to an architectural and landscaping exactitude of its original construction but Matt and Bi Ba's good friends, Steven and Janet Eskind, were not there to share in either the resurrection of the house nor their lives. They were dead and he blamed himself.

The West Los Angeles couple, especially Matt, taking the high road of emotional pain without professional counseling was extremely difficult. The Eskinds had been killed by terrorists and were now a memory of a past littered with heartache and death. Matt sat in the media room overlooking the Bel Air Golf Course contemplating moving on to a new life void of the Papaz's Group history.

He was hoping for a clean slate. A respite from his power and wealth. For the first time in more than a year he was happily looking forward to going on a real vacation with no obligations nor responsibilities that had been the basis of his life for the past eight years. He hearkened back to earlier times romanticizing a more normal life. He did not want to continue the responsibility of making decisions about mankind's fate and geopolitical problems troubling the power elite.

When Bi Ba entered the house, she noticed him sitting in the large room.

"What are you doing home? I didn't expect you until seven or so. It's only 3:30 PM. What are you doing here?" She continued questioning him, "what's going on? You even have a different look on your face."

Matt tried to explain but felt extremely inarticulate. He could not express why or how he was reflecting on the past. He just knew the anticipations of a more normal future felt good. He looked down at the golf course below as if he were speaking to it.

"Sweetie," as he lifted his head, "you know I don't usually come home until after you're here. We never discussed it. I've never said anything about it but to be truthful I have never come home early until today because I felt lonely and I didn't want to be in the house all by myself."

He looked straight into her eyes, "I didn't want to be here alone. You're my rock. You are my anchor. Being alone and dealing with all those memories, especially Steven and Janet, is just too much for me. Today something happened. I ran into a guy named Mike at the gym. I hadn't seen him in about two years. It was as if we had not missed a beat. It's funny, he said all the right things. You know, you look good. It looks like you've been working out. The results are evident. You haven't changed a bit. But here's what really struck me. He asked if we were still traveling. He remembered I was talking about us going to Turkey. He asked how our trip was. Mike said he thought he would like to go there someday if he could convince his wife. Could I help him? I got excited about the thought of traveling again. I decided to come home and look at some of our pictures. Obviously, I didn't make it that far. I came down to the media room where I decided to have a drink. When you got home I was just gazing into space looking down at the golf course. Today is literally the first day I put all the gang and human trafficking stuff behind me. I was just sitting here mentally creating a great trip for him. Hard to explain but it's almost been cathartic. Somehow, I stopped developing stuff for him and started working on a trip for us. I don't want you to say no. I really mean this. How about us going to Turkey? I can make some calls and we can leave in about a week."

Bi Ba did not object. She was just as enthusiastic as Matt about going somewhere. She waited for a whole thirty seconds to respond.

"Sounds great but there is something more pressing right now." She had a devilish smile on her face. "I just walked in. I need a shower. You worked out and by the way you look like you haven't cleaned up yet. So, as you once said, let's get cracking."

She grabbed his hand and led him to the master bedroom suite and towards the 6' x 6' shower in the bathroom with an adjacent wading pool. She took off her athletic shirt and bra and pulled off her pants.

She looked at Matt and said, "We haven't done anything like this in a long time."

She started to laugh as his erection started to bulge in his pants. She grabbed his penis and said, "Does it still work? They had not had sex in months. Take that stuff off she demanded."

She pulled his pants down to his ankles. Bi Ba grabbed his penis. She led him to the sink where she washed it.

"Before we get into the shower I want you in my mouth."

He didn't object. Standing over her as she was on her knees pleasuring him Matt pulled her up. They migrated into the shower and turned on the water. They sat on the granite bench foundling each other. She grabbed his penis and leaned over and put it in her mouth again. She sucked it deeper and deeper.

The sex in the shower was primal. It was driven by hormonal release as much as breaking the feeling of being in despair because of the lack of intimacy. The recent tragic events in their past had weighed heavily upon not only their emotional lives but their sexual life. They had made love infrequently and when doing so it was mechanical at best. After leaving the shower and drying off they walked back through the bathroom's double door and entered the master suite. They dove under the covers of their king-size bed and making love until they fell asleep in each other's arms. The sex and following tenderness where the first displays of real affection either one had felt in more than a year. They had been opposed to psychological help after the Papaz Affair.

Matt was adamant about not spilling his guts to some pseudo-professional who only spoke in what he called psychobabble. He did not want to be vulnerable to someone who was not in their inner circle.

Bi Ba felt the same way but had deeper seeded misgivings about discussing some of her antisocial behaviors with a professional. The stress placed upon her because of circumstances beyond her control months earlier made her do violent and reprehensible acts. She felt guilty about what she did as a defense mechanism to the threats of people she called evil. Guilty because she was so brutal to other human beings. She did unspeakable things. She did not know how to mentally rectify her feelings of being a good person and doing murderous things.

They both wanted to clear their minds by participating in their own healing. Going it alone and not being subject to someone else's definitions of psychological normalcy was what they were seeking. The lovemaking brought them both to a point of opening up to the horrors of the past. Neither one at that moment wanted to discuss what had taken place but they knew they had moved past a barrier. Finally opening up to each other and the sun shinned brighter and the air felt fresher.

After waking Matt was quick to discuss their impending trip to Turkey.

ISTANBUL

He said, "Let's just called the trip reconnaissance and research." He laughed, you know R and R. "We have probably been to Istanbul, what? Five times in the last eight years but this time I want to do it differently."

He reflected for a moment. "I want to do some kind of genealogical study. I'm not exactly sure but for some reason the Four Seasons has kind of drawn me in to looking at my family's past. I know you will think this is crazy but I want to research the hotel and see who has stayed there and what type of mark they have left on society. I want to know if there's any commonality between us and other people who have stayed at the hotel. Hard to explain but that place always created some type of visceral response in me. I really want to research its past. I want to see how it is tied to our future. Shit we are rich maybe we will just buy the place."

Part I -- Istanbul

ISTANBUL

Chapter 1

Flight #427 arrived in Istanbul's international airport at 12:45am. Matt Papaz and Bi Ba Lamanas disembarked the Turkish Air Boeing 787 Dreamliner and within twenty minutes were curbside holding their carry-on luggage. Turkish immigrations and customs were a mere formality. The lines were short and not as intrusive as many other European airports.

They left Southern California carrying only handheld luggage, vacationing on the wing -- no preparations and no plans. Matt instructed the driver to proceed to five star Four Seasons Hotel, Sultanahmet, built by reconstructing the former Sultanahmet jail. Now the old prison was one of the world's most famous hotels. Its history including law enforcement depository utilized for nonviolent criminals was the crown jewel of Turkey's prison system. Built in 1919 as an opulent example of dominance over the former Ottoman Empire its excesses made it obsolete by 1926, because the one to one prisoner guard ratio, became too expensive to function as a prison. After its closure, it languished and became an eyesore in the old city of Istanbul. In 1996 a group of risk taking Canadian investors bought the one-time prison and converted it into a high-end Four Seasons Hotel.

Arriving at the city's flagship hotel, Matt and Bi Ba were greeted by an old acquaintance, Sully, short for, Sulaman. Sulaman Suzer was an expediter of personal services to the Four Season's high-end clients. The short forty-year-old man of Middle Eastern countenance wore a dark brown, leather bomber jacket and light beige slacks. Their first meeting in over a year was no surprise. He held out his hand as if he were about to shake Matt's hand, then pulled back the hand. He rubbed his thumb tip over the remaining four fingers showing the rub of money foretold by their arrival.

He looked at the couple and said, "I'm sure you're surprised I'm here my good friends. Little escapes me and my wallet's knowing who might be staying at the hotel."

The three exchanged hugs. Sully laughed, "How may I be of service?"

Matt replied, "It is late. We can always talk about money but it is good to see you also my old friend."

The Turk replied, "I'm sure the hotel bar is closed. So, before you register just leave your bags here."

He waved over an attendant. "Take these to the desk for Mr. Papaz and Ms. Lamanas. Why don't we walked down the street and find a restaurant that's still open?"

"Yes, I feel like something," Matt said.

"We will go to Izmira, their bar will be open and if you are hungry I am sure they can make you something," Sully replied.

It was Matt and Bi Ba's experience that a drink after a long flight settled the nerves and gave them the ability to sleep. They both ordered the traditional Raki with beer chasers to inaugurate coming back to a place always holding adventure and romance for the couple.

Chapter 2

After finishing a little plate of meza and drinks they agreed to meet in the morning at the hotel patio restaurant at 11:30am. Papaz had a few details needing Sully's assistance.

"See you tomorrow," even though it was 2:30am Greenwich Mean Time.

"We'll talk in the morning but I have some things I want you to think about. Do you have a couple of more minutes?"

Sully said, "of course."

"Okay then, I'll need you to get some scholars who are knowledgeable about the hotel history. When it was a prison. I think I may be jumping the gun a little but one of my dad's uncles was a prisoner at the hotel just after it opened, around 1920 or 1921. It would be fun to research it. I am no genealogy buff but he played a big role in my family history as told by my aunt Helen. She was the family oral historian. This may sound crazy but when I was a kid and the family got together for holidays or special occasions Helen would hold court. She would tell stories about the old country. I couldn't speak much Armenian and she didn't speak much English but she mesmerized everybody and held their attention when she

ISTANBUL

related the family's history. Somehow when she was speaking everything came around to a man named Malgan Malgan. You know, both his first and last names were the same. The two same names always intrigued me. I figured he was big in the Armenian independence movement but never knew his real involvement. Could you help me look into it?"

Sully did not even get a chance to answer. Papaz continued, "It's strange because he was a Muslim not a Christian. The way my aunt tells it, he was epic in the movement after the massacres in 1914 and 1915. He somehow stayed in Eastern Turkey for a while. I think he was living in a small place called Harpoots. From there he fled to Beirut or Athens. I am probably not relating this properly but he sponsored members of my family to leave Eastern Turkey and they made it to the East Coast of the United States. What's interesting is he brought people in from both sides of my family. Both of my grandparent's sides. I have a feeling all villages were rather small and incestuous. Everybody knew each other.

Bi Ba started to laugh. "Maybe that's why all your family looks alike."

"Those who got to Ellis Island got there with the given the name Papazian. An immigration agent arbitrarily changed their name to Papaz. That's how we got our name. I think it's better. It sounds Greek. At the time, there was discrimination against Armenians so the family didn't care if their name was shortened if it made their life easier. I remember my aunt said, we were called the Black Jews. I think there was a lot of animosity against anybody in the US in the early 1900s. All the way from World War I to the 1960s. In Turkey before the Great War it became worse because the Turks thought the Armenians collaborated with the British to fight the Germans who were Turkey's ally. That is when they unleashed the massacres. These are just some cloudy recollections I had from being a young kid sitting at Aunt Helen's feet. They stuck with me this long time. She said the Turks where not far off in their thinking about the Armenian's trying to create a separate state but they didn't do it because they were anti-German. Even though the Armenians are our people, she felt it did not absolve them of some fault for the massacres. Some people say the Turks killing the Armenians was a genocide template Hitler followed. There were many people killed in 1914 and 1915. You know this stuff better than me. She said maybe a 1,000,000 - 1,500,000 people died at the hands of the Turks. I want to know how that directly affected my family. In any event, here's where I need your help. I want you to get me the right people in the academic world to track down this guy Malgan Malgan. To show you my gratitude for looking into this. I know you didn't forget. I will buy those rugs you have tried to peddle off on me for almost ten years now. We will buy them. We don't need to go through seeing them and all your salesman bull crap. Bring them to the hotel tomorrow with your experts."

Sully was a rug merchant with a big cliental in New York, however, his real business was information.

Chapter 3

Matt and Bi Ba planned their morning. They would meet Sully's academic team for an hour, have a leisurely breakfast, then stroll over to the Grand Bazaar and meet some old friends doing some lighthearted shopping. They would casually go across from the hotel and have Turkish coffee at Sully's cousins Café. From there they would walk across the Main Plaza connecting the Blue Mosque to Sofia Hoagie and follow the trolley tracks north four blocks to the Nuruosmaniye Gate, a 15th century Ottoman structure housing the bazaar.

The popular shopping area attracted between 250,000 and 400,000 visitors a day. From its construction overseen by Sultan Mehmet I in 1455 commemorating the triumph of the Ottomans overtaking Constantinople, until the present, it has been the largest bazaar in the world.

The Grand Bazaar also called the Buyuk Carsi comprises more than 4,000 kiosks under a covered structure above an area more than two miles square. Prices are not competitive with shops or boutiques in the Istanbul's main shopping areas because of exorbitant kiosk rents. The tourist attraction exists because of its uniqueness, not its prices. Good prices may be negotiated at the bazaar but at a premium of 10 to 12% above the normal fare at modern retail establishments. This is acceptable because of the experience.

For Matt and Bi Ba, the uniqueness of the bazaar and it's hundreds of kiosks specializing in leather jackets and women's purses outweighed the mass of humanity engaged in arbitrage practices. The couple made relationships with many stall owners over the years.

The kiosks and their wares were handed down from generation to generation. The shop keepers were richly compensated for their fourteen to sixteen hour days acting as sentinels over the inventory. On many occasions because of the competitiveness in the bazaar the shopkeepers act animated as barkers attracting any and all tourists passing by their establishments. The kiosk owner's work is arduous and the hours are long but the entrepreneurial spirit is high. In relative terms, they are well compensated, putting them in the top five percent of Istanbul income earners. Many families own multiple kiosks, acting as oligopolistic sellers of a particular product. Most successful merchants want to live in upscale neighborhoods contiguous to the Bosporus. In the city of fifteen million people, prestige and wealth are measured by living near or on the grand waterway.

Matt and Bi Ba spent countless hours in the bazaar the afternoon after their meeting with Sully.

Sully was not a bazaar merchant but lived well. He lived in the Beyoglu district on the European side of Istanbul. He had a beautiful view of the city across from the Golden Horn and the ascending Golata Hill and its historic tower. The area called, New Town, was festooned with eclectic cafés, restaurants for the new rich, nightclubs and bars for the young emerging professional middle class who empowered growth of the Turkish economy. His house was two blocks from the famous Pera Palace Hotel which Agatha Christie used as home in her book *Murder on the Orient Express*.

A cadre of Palestinian and Algerian housekeepers attended Sully's sixteen-room-house. Twelve of the staff were roomed and boarded in a dormitory structure just outside the grand patio central to the house. Sully and his family were good to their staff, disbursing wages and conditions other domestics were not afforded. Even the servant's children were given benefits of private education paid by Sully. The staff could fraternize with his family and benefited by his many relationships in employment procurement and access to the better things in life.

In short order after only eight hours' work, at their breakfast Sully, the masterful merchant of information had impressive intelligence and cursory knowledge about Malgan Malgan. He introduced Matt and Bi Ba to four academic colleagues then started his dialogue.

"Mr. Papaz," he said, "I know information of particular importance to you, in 1984 Malgan Malgan died in Egypt where he acted as a confidant and advisor to Anwar Sadat. He was assassinated by the Muslim brotherhood. His influence and legacy were passed on to his son Alwan Al Bactar who is now in his late forties. Al Bactar has money and has been known to sponsor many causes directed by the Saudi's. He has ties to radical groups. He aids them in tactical operations as well as information. He has reached in many of the banking houses in Europe as well as being a major lender in the Hawalas movement. He has been known to help United States negotiate with radical elements bringing in a fee of more than a million US dollars. Al Bactar has connection with most of the heads of government and militias in East and Central Africa acting as a money launderer. Money is his mistress; his ideology is that of a mercenary. He follows the winds of the established Saudi interest. He is Sunni Muslim and deeply opposed to the Shiite influence of Iran. He even has been known to take a personal Hague with the Saudi royal family during Ramadan. They visit Mecca and the holy Blackstone together."

The academics at the breakfast table were quiet and waited their turn.

When Sully finished Ismet Cul a professor of Turkish history from the University of Istanbul handed Papaz a file and said, "He is just one of many people with ties to the famous Sultanahmet. Even our illustrious president has ties to the hotel."

Chapter 4

Sully broke back into the conversation and said, "I want to get you the best information humanly possible but it will be expensive. It will cost you more than those rugs my old friend."

He gave Papaz an estimate of the cost for his services. The academics were $200 dollars a day per person.

Papaz looked at the bill and said, "You are too kind. You are billing yourself out at $350 dollars a day. That is too low my friend! Bill us out at $1,300 a day and we will go from there."

Sully was taken aback by Papaz generosity. "This is too generous, we will discuss this matter later when you are happy with the information. I have developed a strategy. First, we will investigate Alwan Al Bactar by looking at his Middle Eastern partners, his operatives in government and his friends in the underbelly of the Islamic radical movement. All that information is easily obtained. It is very public because of his long history in fighting against our oppressors. He is a hero to many."

It quickly became apparent Alwan Al Bactar was living a life like Yassar Arafat, freedom fighter. The Young Turk walked the knife's edge of a moderate versus a radical Islamic terrorist. His rhetoric and deeds were not always parallel. He was not predictable and he was lethal. He never slept in the same safe house or bunker for more than one night. Al Bactar had plastic surgery on four different occasions to defeat identification by facial recognition software. He fluctuated in weight between 130 and 185 pounds intentionally. He died his hair, mustache and beard, hair on his hands and eyebrows different colors at least once a month. He wore different sized specially fitted shoes and an array of hats and scarves. He rarely wore the same jewelry twice even though he obtained an extensive watch collection from his many victims over the years. He only wore them at night allowing him the recollection of his kill before he went to bed. There were many rumors of his strange ways. He was a true chameleon. His color changed as a response to the environment. Alawan Al Bactor created his own environment. He did not adapt to an existing schema of someone else's construction. He was an existentialist who needed complete control over anything and everything connected to him.

"Obviously, there is much work" Sully said. "Your relative Malgan Malgan bore a lethal son. There is little information about Malgan Malgan because he immigrated to the United States in the later part of his life. We will hire an American firm to look into his activities while he lived in the U.S. Here in Turkey I will employ four researchers to look into Malgan and Al Bactar, two for each person. We have to be careful not to threaten Al Bactar in any way. He is leery of reporters and has never been interviewed. I don't know what he will do if he finds someone looking into his past. I will hide my inquiries the best I can. Using my sources the most I can get for you is a cursory analysis. He is very cautious and angrily reacts to the outside world."

"As far as the other inhabitants of the Sultanahmet hotel, we will look at them and their ties to the city. The present Prime Minister of Turkey comes to mind. Tayyip Erdogan was the mayor of Istanbul and stayed at the hotel on many occasions. He might be interesting to look at. It will be easy to research people like him so obvious in terms of how important they are to Turkey. People of note will make the research simple. Please let me give you my opinion on some other matters. Our analysis may change depending on the political winds. Turkey, even today, is not totally free when it comes to speech. If we go too far there is a price to pay. Here is what I think we can do. We must tread lightly and be smart about the process of considering Al Bactar or any other major political players. Maybe we should direct our research in a lighter way and not be 100% academic about it. We will make it interesting. Not as high-powered as what you would find in university circles. I'll tell you more about my thinking tomorrow. I'm just throwing some things out to you that you might want to address when we have our second meeting. We don't want to offend the wrong people."

The breakfast took longer than they anticipated. It was now almost 12:30pm. Matt and Bi Ba agreed to meet the next morning with Sully and his team. From this point on the day was for recreation.

Chapter 5

Matt Papaz and Bi Ba Lamanas slept well the night of their arrival and woke at approximately nine o'clock to sun shining through the skylight above their king-sized bed. After tidying up and showering in the Muslim style bathroom they ventured out to the restaurant through the hallway and stairwell.

After exiting Suite #207, they followed the exquisite 18th-century beige Iznik tiles and Byzantium artifacts covering the narrow mosaic hallway. Interspersed between the rooms were faux cedar Islamic designed doors approximating the old openings to the celebrity jail's holding cells. Each opening had ceiling fixture throwing off a dim orange-yellow light. The hallway looked like a sultan's palace passageway. It took five minutes to reach the hotel's rooftop patio but the view of the Bosporus and Sofia Hogia with sun peeking through low hanging gray marine clouds was spectacular.

Matt made a gesture expressing his desire to enjoy the view a couple of minutes. They walked to a table set with biscuits, croissants, fruit, tea and coffee for the third floor guest. Matt took it upon himself to fill a white porcelain plate with fruits and made two cups of tea. Their table sat at patio's edge overlooking the beautiful city. They decided getting away from their mundane life of the past

18 months was a good choice. Sipping his tea, Matt rose, walked to the other side of the patio overlooking the water and started watching a large supertanker pulled by a tug boat fleet.

Bi Ba looked up as totally out of context Matt said, "I'm looking forward to meeting with our team. This should be fun. Nothing serious, nothing of consequence, just fun looking back at my family's history and trying to tie it to whatever we can come up with here in Istanbul. I think it will fill in my family history after coming over to America."

He suddenly got up and asked Bi Ba if she was finished with her tea.

"I'm fine. I'm ready to go," she said.

They walked down the stairwell to the first floor encountering a beautiful octagular fountain that once adorned the front spa on the main corridor leading to the great palace library of Epiesus palace. They walked through the lobby filled with a beautiful orchard displayed on a long mahogany table. Walking past the gift shop another corridor filled with artifacts and modern Turkish artists' works led to a right turn and followed a much wider walkway previously utilized to take prisoners into the prison central courtyard for recreation. The walkway circled the hotel's inner perimeter leading to double glass doors taking guests into the Garden. Walking through the perimeter's hallway made Matt reflect on the fact that seventy-five years ago, this was a major inmate passageway.

Each newly remodeled room was a large holding cell for some celebrity prisoner in the early 1900s. The hotel rooms today were anywhere from 350 to 500 square feet. When the building was a prison there were 200 cells approximately 80 square feet. Matt reflected, at some point in time he had picked up a factoid that stuck with him. In the United States as determined by the Supreme Court in a ruling dealing with cruel and unusual punishment cells for a prisoner had to be at least 24 square feet and have an opening to sunlight at least one hour per day.

These cells were virtually three to four times bigger and analyzing the hotel's architectural structure he concluded the cells had been flush with light as well as the visual old city trappings. It truly was a prison for the wealthy nonviolent criminals. He giggled to himself, "A country club with a large courtyard."

As they continued walking, his mind fluttered back and forth between his past and the present power and wealth circumstances. He asked himself about the relationship between methods used accumulating his wealth and how he and his friends evolved from nonviolent to violent behavior. Should he be in a prison such as this? Leaving the hallway, walking down some steps to the patio they came to a glass solarium structure built for breakfast and lunch.

He told Bi Ba, "You know just walking through the hotel and reflecting on how it might have forged my history is fun. Hey, there's Sully and his team. I wonder, how long they were waiting."

As Matt and Bi Ba approached the table, Sully rose to greet them and introduced his team.

ISTANBUL

Sully and his academic team met in the hotel's lobby thirty minutes before the scheduled breakfast with Matt and Bi Ba and worked out a division of labor and waited for Matt and Bi Ba in the hotel restaurant glass enclosed patio area.

Excited about his research approach, Sully rose to their approach and asked, "Would you mind if we discuss the project before having breakfast? Maybe we could have coffee while we discuss preliminaries then eat."

Matt and Bi Ba answered, "Sure, whatever fits your agenda."

Meant to arouse Matt and let him know they were in a better place than a year and a half ago, she smiled and said, "Let's get cracking."

Sully spoke of his non-academic research approach. Matt and Bi Ba wholeheartedly agreed a pedestrian passage from family history to a more entertaining rationale would suit their needs.

Matt looked at Bi Ba and said, "This is exactly what I want. It should be fun. Nothing too serious. Nothing so important it deals with life and death."

Sully said, "Excuse my interrupting, but this approach is ideal. It gives us Turks a chance to embellish and weave historically significant stories into your application. Turks and Muslims are storytellers at heart. Our responsibility is finding your personal narratives. I think we all agree it's going to be fulfilling and a wide variation from academic accountability."

Tekin Sevki from the War Academy, a heavy set, chain smoking, poorly dressed, academic interjected, "It will be enjoyable not being scholarly and allowed to develop themes as if I were a fiction writer. It will feel great not having responsibilities of absolute truth and not always using scientific methods uncovering information. I think, if we do this correctly, a beautifully constructed story encompassing a truthful explanation of your family and acquaintances or relationships made in Turkey. I think I speak for all of us when I say, we will not create anything embarrassing, inappropriate or too far from the truth to be acceptable by people."

Everyone agreed but most importantly both Matt and Bi Ba felt good about it. The group's findings would image reality but be based on a theatrical version of the truth. The American couple's lives had been too serious for the last eighteen months and this furnished a needed diversion.

Matt felt it was time to have fun, a perfect time to enjoy his stay in Istanbul. The prize would be a wonderful trip coupled with some lost historical facts if opening their past were not attempted. Bi Ba felt every trip was a passage in time she reflected upon and used as a stepping stone into the future. For her the past always encompassed the body of work or experiences propelling the present and giving her a desire to attack the future. The past presented a roadmap and Bi Ba felt the past five years for the most part were too serious. This exercise would create a more upbeat evaluation of life and hopefully propel them to make easier future choices.

She hoped the product from this research and experience would be pure enjoyment acting as a guide to happiness. It wouldn't be so serious as to cause any injury or time and energy loss, if they were not successful. Everyone at the table agreed and verbally signed off on the project's approach to be enjoyable. It wouldn't be opened to any serious or threatening implications.

Mustafa Sabi was tasked with researching Malgan Malgan and his son Alwan Al Bactar. Once started they would have two additional associates working exclusively on the Malgan Malgan family.

Ismet Cul, his colleague from Istanbul University worked on finding other inmates from the model prison during its first and only decade of existence, 1916 to 1926. His goal was finding inmates with memorable lives after their incarceration at what many believed was a holiday jail. Cul was looking for tangential intersection points between inmates and Papaz, whether business or family related.

Celal Cindoruk from Ankara University and Tekin Sevki from the Turkish War Academy researched the Four Seasons Hotel guest registry from its inception in 1996 to present, directing efforts at people staying in suite #207, the room held for special guests. During their many Istanbul visitations, Matt and Bi Ba only stayed in Suite #207.

Sully processed the project and presented a narrative showing how each selected visitor staying at Saltanahmet possibly crossed paths with Papaz. He also presented conspiracy theories with circumstantial evidence tying together a theatrically entertaining script for Matt and Bi Ba. The project used academic scholarship research trappings coupled with the right of literary license. Information extrapolation creating interesting and entertaining scenarios was the major team goal. The project was not an academic exercise preceding an academic genealogical study for delivering a paper to an institution or association. Truth blended with exaggerations, estimates, folly or any other vehicles creating a docudrama worthy of an oral historian like Papaz's Aunt Helen. The historical events docudrama of the old jail and now luxury hotel residents would be enjoyable reading for Matt and Bi Ba.

Matt Papaz was estranged from his family for more than seven years without one scintilla of communication and his future was expected to be the same. This document was solely for his and Bi Ba's pleasure.

Sully planned subjective historical research as the project hallmark demonstrating their work by its entertainment value. Papaz's Aunt Helen held a venerable family position, not only for historical accounts, but because she defined the Papaz family historical characters with human qualities. Being an oral historian was not always precise but people like Helen made it spellbinding for the listener. In the future when Matt and Bi Ba did have a family he would play the role of Aunt Helen, although his family history stopped and started with him.

Sully's academic team presented names and historical events coupled with hypothetic accounts weaving points of separation stories between Matt and his brotherhood residing in the jail/executive hotel. His team emphasized rationales the academic community probably called heresy.

ISTANBUL

Chapter 6

Three days passed before Papaz heard from Sully again. His Turkish friend made an appointment to meet at the restaurant Sultanahmet a few blocks from Matt and Bi Ba's hotel.

The cobblestone street traveling from the apex, old city's Sultanahmet district, toward the Bosporus and the spice market, outer boundary of the famous Topkapi Palace compound, were fifty foot walls built upon an enormous granite block pad acting as the palace foundation. Leading down by the water's edge, the wide heavily traveled cobblestone street traversing the wall's bottom was crowded with retail stores and restaurants frequented mainly by tourists.

As Matt and Bi Ba walked toward their meeting, Matt slowed, peeking into a luggage store filled with assorted knock off bags, purses, suitcases and briefcases of all sizes and colors. Standing behind a desk with a 1950s cash register atop plastic bags filled with bright red and blue table cloths, the merchant was smoking a cigarette with his left hand and had an old stained coffee cup he used as an ashtray. The shop was in total disarray but the proprietor had full knowledge of every item and its whereabouts.

Stopping to look, Matt said, "Let's look. I want a leather journal binder, paper and pen so I can take notes during discussions with Sully."

Bi Ba felt pushed for time and told Matt, "Just don't negotiate. Pay the guy what he wants."

Matt functioned better with pen in hand. He felt naked without it. Quickly consummating the sale, they returned to the street and started looking for Sully who would already be at the restaurant.

A trolley traveled from the Bosporus up the hill past Serve Plaza, home of the Blue Mosque, Hogia Sophia and the Hippodrome. The trolley line started at the water's edge near the spice market and its final destination was the Grand Bazaar. The C shaped route of the trolley traversed the old European side of the city.

Sully had made reservations at the restaurant knowing his friends loved the atmosphere of the ancient archeological sites on Istanbul's European side. He arrived early and ordered meza and Egyptian made, Stella Beer for the three of them. When Matt and Bi Ba walked into the restaurant, the host recognized them by Sully's description. They were escorted deep into the restaurant where Sully sat on the floor belly up to a low table. He was staring at twelve different exotic Middle Eastern tapas dishes. Lending to the ambience of the 300-year-old restaurant a three-piece band was playing soft background music. Matt and Bi Ba felt at ease dinning on the floor eating with their hands as was customary in old Istanbul. They exchanged pleasantries with Sully and thanked him for furnishing the opportunity of looking into the Papaz family history.

Bi Ba said, "We've had really nice three days just relaxing and doing touristy things for the first time in a long while. Probably the first respite we've had in a year and a half. I can't tell you how great it's been that we've had no engagements, we've had nothing planned, and we've had nothing of importance to do since we've been here."

She laughed, "But there is a price for leisure. All we did was shop. We bought gifts for some acquaintances and friends. We are lucky to have a freight forwarder friend here in Istanbul who sent an agent with us so we can ship all the stuff home. Sully, we have a big van with driver and the agent. Quite an extravaganza but it is fun. I know we're obnoxious but so what? It's great fun."

Matt interrupted, "How are things going on your end with our silly requests? How are we moving along on the project?"

Sully responded, "We have a problem! Let me restate that, I have a problem. Your anonymity is and will always be intact. Let me put this in the simplest terms. Once I started to ask about Malgan Malgan and his son Al Bactar some of my relationships here in Istanbul and some of my sources for information have changed. I and they have been threatened. Al Bactar under no uncertain terms expressed his misgivings about anyone trying to find him or inquire into what he and his movement are doing. His people let me know my life could be endangered if I pursued my investigation. They even threatened my resources. Somehow his people have also tied my inquiry to those of Mustafa Sabi and he had a visit from three Arab mercenaries, as he called them, and they told him to back off. They said they will pay me a visit and if he cared about his life he would find other employment. These people are very dangerous. They are in the shadows just like Al Bactar. The only reason I am alive, and for that matter Mustafa, is because of my relationship with the Saudi royal family. It was a warning I must heed. Like I said, these people are in the shadows. They don't use electronics at all. No computers, no tablets, no phones either land or cell, nothing at all. They even use deliverymen to facilitate the mail and in some cases, they use carrier pigeons. They use dogs to carry written communication. Money is moved by hawalas. They don't wear European clothes of any type. They only dress in Muslim clothing. None of them ever travel in motor vehicles. He and his associates still use the old Silk Road. Al Bactar's men sleep in the way stations at night. We don't know where he sleeps. They act like Bedouins. They use camels, they use donkeys and they use horses. They're living as their forefathers did. It will be difficult to find them. I also think they consider their way of life as romantic, holding great power over the more illiterate, fanatical religious people in their world. In any event, they have come to see us. They knew Sabi was working for me. That itself shows their reach and I am fearful. Al Bactar and his men have what we call long arms."

Sully stopped to recover his breath then continued, "Let me tell you how I plan to use this to our advantage. Here's my plan. I want you to know you are safe and you will not be involved in any of this. I have never met Al Bactar but I know people who have. They say he is both ruthless and brilliant. When his men talk to me I will humbly tell them I have been hired by the American National Security Agency to look into his activities. I will tell them it is a diversion. All the world powers active here in the Middle East use the same sources. Al Bactar knows America respects his activities because he acts as a surrogate for the Saudi's. I will tell them my findings for the Americans are shallow and nondescript and will not tie him to anything except being supportive to moderate causes. This investigation is to please the ultra-left wing in the U.S. My work for them and these back-channel investigations are benign and Al Bactar is aware of it. If he thinks I am truthful, he will let me write my research and present it to the Americans. My life will be spared because I will be an asset to him. If he thinks I'm hiding anything from him his people will kill me on the spot. He understands the games the National Security Agency plays and he will try to use me to his advantage. The Middle East moderates need U.S. political support. His needs is not to be labeled a terrorist. My work can benefit him. He knows my creditability with the NSA and I can and will help his cause. Al Bactar knows all I do is sell information and I work for all sides. He's not a terrorist but he also knows the NSA is not dangerous to him because of his Saudi ties. I am safe as long as he believes I have no other agenda than taking money from my American friends."

"As for our relationship. His people know we go back many years. They know we had breakfast at the hotel. That will mean they know my academic friends came with me. I will tell them I co-mingled our breakfast with my academic friends to impress you and solicit new business from you relative to your charitable foundations and your real estate hedge fund. Al Bactar has no way of tying you with Malgan Malgan. Your knowledge of him comes from your family. Al Bactar, I must assume, has no communication with them. I'm going to tell him you were thinking of buying the Four Seasons Hotel from some Canadian owners. I wanted you to meet my academic friends giving an historic view of the hotel's importance and prestige. Knowing what I know about him he will think I am nimble and using my relationships with Cul, Sevki, Cindoruk, and Sabi wisely and I am not a threat to him. Sabi is so scared he has asked if he could leave the project. You have my word your name will only come up in relationship to buying the hotel. You are safe. It is my suggestion we terminate the Malgan Malgan and Al Bactar portion of our research. If you like, I can still look into the hotel. We can give you historical background of its time as a jail and the people visiting the present-day establishment. I don't perceive that continuing this line of research will put you in jeopardy. I don't want to tell you what to do. As for me, I don't need to be in jeopardy over our relationship, however, I think you don't need to pursue your family ties in Turkey any further."

Sully was frightened. Everything coming out of his mouth started with 'I'.

He continued, "I don't want this man coming after you nor me. His tentacles reach across the seas and across the desert. I don't see any reason why we should endanger ourselves and create an adversary. So, I must tell you I cannot be part of the investigation of Al Bactar."

Matt and Bi Ba said they agreed.

She said, "Let's meet tomorrow morning at the hotel."

Matt suggested, "Let's make it look like business as usual, bring Cul, Cindoruk, and Sevki. Backing away too fast could set off red flags we don't need. I am sorry we endangered you and your colleagues. You must know it certainly was not our intention. We just wanted to enjoy discovering the Papaz family history."

"Maybe we continue working together but the second anything changes we must act to protect ourselves," said Be Ba.

Both she and Matt knew how easily things migrate to the dark side. Vowing to do everything in their power, they each left the meeting concerned for not letting life slip into another dangerous Papaz adventure.

Chapter 7

Following their two-hour lunch with Sully, Matt and Bi Ba left the restaurant walking toward the spice market. They followed Vezirhan Circle trolley tracks to Eminonu District's Galata Bridge. Their walk was almost void of conversation. Both were silent about Alwan Al Bactar making the forty-five-minute journey extremely awkward. They wanted to discuss the probabilities of what Papaz later called the mess, but each held opinions until for a more private, opportune moment to discuss the dilemma.

Arriving in the Spice Market, they walked from kiosk to kiosk looking for Turkish delights as well as Middle Eastern spices they could bring home. Matt wanted some authentic cikolata or Turkish chocolate. Bi Ba surprised by all the spices coming from China. To her the world had become a marketplace for cheap Chinese goods. Globalization and cheap knockoffs permeated the product authenticity in the venerable old market. They shopped for an hour before walking into a coffeehouse and planned the remainder of the day.

Matt suggested they take a cruise down the Bosporus which left from the Galata Bridge Marina in twenty minutes. The TL25 ferry would take them for a three-hour cruise to the village of Anadolu near the Black Sea opening.

After boarding the vessel, they declined seats in the glass covered passenger area. Sitting in the uncrowded open backside of the ferry, they experienced balmy temperature in low seventies Fahrenheit, cloudless sky and virtually no wind. During the three-hour voyage, they saw the Maiden Tower, the 16th century Dolmabahce Palace, Orakoy Mosque and on the water's edge were the two main military fortresses, Anatolian and Yoros. They disembarked at Anadolu and taxied back to their hotel. The topic of Al Bactar was never brought up.

Later, Bi Ba said, "The inability to talk about our pending problem made the afternoon cruise so uncomfortable. I didn't enjoy what should have been a beautiful outing."

The subject was finally approached as their taxi approached the Sultanahmet District.

She said, "I wanted to discuss Al Bactar but I'm afraid it will become a self-fulfilling prophecy. Discussing him might lead to dealing with him. If his name never came up I could hope he never existed."

She knew that line of thinking was immature and pure folly but her current emotional state did not allow dealing with another major problem.

Matt said, "I don't have words to portray descriptions of how troubles follow me. For that reason, I was silent"

He sarcastically laughed, "It's flies to shit theory all over again."

When they finally talked, their only hope was somehow Frederic could intervene and communicate to Alwan Al Bactar making clear their interest was not in him and didn't threaten his existence or political philosophy.

They exited the taxi three blocks from the hotel. On a side street, Matt had seen a backgammon set in a curio shop window. He wanted to purchase the Middle Eastern game without major arbitrage and have it sent home by their personal freight forwarder.

Leaving the shop with the overpriced board under his arm, he addressed Bi Ba, "May I say something about Sully?"

"Sure," she said.

"Both of us know, he wants to get us out of this thing whole. That seems improbable at best. I know it's the Middle East but the NSA thing seems dubious at best. It borders on sounding ridiculous. All I want is get the hell out of Turkey, but it doesn't seem possible because if we are running it will just make our intentions appear more dangerous. Al Bactar will react badly to our quickly leaving Istanbul. Just talking off the top of my head but we must have Frederic consider buying the hotel as some kind of subterfuge. If the financials make sense, it can't hurt looking into purchasing the property. Maybe it will get that crazy fanatic to back-off us."

Bi Ba said, "Matt, I'm sure Sully thought it through. He might seem full of BS but he's not crazy. He has more to lose than we do. In the short run, he's been targeted. I don't want to sound callous but I know he can't defend himself and at least we have the ability no matter how hard it gets to get through this. As far as the NSA thing is concerned there are many inconsistencies in what he wants to do. There are false equivalencies, who he thinks he is and his importance in some grand scheme of things. I wouldn't be surprised if he doesn't know a staff member of the royal Saudi Arabian family. Let alone a prince or whatever. I like him, he's entertaining. I wouldn't say this to him but he seems like a Turkish wanna be. All the ways he portrays himself doesn't seem realistic. Whatever we do, we must disengage ourselves from Al Bactar and his father Malgan Malgan. We must make Sully incidental to what we are doing here. Whatever it takes for us to disengage Al Bactar from having any interest in our activities is what we have to do even if it means buying the hotel."

She got quiet and shook her head, "I can't believe how this stuff just follows us."

Matt responded, "Yeah, you're right. This one is so bazaar I can't tell you how screwed up this makes me feel. We might be in trouble again, so we should call Frederic as soon as possible. He'll probably be beside himself on this one. He will think it's just one more screw up on my part. Without him what would we do?"

She sarcastically laughed, "Without him we wouldn't be around so it wouldn't be a problem."

Matt responded, "I'll ask him to involve Guzman if it makes sense. In the meanwhile, maybe we should get out of Istanbul for a couple of days. I would like to go to Bodrum. It's really beautiful this time of the year. It's only an hour and one-half by private plane. I will have the hotel charter a plane. We can stay at the Kapinski for four or five days. I think it'll be fun. I'll also have the hotel look into chartering a sailboat. You know one of those French Beneteau's. Maybe eighty or eighty-five feet with a captain and two or three crew people. We can kick back in some small villages right off the coast."

"The diving is supposed to be spectacular," she said.

"Someone mentioned it's very much like Ross Mohammed in the Red Sea near Sharm el Sheilk. It should be a lot of fun. Allegedly, there are archaeological sites in shallow reefs close to Bodrum. Certainly, it will be a diversion from Al Bactar until Frederic can work something out."

Bi Ba continued, "Do you think we need bodyguards?"

Matt said, "We'll leave it up to Frederic."

They agreed getting out of Istanbul in three or four days was the right move.

"Later tonight I'll call Sully," Matt said. "I'll make him aware of our plans and tell him we're using the hotel to make all arrangements. After what he said about Al Bactar not using anything electronic I don't think our phones will be tapped but I'll be careful. I just don't want to frighten Sully. I really don't have a take on what he will do. We certainly can't let him know we are overly concerned."

"When you speak to him tell him we trust his instincts. The NSA diversion thing seems probable," Bi Ba suggested.

"You're right. He does seem like a wanna-be but we will let time play its course. We'll find out soon enough."

"When you involve Frederic, ask him to contact Giselle so we can use all of her resources."

He sighed, "We don't need this shit. I can't believe it's happening again."

"Call Frederic." Bi Ba insisted.

"He must contact Al Bactar through whatever channels necessary and let him know we are not in any way, shape or form interested in him." Matt continued, "Sorry sweetheart, I promise I'll make sure nothing happens."

Chapter 8

Frederic's reaction to their new predicament was not judgmental as Matt assessed.

Matt was dully surprised when Frederic said, "Listen old Buddy, this stuff happens. It's the Middle East and you're rich. Something like this could be a kidnapping but it doesn't sound like it has gone too far and we should be able to clean it up. I will have Gisele all over it. Don't worry, I'll send a few of Alvarez's men to Istanbul. Don't do anything out of the ordinary. Tell Bi Ba not to worry. We have all kinds of assets who can reach this Al Bactar. I am sure Arnouk has worked with his money and of course we have Kasogi. I think it's a good idea you guys hang out in Bodrum like you said. I have everything I need. I'll get back to you as soon as I can."

Matt thanked him, "When we go to Bodrum maybe you and Gisele might want to come over for a few days. At least think about it. You need a vacation. You can meet us there or in Istanbul. Come over, I want you to see the Four Seasons. If we must buy the place it would be nice if you saw the property. It will be great if you guys come to Bodrum."

Frederic reached out to his sources, was given assurances there would be no complications, but he still felt uneasy. He always had a recurring strange little feeling in the pit of his stomach before challenges turned into obstructions.

By the time, Alvarez's men arrived in Istanbul all reservations for Matt and Bi Ba's stay in Bodrum were set.

In Istanbul, the Four Seasons chartered a plane for the American couple, made arrangements with Moorings, a British sail and powerboat leasing and renting company. A boat at their disposal in a slip at Bodrum's famous small yacht harbor gave Matt and Bi Ba a pleasant anticipation.

Their plans included staying at the Kapinsky Hotel, a luxurious health spa, devoted to sport and thalassotherapy center activities. Thalassotherapy, therapeutic use of the ocean, its climate and marine products like algae, seaweed and alluvial mud, established on the principle corroborating repeated exposure to sea air and immersion in warm seawater, mud, clay, and protein-rich algae helps restore the body's natural chemical balance. Seawater and human plasma are very similar. When immersed in warm seawater the body absorbs the minerals it needs through the skin. The Turkish baths and gymnasium housed in the lower floors of the spectacular hotel specialized in a holistic healing approach. The different spas specialized in Asian massage rooms, resting rooms and a full-sized gym as well as the thalassotherapy center. These facilities and the best trained staff in the Middle East were all part of a personally tailored revitalization treatment package. The hotel and its amenities were perfect for Bi Ba because she felt she needed time to pamper herself and get rid of the tough guy image she took during the last few years. In reflection, she noticed all her spare time was consumed by martial arts and physical training.

She told Matt, "Going down to the Kapinski is a really good idea. It will give me time to take care of myself for a change. I know there's nothing you won't do for me but being there is really what I need right now. I need to pamper myself. It is almost as if I want to wash off the dirt from the last couple of years."

The spa specialized in treatments for her muscled body. Deep muscle massage coupled with ice baths, saunas, and steam rooms were meant to revitalize her body. Being physically fit was only part of the equation. Letting your body be pampered and having time for self-reflection becomes the psychological cleansing she needed.

In the men's gym, Matt arranged a personalized trainer specializing in a new physical therapy called Z health, yoga and performance enhancement exercises combining increased joint flexibility and skeletal system suppleness. The idea behind the treatment was to open a person's nervous system and retrain paths and movements along its endings. Simply awaking the neurons created greater body flexibility and joint suppleness and increasing a person's quickness and movements generating greater strength and stability. Matt looked forward to working on his quickness and strength pushing him closer to his genetic potential. A simple thirty-minute exercise program was planned to enhance his already superior physical abilities.

Arriving at the Kapinsky, they planned to stay on the hotel grounds for two days until they could meet up with Alvarez's men who would fly to Bodrum on their own and work out an arrangement for their protection. Once they were introduced to some local bodyguards complementing their protection team, they had free movement.

After all security measures were in place, Matt called the concierge desk to reserve dinner reservations in Bodrum proper, a twenty-minute drive from the hotel. He arranged their pick-up at 8:30pm and a drive to the Bodrum Marina City Club, directly below the old St. Peter's Castle.

Riding along the seacoast in the late afternoon was beautiful. They reached La Pasion, the city's finest restaurant, located next to the Marina Club, the handsome couple exited the limo. One bodyguard escorted them to the hostess desk. A greeter was waiting for them at the entrance to the Mediterranean-style eatery. The owner of the restaurant, Hurat Sisi, waited for his guests who were sponsored by the Kapinski hotel. He walked them up the Moorish stairwell to the second floor seating the couple on the balcony overlooking the beautiful Marina.

A Bodrum custom was to cover all boats with red and white tarps contrasting the boat's teak hauls and decks.

Bi Ba expressed how beautiful the sunset looked with all its vibrant colors. The beautiful soft pink and purple sky tones setting upon the striking white and red boat colors created a romantic atmosphere.

"This place is wonderful," she said. "Matt it's exactly what we needed."

They looked on a Marina area for large sail and power boat slips. It was very reminiscent of Portofino in Italy but without the pretense of money and arrogance. Bodrum was not as affluent as its Italian counterpart but it was much more romantic and had a quality of Southern California. It reminded Matt of Newport Beach just south of Los Angeles.

Within two minutes of seating, an array of Spanish tapas and Turkish beers were brought to the table. Sisi came through the Moorish decor room with Turkish chandeliers adorning the ceiling.

He expressed, "Mr. and Ms. Papaz the pleasure of having you in this restaurant is immense. Your bill is taken care of by the hotel. The chef will introduce himself from the kitchen shortly."

Matt said, "Thank you for your hospitality."

"It's my pleasure Mr. and Ms. Papaz."

Before they left he said, "If there is anything you need while you're here in the Marina please feel free to contact me."

Part II -- Bordum

Chapter 9

During dinner Matt looked across the table where four men were sitting behind Bi Ba and said, "I feel something isn't right. There are four guys behind you and they just look out of place. I'll be back in the second. I'm going to go over to the bathroom and on my way back I'll check them out."

The four men varied in age between twenty-five and thirty. They were opulently dressed in obviously European upscale brand suites. Their table had no alcoholic beverage but everything else about them suggested they were four young professionals having a business meeting. This area of the city was a tourist destination at night, causing Papaz to question the group's purposes being in the restaurant were out of place. It was his sixth sense.

He told Bi Ba, "They make me feel uncomfortable like something is wrong."

His usually correct powers of investigative deduction were so acute, Bi Ba said, "When we leave here if you're right they will follow us. We should walk over to the peninsula and sit on the water side and have some coffee and dessert or something."

"We certainly are well protected so our safety shouldn't be a question."

Matt got up again and said, "I'll tell one of our guys."

After he came back they finish their food and called the waiter thanking him for his service. Matt gave the young man an equivalency of a one-hundred-dollar tip. When they walked down stairs he thanked the manager and gave him a tip. As they left, one of the four men asked their waiter for their check.

Matt and Bi Ba left the restaurant, crossed the frontage road from the Marina slip side and walked over to the retail shopping center. The Karada shopping district, a cordoned off pedestrian center without vehicle traffic, was more than ten square blocks of shops and restaurants at the old castle base.

Bi Ba wanted to follow the marina's cobblestone street going to the peninsula's backside opening to the Aegean Sea. After walking for fifteen minutes, they found an inviting coffee house called Arslan Café, a meeting place were locals smoked, played backgammon and drank coffee.

They entered the café and walked past the coffee bar through sliding glass doors leading onto a patio overlooking waves crashing beneath the teakwood deck among the support pylons. Bi Ba found a table sat down as Matt went back into the café to order some drinks.

Sitting at the water's edge with young people in their twenties was refreshing to Bi Ba. The area on this side of the peninsula away from the marina and its upscale tourist boutiques that featured jewelry stores, leather goods stores, curio shops and bistros was romantic reminiscent of her college days when she hung around Martha's Vineyard. Sitting there, she realized how unique

Bodrum was. Its peninsula was no more than a mile wide at the point of St. Peter's Castle and the Marina. They walked from an exclusive restaurant sitting in front of slips housing beautiful boats through a pedestrian shopping center to this seaside patio café in less than fifteen minutes.

The romance of Bodrum beauty was shattered when she saw the four Arab men had just entered the cafe and were standing in the same line as Matt who was ordering coffee and desserts. Up until this point she felt safe because they had been escorted from the restaurant to the café by a security team of Alvarez's men and their Turkish complement.

The sighting of the four Arabs was very disconcerting. Just as Bi Ba spotted the four men, Papaz also caught sight of them. He waited in line, finished ordering his drinks.

Deciding to take the offensive, he walked up to the four men and said, "It's pretty clear you're following us. Why? If you have something to say or something to do, then do it."

One of the four men looked him right in the eye and said in fluent English, "You're right. We do want to speak to you. Neither you nor your woman are in jeopardy. We don't want to hurt you. If we felt otherwise you would be dead by now. All we want to do is talk. We will order our drinks and meet you outside."

He was very forceful, not only his tone of voice but also his demeanor. Papaz walked to the outside patio and sat at their table. He didn't need to tell Bi Ba about their friends as they waited for their drinks and the four Arabs who demanded their attention.

As Matt and Bi Ba's antagonists walked onto the patio they took a table sitting next to the couple.

Another man joined them and spoke for the group, "We don't want to harm you. All we want to do is talk. My name is Tarek Al Nassar. Don't be alarmed. I am sure you know who we are. We are here on behalf of Alwan Al Bactar. I will say it again, looking at Papaz, you are not in danger. We have no weapons and we have no intention of hurting you. Please tell your men to be careful. We are not a threat. Like I said before, we wish you no harm."

Alvarez's men had surrounded the patio.

Papaz walked to their bodyguards and told one, "Everything is okay. Don't overreact. Just be aware of the situation."

By the time, he arrived back into the patio, drinks were on the table.

One of the men demanded, "Why are you in Turkey? What do you want to know about Al Bactar? Why?"

Al Nassar cut him off and said, "We only want to know your intentions. This is a very dangerous part of the world. Why are you asking about Malgan Malgan and his son Alwan Al Bactar?"

Papaz was good on his feet responding instantaneously. "We might be out of place in your world but we mean you no harm."

He was good under pressure. "I'm sure you know much more about us than we know about you. So, let me add a little bit more about who we are and what we are

ISTANBUL

doing here. You have heard of our medical foundations in East Africa and in South America. I am sure you are aware of our charitable foundations in Mexico and Central and South America. You know about our work in the inter-cities in the United States. You know everything about us! We are open and transparent. We are business people as well."

He figured he would use his cover as an investor who was interested in the Four Seasons in Istanbul. "Our primary purpose for being here is we are looking at high-end hotel properties. It is a convoluted story but it is the reason I have inquired about Malgan Malgan and tangentially his son."

Papaz used multi syllable words talking down to his advisories. "Malgan was the second cousin of my mother. And had a history with the hotel we are negotiating to buy. Your sponsor Alwan Al Bactar is only of interest because he is my cousin's offspring. No more no less. You can look at our civic record and you will see it has been our mission to help the poor and the disadvantaged. They are as much in need of our help here just as they need help from Al Bactar. The main differences are we are driven by money and your sponsor is driven by commitment and honor to the poor people living in his world. We are not as courageous nor do we have the same personal investment as Al Bactar. We only place our monies in jeopardy, he places his life in jeopardy. We have not and will not open ourselves to more danger than the loss of our money. We are different than Al Bactar. Like I said he is a man of honor and has made great sacrifices. Money is a cheap way of commitment for us. You must know his philosophy and our philosophies of helping the poor are very much aligned. So, we have not been, nor will we ever be a threat to him. Our only reason for opening the past was of coincidence in buying the hotel and looking at his history. I am Armenian by dissent. My family comes from Harpoots. My thoughts were if we purchase the Four Seasons it would be interesting to look at its history and how it affected my family."

"In the United States discussing our business trip with some family members I became aware of Malgan Malgan. Until then I had never heard his name. I certainly am aware and have been aware of Alwan Al Bactar. He is known throughout the world. Some people in my country see him as a terrorist. Some people see him as a freedom fighter and the protector of the poor. He is loved and he is hated. He is very controversial. I am in concurrence with his goals but I must be honest I am not in synchronism with this tactics and strategies to reach these goals."

"As soon as we arrived in Istanbul we were greeted by an old friend, Sully Suzer. I asked him for help. He has worked with me on many other occasions but only in regards to business. I asked him if he could find some academics we could hire to do a genealogical and historical survey of the hotel from its inception as a jail to its present status as an A property. Obviously, this has led us to bringing up your sponsors name and his history. Like many things in the Middle East, activities become clouded and convoluted none more so than my friend Sully who we found out was working for the NSA. We did not intend to stir up a bee's hive nor bring up anything political in nature. I assure you, we will close down our research and not cross the path of Al Bactar. We are not a threat. If the truth be told, I can and I will help him in any transparent way not affecting my standing as a businessman or philanthropist. I would be glad to aid the cause of your sponsor if we can figure a way to do it and protect me politically. Let me be as forthright as I can. I will not consider nor will I help in any way subjecting me to security agency oversight leading to or suspicion of involvement funding any type terrorist activity. If our monies appear as being clean and go into clean projects advancing the poor living standards, I would like to aid the son of my cousin. I must always be seen as a person taking political neutrality but also someone who works for the cause of the poor. My life's work and my heart are consistent with Alwan Al Bactar positions, only tactics differ."

"I have asked you to listen and you have been gracious enough not to interrupt. I respect that. Now let me sum up my feelings. I am not nor will I ever be an adversary. Our intentions have been simple and family-based. From this point on we will stop any further investigation of Alwan Al Bactar and his father. We wish you well in any endeavor and, as I said before, if we can be supportive and a benefactor in this political climate without facing injury or reprisal then it would be our honor to do so. Now gentlemen, you've heard what you came for. I am asking you leave so we may have our coffee and go back to our hotel. Please give Al Bactar our regards."

Russell C. Arslan

Chapter 10

As soon as Papaz opened the fourth-floor suite door, he noticed a note resting on their living quarters couch.

Pointing to Bi Ba he said, "That wasn't there when we left."

She agreed, "If it was left by the hotel, someone would have notified us at the concierge desk when we arrived."

She wanted to say, how in the hell did anyone get into our suite but knew better of it. The hotel's security was minimal and apparently so was their security's team.

Papaz opened the hall door and called over one of Alvarez's men and discreetly told him someone had broken into their room. He said, "Bi Ba and I will go to the lobby for a drink. Make sure your men sweep the room for bugs and find out how the hell this happened."

Within fifteen minutes he got a call from a member of the security detail saying, "The room is clean and you may return up-stairs."

After opening the door, he walked over to the couch, picked up the tan colored envelope sealed with a red wax crest and opened it. The note was in bold cursive letters.

He read aloud to Bi Ba, "Meet me at the bar downstairs by the pool. It had a three-word signature, Alwan Al Bactar."

Bi Ba walked in front of Matt over to the double French doors opening to the suite's patio balcony overlooking the pool area and the beautiful Barbados Bay. She could see the bar and some of its guest. No one stood out.

She said, "We might as well go face him now."

Matt replied, "Now is as good as any time. What do you think he wants? If it is really him."

She walked back into the contemporary suite designed with antique Middle Eastern art, modern day Turkish paintings and other artworks displayed throughout the living area. She walked over to the front door, opened it and called one of the security team and whispered in his ear, "Send two men down by the pool's bar ahead of us. You guys are going to come with us. We are going down to the bar."

The six were grouped two in front and two behind Matt and Bi Ba as they walked down the corridor's hard wood floor leading to a magnificent spiral staircase anchoring the hotel's centerpiece floor-to-ceiling eighty foot solarium. Ascending from the pool area to the fourth floor, the magnificently constructed stairwell was Bodrum's most prestigious hotel lobby's beautiful architectural signature.

They walked to the basement and through an indoor bar area designed looking like a large magnificent tent in the middle of the desert. The wall coverings were kilim, canvas pieces from actual Saharan desert tents. Adorned with canned wall fixtures light emanated through intricate, ornate carvings allowing the burning wax candles to show through. The floor covered with Turkish balouch rugs mostly in the burnt orange to red color range. The tent smelled of coriander and turmeric spices, had a heavy scent presence of barbecued meats being served with hummus and rice and placed on each table as a Meza for the club's guest. After walking through the crowded club, they reached the outside pool area and its bar overlooking the bay. They walked over to the mahogany bar, sat at a small Iznik tablecloth draped iron table with a small lantern acting as a candle. Four tan wicker chairs encircled the table. It was one of many table and chairs sets in the hotel's large pool area. They were now sitting at the sandy bay water's edge, giving them a strategic viewing position for the beach and the hotel. The crescent moon sky had no cloud remnants blocking its rays. The breeze coming softly off the water cooled the balmy night. In the background, they heard soft tones of Middle Eastern music coming from the tented Sultan Club while they walked through coming to the pool. The two were holding hands at the table waiting for their adversary. They could not help notice the beautifully romantic bay but it was secondary to their safety and well-being. They both felt conflicted. They were in an idyllic setting sharing each other's company and cognizant they could be in danger. Ironically, they could be in danger not for anything they had done but for the circumstances of asking the wrong questions at the wrong time.

Papaz caught the eye of one of the bartenders. The young man came over and asked if he could get the couple some drinks. Matt said, "Yes." asking Bi Ba what she wanted.

"I will have a double Raki and a water back. I think I need something strong," she said, looking at Matt. "What are you going to have?"

"I'll have the same. We're going to have a guest. He should be here shortly. You can bring him a bottle of water with no gas. You might as well bring it with our drinks. As soon as he comes to the table I would like you to come back and ask if he would like something to eat."

Matt knew religious Muslims didn't drink. The two sat sipping their Turkish Raki for almost 30 minutes before Matt noticed a small zodiac boat coming into his sightline from deep on the bay horizon. As the small craft size enlarged, as it approached the beach it became evident there was only one person aboard. It took more than ten minutes for the boat to pull onto the shore. When the zodiac front lodged deep into the soft sand a man straightened from a sitting position, walked away from the dinghy directly to their table. He was small in stature, maybe five feet, eight inches to five feet, ten inches tall but he walked with such power and suppleness he expressed dominance over his environment. Uniquely handsome with coal black beard, dark Middle Eastern features and surprisingly prominent deep green eyes. His desert musk smell would have been offensive if it did not fit his warrior persona.

Standing at the table's edge he said, "I am Alwan Al Bactar. My men came to me and told me we should talk. They stake their lives on this meeting. They say I am safe and you are no threat. They tell me you have some information about my father and that I should engage your company before you go into the wind."

As he started to sit he looked directly into Papaz's eyes, "I want to know about him."

He grabbed the bottle of water from the table and poured it into the glass and said again, "Knowledge of my father is very important to me."

Matt replied, "I did not know your father but I certainly know of him. My accounts are not firsthand and only a version of what I have heard over the years. I came to know him by his sister. Her American name is Helen but her Armenian name was Sidune. Your father came to America from the old country, present day Harpoots with my aunt and two others. We know he was arrested and placed in the old Sultanahmet jail for separatist Armenian activities. He was a member of many radical organizations clashing with government troops in Eastern Turkey near Ankara. He started the first major Armenians separatist movement in his early twenties when he was imprisoned for his political activities. My aunt said he was in jail for six months. Like I said she mentioned something about the Sultanhmet jail. From late 1920s through most of the Great Depression early years he led the separatist movement both in Turkey and Russia. He was forced to leave Turkey in the early 30s. This is a rough sketch of who your father was."

"There is more. A British as well as a Turkish bounty was on his head, when he came to America by way of France with the help of a cousin whose last name was Asnavor. He came to California and stayed in Fresno with another cousin, Elia Aslan, a farmer. His cousin Elia was quite successful producing watermelon and honeydew melons. Elia and his brother Aslan Aslan took

Malgan and his sisters under their wing. Your father ultimately became the superintendent of their 3,000-acre farm. The farming operation was very prosperous even in the first years of the Depression. Both Elia and Aslan were in their early seventies when your father first came to America and Elia had no children and Aslan had no use for his so your father inherited the whole operation. His success as a businessman and farmer allowed him to bring over thirty family members to America from Turkey during the next 40 years. Your father also helped create a very important California Armenian organization called the triple X. It was named after 30 Armenian men in Fresno, California who were discriminated upon, couldn't find jobs or housing, and through their efforts and hard work became successful and bonded as brothers to help other Armenian emigrants. As a group, they are responsible for bringing more than 600 Armenians from Russia and Turkey to America. Your father basically stayed in the United States and used his money to help others until approximately 1970 when he decided to go back to Turkey. That's where he met your mother and they had a son. That son was you. He married your mother and stayed in Turkey for two years. He did not bring you to America because both your mother and reluctantly your father felt it was better for you to be brought up in Eastern Turkey because of the advantage of family. He loved America but he felt many things had changed after World War II and it would be better for you to be raised in Turkey. That's where his heart was. Because of medical problems he came back to America but had intentions of returning to Turkey and living out his remaining life with you and your mother. By the time, he overcame his medical problems and returned to Turkey your mother had passed away from tuberculosis and you were taken by a cousin to Beirut. Malgan had no way of finding you because your cousin gave you up. You were passed from one foster home to another. He tried to find you, he hired people to find you, and even solicited the US Consulate in Ankara to help in this endeavor. He gave you up for lost."

"He became a consultant to Anwar Sadat in early 1980s and when he traveled to Egypt he came to Turkey on two occasions looking for you, obviously to no avail. After his death, his American family tried to bring you back but as our Aunt Helen said, you were gone and there was no trace. Most of this took place between approximately 1976 and 1984. When your father came back to America one last time about a year before he died he had another child. A child out of wedlock but your brother's name is Stanley Malgan. He is a lawyer living in San Francisco California. After your father was assassinated in Egypt. Stanley sold the large farm and other family businesses and became a wealthy person. I met him only once but he struck me as foolish and impressed with himself. My mother was close to your father and spoke well of him but never had anything good to say about his illegitimate son. Your brother's mother is no longer alive and I have no recollection of her or her history. My mother always said your father was a person of conviction and purpose and your brother was an embarrassment to the family name. Your father helped the Armenian community by setting up old age homes, three of them in California, and your brother took his estate to court and tried to liquidate the properties for his own benefits. He failed and the homes are part of your father's legacy. Your father also created many jobs for Armenians in Central California by purchasing some retail farming supply companies and hiring only immigrants. Your brother tried to take that too but again he was unsuccessful. It is evident you have your father's DNA and Stanley Malgan does not. You and your commitment to your people, not only Armenians but the poor and disenfranchised in the Middle East, are a modern-day replica of what your father did when he was a man of your age. Your instincts to help others are applaudable and you carry your family's heritage well. Matt extended his hand across the table to shake Alwan Al Bactar's hand."

Looking at Bi Ba he continued, "It is our great pleasure to meet the son of my cousin. What I know of you tells me you are honorable but I think the price of your convictions are very high. As I mentioned to your men, I too have convictions but I risk nothing but my money whereas you risk your life. It is rare to meet a person of your quality. May I say it's an honor? I really can't tell you much more about your father and your brother except I am proud to be related to Malgan Malgan and of course to you. When we came to Istanbul and entertained the thought of buying the hotel I wanted to see for myself who Malgan Malgan was. This is how we have arrived to this point. What I'm going to say is a little off base but please let me finish. I told you that we might purchase the Four Seasons Hotel. If I do I want to have a hall or a room or museum that it is dedicated to people who were jailed there, or stayed there, or who worked there that had some influence upon my family. In California, there is an old historical hotel called the Hotel Del Coronado in San Diego. It is truly a historic landmark. On its lower level the owners created a museum respecting the men who built the wonderful structure. I want to do the same in Istanbul if we purchase the hotel. I want to dedicate it to our history. I think the political climate in Istanbul and Western Turkey is opening up its Armenian past. Your father is a person I want to spotlight. He was a great man. I am sorry I am so long-winded but that's how all of this started. Now, hopefully you will have a clearer picture of why I wanted to hire Sully and his academic friends and what I wanted them to do. Part of their task was to choose anywhere from twenty to twenty-five people who stayed in the jail, or the hotel, or was an employee having some influence on our family. I never intended to meet you. I will be the better person for your acquaintance. I have spoken too much. It is your turn, my cousin."

Chapter 11

When Alwan Al Bactar finally spoke, it was surprising to both Matt and Bi Ba that he was articulate and succinct. His voice resonated in the soft wind deepening in his baritone speech. It was unusual for a Middle Eastern man not to speak in an Asian high pitched manner. Looking at his surroundings as if he were doing reconnaissance he finally spoke.

"You are the first European with knowledge of my father I have talked to. I accept, you did not know him. I appreciate you were honest with me. I know you were brief in your description. There is much more I would like to know but this is not the time. I must make myself clear. I am nothing like my father. Times have changed and so have the ways of the oppressed. I have killed people. I have tortured people. I have kidnapped people for money for our cause. So, no I am not like my father. I am a person who lives in the present and must deal with hardships the oppressed must endure at the hands of tyrants who rule our lands. I did not follow my father's past because of his history. I followed his path because it was the path to justice. Because of your wealth, where you were born and who you were born to. Because of how you were brought up we are different. You are more sophisticated than me. I am a simple warrior of the desert. I would use your ways if I were a person of your world. I have to use my own devices to fight the war of impoverishment in my world. You and my father are quite similar. You fight a war relative to your wealth and so do I. I am by nature a warrior and must strike fear in my enemy. I am weak and outnumbered so I must create fear in my opponent by doing what is not acceptable to him at the point of most damage. You pay others to do your bidding and do it in a political and financial world not nearly as violent as the world I live in. My father was the same. I must kill to bring justice. I am a Muslim and I follow the teachings of Allah but I am also a realist. I break from my religious teachings and create ways for my people to oppose the oppressor. My actions are often blasphemous but if it frees my people then the number of crimes I commit or the number of people I kill are meaningless."

"As for my heritage, I am Armenian even though I do not practice Christianity. My people faced Turkish oppression pushing us to commit terrible crimes. Just look at the massacres. Do you think there are any changes in central Turkey even today? Look at our brothers the Curds. All they ask is an autonomous state and they are stalked and killed as if they were animals. Freedom for my Armenian brothers is our cause. It is no different from Palestinians, Curds, or any other poor and oppressed people. Many of our problems are remnants of the old British colonial world established prior to World War I. The Middle East faces the prospects of the weakened poor versus the strong and corrupt. I am proud to protect the weak because I am on the side of justice. Freedom fighters like me must hide in the dust storm swells. Our warriors engage the enemy blended with civilians as if we are the subjugated not the worthy adversary of the corrupt. We cannot confront the aggressors directly, they are too strong, therefore, we must use terrorist tactics. What makes us different is we have a just cause. I must define justice because my life is at stake. I will die for my people but I will define what is righteous and must be done. I will not let others define justice, righteousness and morality. I know I will not live to an old age as my father did because my life as freedom fighter is short and violent. I have a child and a wife but my existence does not let me father my son or husband my wife. I will die young but the cause of justice for the impoverished, my people who have so little and are treated like cattle, will be won by men like me."

He stopped speaking for second and reflected. Completely changing the subject, he said, "I am pleased to meet you my cousin. What I understand you may not. Yes, we are much alike but how we live and our backgrounds make us differ as to how we approach justice. If you lived in my harsh world you would be like me. You would be labeled a terrorist and you would die to help the poor. We are no different, you and me. You are only more sophisticated. In my world, there is only one way to affect change and it's through violence. You are years ahead of me in sophistication because of your circumstances. My world is physical because the only thing I can give is my life. As you told my men in your world it is your money you are willing to give. It is only your money you told them. For me it is only my life. There is no other difference between us. In our backgrounds the price of failure is different. Not the intent of our actions. We are the same my cousin. My men told me you would sponsor or finance some of our work. I am grateful but I cannot let your money and your world influence mine. Your world's tools, it's money and its political power cannot play a role in the destiny of my people. My weapons are my labor and my life. I thank you for the offer but it would be wasteful. Money to buy a home when I live in the desert would be foolish. Money to buy a car when I ride on my donkey or horse would be foolish. Money for my cause when people need understanding and true justice would be foolish. If I ever need your help I will seek you out. The honor of our meeting is mine my cousin. My father would have been pleased to have known you. I have a request, I would like you to further pursue my father's history and I would be honored if you share that knowledge with me."

Alwan Al Bactar looked at Bi Ba, "In my culture we are not as developed as yours when it comes to women. You are much like my wife. You are his soldier for the poor and a worrier of the desert."

He got up from the table and stepped onto the white sand. He pulled the zodiac back into the water. Alwan Al Bactar stepped aboard the rubber craft and started the engine. He sped away with the same urgency as he arrived. Matt and Bi Ba watched the small craft got smaller and smaller as it moved towards the horizon on Barbados Bay. Neither Matt nor Bi Ba said a word until Alwan Al Bactar had disappeared over the horizon.

Matt said, "What the hell was that? He was nothing like I thought he would be."

She responded, "You're going to be disappointed in me. I don't know how to say this so I'll just come out with it best way that I can. We, you and I have probably killed more men than him. We have probably kidnapped and tortured and been involved in more mayhem and reckless violence than him. If he is supposed to be one of the world's most feared terrorists what does that make us? I don't know if I'm disappointed in him or overwhelmed by what," she paused for a second, "what ass holes we have become. Man, he was right about one thing. Your money and your way of life are different than his but that crap about not being a warrior because you are affluent and sophisticated is no more than bull shit as far as I am concerned. Floating in and out of here on his zodiac and those green eyes, wow, what bull shit. Give me a break."

"Tomorrow we are out of here," Matt said. "I have not heard from Frederic which usually means he's not coming. When I get back to the room I'll call him."

Chapter 12

The next morning, they wanted to have breakfast on the hotel first floor patio overlooking the pool and the bay area. It was a late for them, already 7:45am as they walked from their room to the restaurant talking about their day. Grabbing a cup of tea in the lobby to drink while walking to the eatery.

Matt told Bi Ba, "We're in no hurry, the boat isn't leaving without us. The captain said it would probably take a little under three hours to get to Gumusluk."

Bi Ba added, "I can't even pronounce the name of the place, but there are some incredible archaeological ruins under the water no more than 500 feet from shore and no more than twenty feet of water."

He said, "We can free dive we don't have to scuba. I think."

She continued, "It's either a Temple or Roman spa. The water is supposed to be so clear you can see forever."

"I'm really excited about this, there are supposed to be lots of sea turtles. Anyhow, it's going to be great. The captain set out the day for us. When we get there, we will dive for a while. A professional diver will be there to take us to the ruins. After we dive we have the option of either eating on the boat or mooring in a front slip at one of the many restaurants."

He said, "For the night, we can either stay at the hotel or on the boat itself. I got the impression, he's not impressed by the hotels. In any event, if we sail over there it's three hours. If we go by motor, we can probably get there in a little over an hour and a half. He made it sound like we don't have to make any decisions until we get there."

Bi Ba said, "I'm assuming, since you didn't hear from Frederic, they are not coming. Hopefully he will meet us in Istanbul on our way back. He usually wants to look at properties before you guys invest in them. This will give him a good reason to meet us next week. It will be nice to see him and Gisele. It will be a lot of fun."

Matt said, I'll call."

"Right this second?" Bi Ba said, "I am in no hurry to get down to the marina so if you don't mind, let's have a leisurely breakfast."

Walking past the hostess station, they were told a table was reserved for them on the outside patio overlooking the beautiful horse shoe bay. The breakfast was a continental breakfast that was more like a brunch with four massive stations for food.

Matt said, "I'll drop off my tea at the table. Why don't you just get in line? I'll see you in a couple of minutes."

Bi Ba proceeded to the station with a sous-chef and ordered a vegetarian omelet. Matt advanced to fruit, yogurt, and cereals. After filling his plate, he returned to the table. She browsed through waffles or French toast choices and syrup and sauce assortments but declined, saying she would return after eating her first course. There were two other tables or food stations, divided into meats and cheeses with the final table reserved for bakery goods, pastries and Danishes.

Matt sat down first. A few seconds later Bi Ba arrived. Simultaneously, a young Turkish man wearing a dark blue pinstripe suit, white dress shirt and no tie, with dark brown shoes appeared at the table and sat.

In broken English, he said, "My name is Ozgur Ozkan, I am from the twelfth prefecture in Istanbul. May I have a couple minutes of your time?"

He was at a disadvantage. He was not proficient in spoken English but his comprehension of the language was sufficient for him in most situations.

With deep thought and concentration, he continued, "We understand you had a guest last night."

Before he could say another word, Matt in an aggressive, assertive, controlling manner started speaking and cut him off. Controlling the conversation, "Yes, we did have a guest last night, if you want to call it that. Right here in the hotel. We were sitting," he pointed to the bar area of the pool next to the sandy beach below. "We were sitting at the second table to the right of the bar, when a zodiac came in off the water, motoring the craft right into the sand. It felt like he appeared out of nowhere."

Matt pointed showing Ozkan the rubber craft tracks. "That's where he pulled up. That's where he got off. He walked straight over to our table," Papaz looked at the inspector, pretty much like you just did. The man obviously wanted to talk to us. It was evident he knew who we were. He introduced himself and asked if we were interested in Roman artifacts or any other kind of archaeological antiquities. He knew about us chartering a boat for the next four days. He even had knowledge of our itinerary. He said he heard we were not collectors but we were people of means who might be interested in high quality art."

"He talked to us for no more than fifteen minutes and we told him yes, we were interested in art but no we would not buy from him because we do not buy in the illegal black market. If he could bring his art to an established dealer with a government seal and the proper paperwork I would buy from him if we like what he had. That was all, no more no less. He got back on his zodiac and headed out to the open sea. Now, that's all I have to say. I'm asking if you don't mind please leave so we can have our breakfast in private. We have met your demands and I've answered your questions."

He effectively dismissed the Istanbul police inspector. Ozkan did not know what to say. He was at a great disadvantage because he didn't have the ability to articulate his position in English and he was taken aback by the fact he was dismissed.

He got up and said, "You have outflanked me."

Papaz wasn't exactly sure what he meant by outflanked but knew he had effectively ended the conversation.

The police officer said, "We will meet again under different circumstances."

The name Alwan Al Bactar never came up and was the reason for the visit. The Young Turk said to himself, he won the first round but he won't get out of Turkey without talking to me again. He walked away from the table through the restaurant to the large centrally located staircase in the hotel's solarium where he continued to the lobby and out the front doors to a waiting police car. It would take him to the airport for his trip back to Istanbul.

Bi Ba looked at Matt and said, "It's pretty clear you didn't need my help. I didn't have to say a word. You verbally cut him off at the knees and didn't give him a chance to get one word in. That was really impressive but I think you might've been a little harsh. I hope you didn't piss him off so much that he will continue to come after us."

Matt responded, "He won't come after us because we have no relationship with Al Bactar and that's all he really cares about. Sure, I pissed him off but no one is going to come after us if we're going to buy the hotel. The investment is too large. Maybe $100 million dollars. No one will want to jeopardize a foreign investment of that magnitude. For all intents and purposes we don't have to worry about this guy. Al Bactar's problems are with the Arab states and not with Turkey. He is actually pretty much aligned with the Turks. Turkey and the Arab states are separate entities with separate languages. The Turks offshoot of Sunni Islam is not as radical as the Arabs and really imposes no threats to Al Bactar's belief system. This Ozkan guy must be part of Turkey's national security operations or something. He is not local police. I'll tell Frederic to get him to back off. I know I came on strong but believe it or not it was for a reason. Frederic will have a lot of pull inside of their national security apparatus. I will talk to him about this and let him deal with it. If we sound like we're pissed off it might sound like it can jeopardize the purchase of the hotel. They sure as hell won't want that."

"Frederic will clear it up. Now that the Turkish low level irritant is gone let's finish with breakfast. Unbelievably, I'm still hungry. I'm going back for a waffle. Is there anything you want?" Bi Ba said.

She went with him to the food bar. After breakfast, they went to their room and cleaned up. They met their captain and crew in the marina at approximately 11:30am.

Chapter 13

Inspector Ozkan made a call to Istanbul headquarters as he left the hotel. He called the district terrorist activities administrator, commander Arin Ates, asking if he could use other tactics to interrogate Papaz because he was not cooperative.

Speaking in Turkish Ates said, "He wasn't forthcoming and I have every reason to believe he is lying. We have pictures of him with Al Bactar at the beach and he boldfaced lied to me. He told me he was approached by a merchant who sold questionable antiques. He was very clever and gave me Al Bactar's description. I am on my way to the airport coming back to the office but I am asking you to give me more resources and allow me to detain Papaz for a proper interrogation."

Commander Ates replied, "It's your call. Do what you need to do. If you want some military assistance go directly to the Bodrum Peninusla's Gocek naval base. I'll have everything set up for you. I will okay any interrogation methods and as many men as you want. You have an open check as far as I am concerned. Use your own discretion."

Ozkan would now have his chance with Papaz but this time he would not be bullied and he would control the conversation. He thought to himself, this will be an inquisition not an interrogation. I have the full weight of the Turkish National Security Service behind me. Anything I want to do I have their blessing. And that, eshag, (a Turkish slang word for ass hole), will pay the price for treating me with such disrespect. Ozkan ordered the driver to drive to the naval base where senior officers were waiting to expedite his demands. The twenty-five miles drive up the Peninsula north wing took ninety minutes.

Matt and Bi Ba finished their breakfast and arrived in their suite at 10am. Matt sat on a living room sofa and said, "I'm calling Frederic to see if he and Gisele are going to meet us in Istanbul."

He made the call and told him about his interesting encounter with the inspector. He related what had transpired during their breakfast and said, "I was maybe a little obnoxious but the guy is a piss ant. I don't need any more trouble from him. Persuade someone we are benign and get him off our asses. Bi Ba thought I should get a hold of you as soon as possible because I was really harsh and dismissive with him. She said I was my old aggressive self. I did not threaten his life or anything but I embarrassed him. To be honest, I dismissed him from the table and I know he didn't buy my story about a merchant selling antiquities."

Frederic said, "Okay it sounds like he's got a hard on for you. I will get on it as soon as Gisele gets back from lunch. I just called her office said she won't be back for two hours. She's still at her Paris office and has to be there for four more days. She has contacts with Abdullah

Gul, president of Turkey. I will have her get on it right away."

Frederic changed subjects, "How about if we meet up with you guys in Istanbul when she's finished with the project she is on?"

Matt didn't even have to invite his friends to meet them on the second half of their trip. Frederic continued, "I will contact the hotel so we can inspect their financials and get a walk around. Let me get back to this guy Ozkan. Do you think he will come back at you personally or just professionally?"

Matt said, "I don't have a clue but he was pissed."

"Just in case I am going to beef up your security. I am going to have a boat follow your yacht as you guys cruise down the peninsula. They will be close enough to give you all the security you need. I'll have the security team get in touch with your captain so they can work things out. At least, you will have more protection and always be in sight. Tell your captain you want to stay close enough to see the land. We'll have people following the boat in highway vehicles."

As he was looking at area maps he Googled. "If there is anything else I will let you know. Talk to you soon."

Matt thanked his friend and said, "It will be nice to have a couple of quiet days before we see you guys.

Ozkan arrived at the naval base and was taken to headquarters. He moved rapidly acquiring a team to help him apprehend Matt. He commandeered two small gunships patrolling the Peninsula waters. His attention was drawn to a translator and some shore patrol officers for help in the capturing Papaz. This plan was simple. He would intersect the yacht at sea. After viewing nautical charts and information from area military planes he knew the exact location of the Bodrum Dream at all times. Ozkan determined exactly when and where his team of twelve heavily armed Marines would go aboard the yacht. After apprehending Papaz the two gunships will tow the yacht into Gumusluk's small harbor. If everything works out at two-hours past midday, he would maximize Papaz's capture to the most public exposure. He wanted the highest humiliation level created for the arrogant American. It would be equivalent to that of a perp walk used on high profiled type criminals.

At 11:30am Matt and Bi Ba arrived at the Bodrum Marina. The eighty-six-foot sailboat was tied in a temporary slip in front of St. Peters Castle. The captain and crew of three plus a professional cook were waiting for the couple. They were all dressed in white shorts, white deck shoes, and white short-sleeve polo shirts. As soon as Matt and Bi Ba exited the hotel's 660 series black Mercedes-Benz the three crew members grabbed their bags from the driver and escorted their guests into the fenced off area of larger slips for oversized power and sailing vessels. They walked a narrow wooden walkway to mid ship. Bi Ba was astounded by how large an eighty-six-foot sailboat really was. The Bodrum Dream comfortably slept eight people. There were four staterooms, one master and three smaller, all with their own bathrooms and showers. There was a large galley and the craft's central cabin were spacious. The deck's size under the enormous sailing mast impressed Papaz. The Bodrum Dream had the latest electronics and safety features. The captain was the only member of the crew who slept on board, if Matt and Bi Ba decided to stay overnight on the boat. The other crew members would put ashore and sleep in the peninsula small towns or villages. Fitted with an extensive bar the boat's chef trained at the Istanbul Culinary Institute, one of Europe's most prestigious schools, having a four-star Michelin rating.

Captain Murat Yetkin told Papaz he had talked to the local meteorologist and the winds would not pick up until much later in the afternoon so they would not be sailing out of the harbor. They would be using the boat's massive twin engines powering their way to Gumusluk. The couple would be on the water less than two hours before they arrived at their diving site, the Roman ruins of the ancient city of Myndos on the outskirts of Gumusluk. The captain told Papaz he had hired a professional photographer specialized in aquamarine photography. They picked him up in a small village fifteen minutes from the diving site, the only stop before they went into the water diving with the fish and Roman ruins.

Captain Yetkin explained, "We should get to our destination no later than 2pm if everything goes well. There is something else, I have spoken to one of your security officers and there will be a second boat with six men traveling behind us. They will stay 1,000 meters either to the side or behind us at all times."

Papaz thanked him for his understanding. "We had some trouble last night at the hotel and it just seemed appropriate we have a security team follow us. They will not interfere with anything you do and they won't make your job any more difficult."

The captain said, "I understand and it is something that happens quite often in the Aegean. I have planned some things you and your companion might enjoy."

He did not know what to call Bi Ba.

Overhearing the conversation, she said, "Just call me Bi Ba."

He continued, "Every day we will have time for diving. It will be our priority. There are small towns and villages you might like. When we approach, then I will tell you what might be of interest. We can pull over to the shore at any time and you can walk around, eat, or do anything you would like. There are many archaeological sites near Gumusluk. If any of them interest you, we can get some guides and professionals to escort you. This area has many restaurants and markets so we can stop anytime you desire. As far as I am concerned there is no set itinerary or time schedule. I am at your disposal and there is nothing you can ask of me that I won't try to provide," he paused for a second gathering his words not to offend the couple. "Of course, that means things legal and acceptable in our culture. I checked the weather, it is perfect but as I said we will be under power much of the time. There is not much wind so we will sail very little. No need to go deep into the sea. We will stay close to shore. My crew and I are here to do whatever you request. I think we are ready to go so please go below and change your clothes and we will embark on our journey."

The three crew members untied the dock lines and the boat backed out of the slip into the marina. A number of large boats were on the water suggesting the small yacht harbor opulence. The predominant colors of red and white punctuated the fleet of wealthy Turkish sea goers. The Bodrum Dream was just one of many large vessels housed in the Marina. It left the harbor powering past the great rock foundation of St. Peter's Castle. The second Papaz Armada boat carried its security team following passed the eleventh century structure at approximately 1,000 meters behind the sailboat. The azure deep blue Aegean waters were before them and the heavily green foliaged peninsula was on their left. They would power for approximately two hours to reach the destination where they could swim in the eighty-degree water covering the third century BC Roman villa on the edge of Myndos.

Bi Ba found a place on the deck where she laid out a towel and asked Matt to apply suntan lotion to her back and spread a towel of his own. The boat's luxury and extravagance and the beautiful surroundings were more than either had anticipated. It was an elixir or medicine for their souls. This was truly the first time in 18 months they were allowed to rest and try to erase the memory of their good friends being killed.

Ozkan mustered the crews for the 110-foot gun boats and left the naval base with dispatch. Their disembarkation time from the military fort was 1:05pm. Naval aircraft monitored the Bodrum Dream with a helicopter and light planes determining the three-vessel's intersection point would be 2:17pm. The craft's convergence approximately one and one half km from the city of Gumusluk small yacht harbor. Sailboat boarding adjustments would need to consider picking up the photographer and winds increasing after 1:30pm. The actual intersection of the three boats would take place near the remains of the ancient city of Myndos was three km from the small boat harbor at 2:27pm. When the Bodrum Dream approached the underwater ruins site just outside the city, the captain cut the engines and told the crew to lower the anchor. As the three men were working, the two Turkish gunboats appeared from the sea's horizon the sun behind them to obfuscate their presence. Ozkan ordered the gunnery officer to fire a shot across the bow of the sailboat. He yelled over a microphone announcing they were boarding the vessel.

Matt and Bi Ba and the crew could not comprehend what was happening. The sound of the ordinance and chaos ensuing with twelve men boarding the boat was a total surprise. Once Papaz got his bearings he realized they were being commandeered to shore by the Turkish Navy. The oldest of the soldiers on board the vessel looked juvenile to Papaz. It did not bode well in his mind having young people who looked barely old enough to shave to be wielding automatic rifles. He heard the piercing voice of Inspector Ozkan before he took a blow on his left temple that took away his consciousness. Ozkan had one of his contingency of men throw water onto Papaz's face to wake him up. Ozkan walked up to him and told him to stay on the ground and put his hands behind his back. He placed a pair of steel handcuffs on his crossed wrists and kicked him forward which pushed Papaz onto his face.

He looked at his captive and said, "You are in my Turkey now and we will finish our conversation. You," he stumbled for the words in English, his interpreter interrupted and said something in Turkish and Ozkan replied. The interpreter used the words dismissed and insulted and said Inspector Ozkan this time had something to say.

Papaz was told he was going to be interviewed in the small jail in Gumusluk and this was now a military matter. Two men pulled Papaz to his feet while two other men politely escorted Bi Ba off the boat. They were placed in separate vehicles and taken to the village's small police station. All the while the second boat of Papaz's armada was 1,000 meters away and could only watch in despair and dispatch a call to Frederic Valence

Part III – Gumusluk

Chapter 14

The two black and white marked police vehicles pulled to the front of the small station. The building constructed in the early 1900s was used as a fish processing plant until 1933. In 1947 converted into a police station. Little more than three hundred square meters, its police station / jail configuration was a central office quarters, four offices and a lobby area. Eight holding cells were in building backside connecting to a docking area. The small city's police department had six police cars, four were still in the garage adjacent to the station.

Papaz was dragged out of the vehicle's back seat in front of thirty to forty townspeople. His bloodied face was from falling forward when kicked by Ozkan on board the yacht ten minutes earlier. This public prisoner remand in hand cuffs and escorted by the military was an unusual occurrence in the sleepy seaside community. People with cell phones were taking pictures and Papaz's arrest became viral in a matter of minutes.

Bi Ba was also escorted from her vehicle into the small police station but was not manhandled. Once inside of the old stone building Papaz was immediately taken into the jail area and thrown into a cell. He landed hard on the cement floor. A Marine brought in an old metal chair and threw him upon it. His handcuffs were still in place with his hands behind his back.

Ozkan ordered the Marine to tie Papaz's feet to the front chair legs with a nylon lead. Then instructed him to tie Papaz at the chest stabilizing his body's top half. For all intents and purposes Ozkan's prisoner could not move. Ozkan calmly and succinctly talked to his interpreter. There was a time lag of thirty seconds before Papaz could hear the English translation.

"You are mine now. Where is the traitor Al Bactar? What is your relationship with him? Where'll he strike next? We have a video of you and him at the hotel. Where is he?"

Before Papaz could respond Ozkan pulled from his pocket a small eight-inch-long rubber hose and hit him across the face.

Papaz's face started swelling and simultaneously he started spitting blood. He could not speak because of the blood in his mouth and Ozkan took that as being noncompliant and hit him more, striking him in the mouth shattering one of his front teeth. He was hit so hard he became unconscious.

The last he had heard was Bi Ba's voice coming from the next cell. She was screaming, "Stop it you bastard. Stop it. Who in the fuck do you think you are? Who in the fuck is this guy Al Bactar? He doesn't know what you're talking about. Some guy came up to us last night at the beach and said he was a merchant. That's all we know. That's all that happened."

Ozkan looked at her and hit Papaz again, this time in the rib cage.

ISTANBUL

She yelled, "You're going to kill him, you are going to kill him. Please stop! I will say anything you want me to say. We don't know anything but I will do anything. Just stop!"

She knew the only person in the cell area understanding her was the interpreter. She yelled for him to get Ozkan to back off.

"Get him to stop. We don't know anything. Tell him to stop."

Ozkan looked across at her with contempt and grabbed Papaz and hit him again as a soldier walked into the small jail holding area and started yelling orders. Someone in military clothing not conforming to the twelve Marines' grabbed Ozkan's shoulder before he could unleash another blow.

Bi Ba could not understand Turkish but he restrained Ozkan. The two men walked out of the cell area together into the police chief's office. She did not know what had happened, all she knew was the beating stopped. Her unconscious partner sitting limp in the metal chair was being relieved from further torture.

Twenty minutes passed before the police chief's office door opened and Ozkan yelled something. His military escort and translator all exited through the front of the police station. A tall very dark military officer walked to a remaining police officer and saying something in Turkish. A young twentyish policeman still in the cell area opened up her door.

She screamed, "What the hell is happening?"

She looked at the military officer and yelled, "Who are you?

Looking at Papaz she yelled, "Get him some medical attention."

The Turkish officer responded, "I am Major Celal Gursel. You are free to go. Take him with you."

In a very controlled and restrained manner he said, "We apologize. We have detained and arrested the wrong person."

He called over another police officer. Looking at Papaz he said, "Get him out a here."

The young man opened Papaz's cell. Gursel then looked directly at Bi Ba, "The government of Turkey apologizes for what happened."

He gave her a card. "If you want to pursue this call my office. It is the office of the president of Turkey. You are very lucky I got here as soon as I did. The military takes cooperating with terrorists very seriously." Looking at Papaz he continued, "He could have been killed and no one would have known. This is Turkey. You don't have the same rights here as you do in Europe. Again, if you want justice or some type of apology contact the president. He knows of the situation. That is why I am here. I convey my countries apologies."

He walked past her through the lobby and out of the door of the small police station. By this time Papaz was semi-conscious and on his feet but badly hurt. The six men from the second vessel were allowed into the jail and they carried Papaz into a waiting car parked on the street.

"We're taking him to the airport," one of the security team told Bi Ba. "We have a plane on the tarmac waiting for you. There will be a doctor accompanying us. We will be in Istanbul in less than an hour and a half.

Ambulances will be waiting for the two of you. It will take him to the hospital."

Chapter 15

The Beechcraft 300 King Air landed at the small aircraft terminal on the domestic side of Istanbul Ataturk International Airport. An ambulance waited for Papaz, Bi Ba and the doctor accompanying them from the Bodrum Peninsula Milas-Bodrum airport. They were taken to the Acibadem International Hospital where a team of government doctors, sent by the President's office waited for Papaz at the emergency ward.

He was whisked directly through admittance and greeted by Dr. Camel Ozal, a trauma specialist responsible for his recovery. Papaz was conscious but in immense pain. The first thing they did was administer an EKG examination and check his vitals. He had to undergo a PET scan and an MRI to determine if he was concussed and the amount of damage to his kidneys. He was also x-rayed to check the damage on his ribs.

The doctors' team determined he was starting to dehydrate. They connected an IV gave Papaz two bags of saline solution and electrolytes. To ameliorate his pain, they gave him OxyContin. The team's conclusions were clear. Papaz was concussed, suffered a broken left eye orbit, shattered left front incisor necessitating a tooth implant, three broken ribs on his left side and right side ribs deep bruising plus various contusions and lacerations to his face.

Matt planned to stay in the hospital two days then he and Bi Ba return to the Four Seasons Hotel, remaining there until he healed enough to fly back to the United States.

Frederic and Gisele's Istanbul International Airport arrival was met by a government limousine taking them directly to the hospital. Both dropped projects they were working and flew to Istanbul to be with their friend. Acibadem International had just built a new wing to their medical complex in which Papaz had a private suite. The room and team of doctors were provided by Turkey's president.

Frederic and Gisele walked to the corridor of the new hospital wing Suite #273. Standing before the door to Papaz's room were two military officers. Both Frederic and Gisele had to show their passports to be able to walk into the room. The first thing Frederic did was stare at Matt.

"We saw the doctor's reports on our way over here. They made us privy to everything while on the plane. The best part is you're going to be okay. He could not contain himself. I'm really sorry but you look like shit. Man, that guy really fucked you up!"

His laugh got louder as he pulled out his iPhone to take a picture. "You look like Mr. Potato head. You said you think you really pissed the guy off. That's the biggest understatement I've ever heard. Like I said we read all of the reports and you will be fine, but he beat the shit out of you. It looks like a lot of pain."

Gisele said. "Frederic, I know you are picking on him to show affection but enough is enough."

Frederic said, "He'll get over it," as he took another picture.

Matt could not say a word because his head hurt so much. He sat there trying not to laugh at some of the remarks coming from his best friend's mouth. He felt lucky that he could find some humor in all of this because it could have really been bad.

Matt mumbled, "I am really glad you guys are here! I guess I'm lucky. I know I'll be okay. I told Bi Ba I didn't want to see what I look like but I think you said it all. Maybe not so much Mr. Potato head. How about Mr. Basketball face?"

He tried his best not to laugh because the pain was excruciating. "That little piece of shit really hurt me. I think if you guys hadn't interceded I would be dead."

He looked at Gisele and thanked her. "I know you went through the president's office. Is there any way I can thank him personally? Is that possible? I promise I won't make things worse. I have a plan. I'll even tell him I was partially responsible because of my reprehensible treatment of Inspector Ozkan at the hotel in Bodrum. I'll say I probably pushed him past his sight line. Something like, most likely Ozkan was elevated to some military strata above his comfort level. He overreacted because I was so aggressive. I'll tell him it was my fault. I should have been more conciliatory towards him when he came up to the table. I will take the blame for the confrontation at the hotel and say it's understandable he was pissed off. All that happened was he was confident in his position even though he was clearly out of bounds. He was opinionated and wrong but never in doubt that I was fostering terrorists' activities. I will tell the president I am sure he will learn from this. He'll be a better officer in the future. I will even ask him not to overreact. Please don't take it out on Ozkan. He was just doing his job. I gave him no alternatives but to interrogate me even though he went a little bit crazy. Finally, I will say something like, Mr. President please don't take it out on him. It was my fault."

Matt changed the subject, "You know for a little guy he hit way beyond his weight class. Man, he had heavy hands. He had to get back to the president. I will ask the President for as much political leniency as he can give Ozkan but I want to get back at that fuck and really hurt him. He made it personal and I'm not exaggerating when I say he wanted to kill me. Let him feel lucky because we didn't press any charges and hopefully the president will ease up on him. But like I said, I want a piece of him. I can and will wait as long as I have to.

Gisele walked up to the bed and grabbed his hand. "Sorry Matt, I know it must hurt but you will be okay. Everything you are thinking must be positive. That way you will get better faster. Make sure you watch out for that OxyContin. It's bad! Being addicted to pain pills is the last thing you need."

He said, "I know."

She continued, "Frederic and I have already decided were going to stay here in Istanbul as long as you and Bi Ba are here. Then we'll decide what to do. The president's office will do anything you want him to do with this

Ozkan person. I like your thinking. I know you have the memory of an elephant and you want part of him. It won't be easy but you'll just have to wait. It's kind of old-fashioned but I like that about you. No one should be able to mess with you without paying a price. I mean a heavy price. I'll tell the president you want him not to reprimand Ozkan because you were off base and you did not truly respect Turkey's deep concerns about terrorism. Your story will remain the same. You met a merchant at the hotel. It might have been Alwan Al Bactar but you didn't know. If the merchant was really him then Ozkan had every right to interrogate you but not with prejudice. I will tell him we understand. All you want to do is leave this misfortunate incident behind you."

Part – IV Istanbul

Chapter 16

Two days in hospital turned into four. Late in the afternoon of the fifth day Matt was released from Acibadem International Hospital and taken by a town car to the Four Seasons Sultanahmet. He knew Sully would materialize either walking through the hotel lobby doors or if not, it was just a matter of hours before his Turkish friend phoned.

Matt was conflicted about what to tell the Turk. He didn't know how far Sully's tentacles reached into the president's office. Did he have knowledge of what happened in Bodrum? That was a vexing question. He wasn't sure if Sully was out of the information loop and if he was, should he be kept there. For Papaz it was a dilemma of conscience not one of security. the president himself had given a guarantee of safety.

Frederic said, "It's always better to be truthful. Well at least be as honest as you can. Let him know in general terms what happened. He is going to find out one way or another if he has all the connections you say he has."

Matt answered, "As soon as he sees me, the shit will hit the fan. I have to tell him something."

"He will be frightened when he discovers Al Bactar saw you. If you give him some semblance of the truth, you have to come up with something believable."

Matt agreed and said, "It shouldn't be too difficult to develop a cover story about what happened. I have to do something because there are too many people who saw me on You Tube being arrested and pulled into jail to think Sully doesn't already know. Everybody thinks they know what took place, especially after everything went viral. I know there's a lot of Internet censorship here in Turkey, especially on Facebook and Twitter but shit always gets out."

"As soon as you see Sully tell him Ozkan went rogue because he hates Armenians," suggested Frederic.

"I'll say all this is because his prejudice against my heritage. He's a Turk. He will understand. It's a better tact to take than mentioning anything about Al Bactar. I don't want to mention Malgan Malgan's son because of the threat. Sully will back off from helping me with the hotel, if he even senses my cousin was near what happened to me. This way he won't feel he's in danger. I know he'll still want to do the project if he sees it as safe. So, I think I will use that as a reason to pursue him first. I'll tell him I didn't want him to be scared off by anything he heard before he talked to me."

Frederic said, "As far as Giselle and I being here you should just tell him we are your business partners and are here in Istanbul to look at the hotel's financials. I'll go along with anything you say about what happened. There is something else. Don't tell him how seriously you were hurt."

Matt listened and agreed. "I'll tell him I look lots worse than it really is. I'll even say you and Gisele and Bi

Ba had me stay in the hospital two extra days as a precaution because of my concussion."

When the town car pulled up in front of the hotel Papaz was surprised Sully was not in the lobby entryway waiting for him. Walking through the lobby towards the registration desk he pulled out his cell phone and made the call. Sully answered the phone at his rug store two blocks from the hotel.

Papaz asked if he could come right over, I want to tell you something before you hear it from someone else. In Papaz's mind, and he felt rightfully so, the hotel's walls had eyes and ears. Some member of the staff would call Sully to sell him information about his friend being battered. The price would be money or a quid pro quo for other information. In any event, someone at the hotel would tell him that Papaz was there and what he looked like. The informer would come up with some interpretation why Papaz was injured. It most assuredly would be incorrect. It was imperative to their relationship that he was the first-person Sully heard the news from. Sully arrived within twenty minutes, saying he was busy with an American interior decorator he had worked with previously. Their relationship was such that when he received the phone call he told the decorator it was important, personal and he had to leave for the night. They could continue their discussion the next morning.

When he arrived at the hotel's front double doors a member of the concierge staff told him he should immediately go to the Papaz suite. Within minutes he was standing in front of the door and knocked.

Matt gestured to Frederic, Gisele, and Bi Ba that he would answer the door. When he opened it his grotesque face was prominent and obviously noticed by Sully who held his tongue but was cognizant of Papaz's condition.

He was surprised and disturbed. Before he could say anything, Matt said, "There's something I have to tell you. Don't be upset. I'm fine. It just looks a lot worse than it is. I didn't want you to hear what happened from anybody else."

Pointing to Frederic and Gisele, he introduced them and asked Sully to sit down.

Sully said hello and acknowledged Bi Ba.

Papaz's rendition of the event on the Bodrum Peninsula was somewhat truthful spun as a hate crime against Armenians by someone who was just totally out of control. The name Al Bactar was not mentioned but his father Malgan Malgan in context to the project was discussed.

Matt stated, "We are going to continue and not let this be an obstacle. It was one man out of control. It just so happens he had a lot of juice and was able to do this to me. I want you to know it stops here. I have talked to President Gul and he has given me assurances. The National Security officer who did this, his name is Ozgur Ozkan, will be reined in and this will never happen again. He has personally signed off on the gallery and museum if we purchase the hotel. Gul is fully aware of Malgan Malgan and some other personalities we might showcase as influencing the hotel and Istanbul. He's good with that. He thinks the Turkish political climate of trying to procure a European Union spot creates a more ethnic diversity tolerance vision alignment which can only help negotiations with Europe. Look, except for my face, I am fine. It's important to me that we continue with the project."

Sully listened intently. His response was settling to the group. He said, "What can I say except I apologize for what happened to you. One person should not reflect upon my people. Many of us have pride about moving into a new relationship with the Armenians and other minorities. For us to become members of the European Union we must liberalize our ideas. I agree with the president. Today we are much more European and sophisticated than twenty years ago. What happened to you is not acceptable. I am appalled and embarrassed."

"As far as the project is concern, we will continue. I think I can speak for the researchers. I know they feel the same as me. When next we meet, I will have some progress to report but that won't be until you are up to it. From my past experiences, I can help you with your face. This is going to sound strange so please hear what I must say. I used to be a wrestler, mud wrestling, with a circus when I was young. It was the only way I could make money. Often, I was beaten severely because I wasn't very good. The wrestlers had a cure for my face swollen, bruised and cut, black and blue, especially under my eyes. They would soak my face in saltwater from the Bosporus or make a solution of salt and sugar brine. I soaked my face as long as I could hold my breath placing my face into the brine held in a large bowl, I held my breath for at least a minute. I did it fifteen to twenty times a day. It took the swelling, the black and blue color off my face, and the salt water really helped with the pain. I am saying this in all honesty. On many occasions, I was beaten much worse than you," and he smiled. "Look how handsome I still am."

He started to laugh and said, "Your face is not so bad. Soak it in the Bosporus water, you will be fine. I'll have some sent to your room in the next half hour."

He got on his cell phone and started speaking in Turkish.

Chapter 17

The conversation with Sully was easier than anticipated. After he left Frederic said, "I like him. He's more than just an expediter. A lot of these Middle East guys are not very good at anything except flopping their mouths. They are all bluster. They talk a lot but don't deliver. We looked into him and I think he can be a real asset to us in some other capacity when he's done with the work for you at the hotel. Of course, that's if you want him to have a role. Initially I think I'd like to place him with Arnouk on some of the money lending stuff. We can see how good he is and see if we can trust him."

Matt said, "Right now, all I really want to do is get out of Turkey. I'm sure you're right about him. The more stuff he does the more impressed I am with him. As of right now I'd just like to keep him on the hotel project with his research team. I'm sorry I sound a little self-pitying right now but shit my face and ribs really hurt. Since you and Gisele are here maybe starting tomorrow we can do some tourist things. I think I'll feel a lot better if I get outside."

Frederic answered, "I know we'll find the city really enjoyable."

"Its great fun and Bi Ba and I are good tour guides. If what Sully guaranteed me about the salt water and brine solution is true, I'll be much better by tomorrow."

"He says it will take down the swelling and discoloration. You'll feel a lot better when you look like a normal human being again."

"I don't know about the pain, though. You know I could be wrong, but I remember reading a long time ago, when Mohamed Ali was going to fight Joe Frazier for the first time, it was 1971, he soaked his face in brine to make his skin tougher so he wouldn't bleed and his eyes wouldn't swell shut. I also remember after the fight he was in the hospital for a couple days because of the beating he took. He looked grotesque. There was something about him soaking his face in salt water to get the swelling down. I don't know any particulars but if it was good enough for him it certainly will be good enough for me. Hell, I took just as bad a beating as he did."

He looked over at Gisele and said, "I think you're right about the pain medication. I'm just going to rely on Tylenol even though this hurts like hell. Like I said, I should be feeling a lot better tomorrow. We will show you guys around. I will wear sunglasses and Bi Ba has already purchased some makeup. I know I will feel better. If I don't look better, so what. What's one more freak on the street? It'll be good for me to be outside. You'll just love Istanbul. Maybe even later tonight we will walk down the street to the Turkish bath house. You guys have not seen one of those yet. Maybe we can talk you in to it."

As Matt stopped to get his breath he had another thought, "There are all kinds of restaurants around here. The three of you can get something eat. I might have to drink my dinner." He tried to smile but it was really difficult. "In any event, you won't believe how good the food is."

The two couples stayed in Istanbul for another five days; part business but mostly pleasure. Frederic set a meeting with the hotel's local accounting firm which went well. The numbers were equivalent to a nine-cap rate, good for an A property hotel in the Middle East. Frederic thought the numbers were good and would present a full-fledged offer to the Canadian owners of the Four Seasons when he got back to New York.

He sent a letter of intent and a five percent deposit. He told Matt the negotiations were simple. "I'll contact some of our other investment partners," meaning, Guzman and the Tijuana Cartel. "I'm sure they will participate. Like I said this should be simple and there is nothing extraordinary about our offer or their demands that should be problematical. It will be an all cash deal. That is the most important thing. They won't have to carry any paper. Gisele thinks it won't be a problem for a foreign LLC to buy a historical site in Istanbul with already existing foreign ownership. She thinks we are solid with President Gul. Turkey is really progressive but more importantly it wants to be a member of the European Union so there are no bribes or extraordinary fees. There is no major corruption to deal with in Istanbul so we don't have that problem. Hopefully I can tie this all up in maybe ninety to one hundred twenty days. When we get back I'll pass everything to our lawyers. They will put it in play. From our point of view, it's a done deal. The big stuff is easy to negotiate, we'll let them have all the small stuff. Like I always say don't sweat the small stuff, it might only be one percent of the total project cost but Canadians like to think they're getting a really big deal. The small stuff is always emotional so when we let them have it they feel better about the negotiations. The things we will give them are small things like indemnifying against any legal costs if there are any problems but it guarantees the deal will get done. Our counterparts in Toronto are not litigious so I don't foresee any major problems once both sides sign off. Like us they want everything to be clean. It might cost $1,200,000 to $1,300,000 per door but that's okay. There will be no remodeling costs and we don't have to upgrade anything at the hotel. I really see an upside in this investment. Between the hotel, itself and what you want to do as far as the museum is concerned I am bullish. Both financially and politically it makes a lot of sense. Maybe because I like this place, I really like this deal. How many other people can say they own a prison hotel? There is not much more. You look at little tired," he said to Matt. "So why don't you rest for a while? We're going to our suite and hopefully get a nap. We will sleep for a few hours if we're lucky."

"If you're up to it later, we'll go out to dinner and see that Turkish bath."

He started laughing, "My treat. I'll bring the straws."

Chapter 18

The day before the two couples were to leave Istanbul, Sully called Matt and said, "I sent over a preliminary report drafted by one of the team. Its content is a narrowly defined work in progress on Malgan Malgan drafted by Professor Celal Cindoruk and his staff."

It was at the hotel early enough for Matt to have access before leaving for Los Angeles.

Papaz told Sully, "Give me his number I will call him right after I get off the phone with you. I want to talk to him even before I get into this thing. I'd like some insight on where he's coming from. This is not a business or academic analysis so if he has a bias I can deal with that. It's fine for him to have an agenda but I just like to know the what and where fors of his thinking. I can't believe how fast his team came up with something."

Sully told him, "There were at least five graduate assistants. They were extremely enthusiastic about the project. You must know young people in university have this special romantic notion about doing an American project, especially research. For these students, it's not the money it's the prestige of working with Dr. Cindoruk." The conversation ended by Sully giving Papaz the professor's cell number.

In Cindoruk's Americanized English, he said, "I had a cousin living close to Los Angeles in a suburb called Encino. I lived with my cousin's family and went to high school, then to Cal State University Northridge, where I got my bachelor's degree in mechanical engineering. Then I went to MIT and got my PhD and decided to come back to Turkey because the academic opportunities were greater."

He said to Papaz, "My findings are preliminary and of course our research is very dynamic. There are many anecdotal stories or other information that might interest you."

Papaz let him talk. He always felt listening was a greater gateway to knowledge than talking himself.

Without being too academic the professor said, "We attacked the project from many different directions. Malgan Malgan is almost mythical in proportion and one of our problems was dialing down the amount of information. We attacked it first from a social media standpoint. I wanted my students to have fun with it. While working on the project I found one of my student's family comes from Harpoots where Malgan Malgan was born. He lived there until he was approximately thirteen. My student's father contacted some of Malgan's family members and they are talking with third-generation Malgan cousins. These people are not much more than town gossips or rumor mongers but they will give us some direction and keep us within a margin of his activities as a young person. It is all myths and rumors but it does at least lay down a path. I directed two of our assistant researchers to the University of Istanbul genealogical archives. There are treasure troves of genealogical information there amassed after the massacres in 1914. It is very much on par with the Mormon Church Genealogical Institute in Salt Lake City, Utah. There's a lot of information at our disposal. It is not only about Armenians but Turks as well. We are also scrolling through all government databases for his timeframe in Turkey. They are sketchy at best but any information can lead us in the right direction."

Cindoruk paused for a minute. "We have a problem only you can resolve. Much of our research is at odds with your Aunt Helen's version of his life. It is commonplace for family historians to embellish and even prefabricate events to entertain their clan. This is how myths and legends at a familial level are generated. Every generation the stories are passed down they become bigger and bolder. Everything we pulled up shows he was a great man and his philanthropic endeavors helped the Armenian and Turkish causes. Our problem is much of her chronology and dates are out of order. Most of the things he did that gave him the resources to help others came after he arrived in America. He was a major sponsor of the Armenian separatists but that was after he made his fortune in America. He, I hope I am not as we say in Turkey poisoning your aunt's well, was almost a Renaissance man. We found Malgan Malgan was self-taught. We have accounts he learned mathematics to the degree of calculus on his own. He read all the great European and American authors and was greatly involved in American and Turkish politics. I want to express something that's very sensitive and hopefully won't be offensive to you. It is my honor and my privilege to work on this project but for my name and the name of my assistants to be attached to it we must separate the truth from myth. There is a great American academic named James Campbell who was famous for his work with American Indians. He discussed their myths, legends, and storytelling and how important it was to their heritage and place in America. I feel our work for your museum should differentiate between academic and mythological details. We are going to separate them but for anyone who goes through the museum they should have the ability to enjoy the myths and legends of this great as long as we're honest about their role in his real life."

Cindoruk paused again, "I must apologize for lecturing you on process and etiology. I just want to present you information that will be worthy of your hotel walls. One of my assistants even wants to put technology into play in presenting the history of your cousin. He wants to create some interactive visual effects. More than photographs but we'll discuss that later. What your aunt remembered from the passage of other oral historians in your family and which she added to by prefabricating some events are only what people want to remember about Malgan Malgan. The past can be wonderful because only the mind can revisit it. Historians who are not academically trained pass on a romanticism that must not be lost especially when we're talking about family or tribe. Especially when we're talking about clan. There is always an aggrandizement when we talk about our own people. The optimist's recounting of events can be naïve but it is the essence of man's best life recollections. We portray Malgan Malgan as a great man because he was. Our research must be in real terms and based on proven facts. The myths and legends about this great man are not going to die so we feel they should be presented as an entertaining element to his history. I think when you see what we have done the two-approach meshing does work."

"When you read the report, there is a section, for your eyes only. To make sure we were on the right track we had to investigate you and your background to find out if there were any confluences in civil or business or political intersections in the two of your lives. We expanded our research to look at some of your charitable organizations, your business interest, and your civic and political stances on major issues. We wanted to see if there's any cross correlation between you and Malgan Malgan not obvious on a cursory inspection. Because of my scientific background, we extensively use some programs used for forensic investigation by police departments to tie elements of information together we would never contemplate doing. Let me give you an example. Your aunt said he was wealthy. In gathering his immense fortune, we found out some of your investments have benefited greatly by some of the patents, that's right, I used the word patents because he was an inventor. He wasn't just a farmer. He made the bulk of its $500 million fortune on patents and something your aunt was remiss in expressing. In academics, we sometimes use the phrase degrees of separation[1] to express closeness.

There is a very small degree of separation between your business pursuits and his innovations. He held more than eighty patents many of which purchased by Howard Hughes' Baker Tool Company, the largest makers of drill bits for mining and oil production in the world. Some of your mining investments in Zimbabwe and Kenya use their technology and equipment and because of that you are not plagued with most African mining interest problems. Your mines' history shows impressive safety records regarding fires and actual mines collapse. Most of his drilling technology patents are offshoots or derivations of his three-point hitch and leverage technology for tractors that he developed in the 1930s. You'll see in great detail how it transforms the use of mechanics on the farm and increased farm production. Many people think he was one of the great minds leading to the 20th century agricultural revolution."

"In the for your eyes-only section, we make clear the degree of separation between you and your cousin is extraordinary small. It was as if a magnet pulled your minds in a single direction. He was an inventor and you are a financial visionary but there is a sameness coupling your society views and created a consciousness. I apologize, I am getting ahead of myself but I'm really excited for you to receive some of this information. Like I said before, everything is dynamic flux and of course I have no agenda except presenting to you in the best of our abilities a picture of Malgan Malgan and how closely aligned the two of you are. When you read the document, you will see we have presented the most objective historical accounts possible. We feel there is substantial connection between the two of you."

Papaz listened for over 20 minutes. The depth and scope of the analysis impressed him. "I hope you know, I will be corresponding with you as soon as I look at your paper. I am bringing it with me on the plane. Hopefully I will have read it by the time I get home. We are going by private jet so I will have access to the internet. If we can work out the timing I will probably iChat or videoconference call you and your associates. I'm really looking forward to reading your take on my cousin and how events thirty years later have had an effect upon me. Your enthusiasm is infectious. I can't wait to look at your work. As well as I know myself," he started to laugh, "You should probably expect correspondence from me as soon as we get to the airport. If I weren't so busy between now and tomorrow he stopped for a second, you might even hear from me later tonight. When I get back after dinner I'm sure I am going to put my head in the project. Your observation about Malgan Malgan being famous for his quote, money, fuels choices, is very interesting to me. Some people want to make money because of their insecurities in life. It sounds like he wanted to make money because it could fuel social change and it gave him the power needed to facilitate making the right decisions for other people."

Cindoruk said, "There's much about the two of you that is more than coincidental. You have lived your lives with such a small degree of separation it is almost as if there is something similar in your DNA. There is a common thread of greatness about the two of you. I know you're busy Mr. Papaz. I will let you get off the phone. May I say it's a pleasure and a privilege to be able to work with you?"

Chapter 19

After a final touring day including visits to the Topkapi Palace in the heart of the Sultanahmet district they return to the hotel in the late afternoon. Upon entering their suite Matt opened the materials sent by Sully.

He told Bi Ba, "If I get started on this stuff, I'll never put it down but I've been thinking about it all day. How about if I call Frederic and see if they mind going for an early dinner and leaving tonight. What do you think?"

She replied, "Sleeping in the plane or sleeping at the hotel doesn't make much difference to me. I know how anal you are. I'm sure you want to get into the research. Sure, it's fine with me."

He called Frederic. His friend's response was simple and concise. "If you guys want to leave tonight, that's great. We can eat or not. We don't care."

Matt said, "There is a place we must take you guys before you leave Istanbul. It's called Lebi-i Deya. It's off Taksim Square on top of the old Richmond Hotel. It has a spectacular view of the European side's old part of the city. I'm going to call the concierge and have him set it up."

Matt called Alvarez to let him know of his plans for dinner. The security team followed them to the restaurant. An extra reservation was made for Alvarez and a task force female member. They were situated three tables from the Papaz party, providing protection both inside and outside for the two couples.

In front of the hotel at 8:00pm, their town car arrived. Aware of the two-car world, the driver accompanied his vehicle from the hotel across the Bosporus to the restaurant. He followed the first car and was followed by a second. A sandwich of identical vehicles traveling to Taksim Square's pedestrian area where they turned at the embankment and parked at waterway's edge. The two couples were delivered to the Richmond Hotel front entrance.

The old hotel had only one elevator going up the dilapidated looking 19th century building's side to the rooftop restaurant. They took the small penthouse elevator then walked up one flight of stairs to the most beautiful setting Frederic and Gisele had ever seen. The whole European side of the city with its glistening lights laid before them. They were greeted by a hostess asking if they could wait for just one minute.

Outside the Lebi-i Deya eating area and bar was a patio encircling the building roof. Tables set for bar and club patron seating to smoke and partake while viewing the Bosporus and Blue Mosque. The beautifully designed, contemporary inside restaurant was Istanbul's first smoke-free eatery.

When the hostess returned, she walked them through the 360° patio into the restaurant and seating them near a floor-to-ceiling fireplace, the eatery centerpiece. While waiting for a waiter to order drinks the head chef came over and greeted them.

ISTANBUL

His English was limited. "You are guests of the Four Seasons Hotel. I have prepared a special meal for you. We call our food Mediterranean infusion. It is a mix of Moroccan and French. It is our pleasure to be of service. Please enjoy yourselves."

He walked back to the kitchen. Alvarez and his woman associate were seated to the left between their table and the long bar.

Alvarez's associate noticed a group of three men sitting at the bar who seemed out of place. They all had close cut military haircuts and filling their clothing as if they were muscled Special Forces. They were more interested in looking at the Papaz table than the beautiful women at the bar.

She said, "I'll walk over to the bar and get a better look."

She ventured across the room and stood next to the three men and ordered two drinks. She picked up on two important things. They were carrying guns and they obviously weren't interested in her flirtatious smile. While she was standing at the bar Papaz got up from his table, walked to the restroom.

One of the three men peeled off his barstool and followed. Alvarez immediately got up and walked at a fast pace pushing through the crowded bar area, he reached Papaz at the men's room door. The three men converged at the same time. Papaz walked over to a bathroom stall and opened its door. The Turk started walking towards the closed stall and Alvarez bumped into him acting the part of a drunk.

He said in English, "Sorry."

The large Turk tried to push him away. By this time Papaz finished relieving himself and walked out of the stall the two men were still confronting each other. The large Turk never had a chance to harm Papaz because three more men walked into the bathroom.

When Papaz got back to the table Alvarez was already sitting down with his companion texting him. Don't look or react. The three guys at the bar want a piece of you. Have dinner and drinks. When you leave two of our men will escort you out of the restaurant.

Matt did not say a word to Bi Ba, Frederic, or Gisele about the incident. After finishing dinner Matt said, "I'll get some cigars." Looking at the two women, "How about a pack of Turkish cigarettes? We have to go out on the patio and smoke and have one last Raki."

They paid the bill, walked out onto the patio, sat at a table and ordered the traditional Turkish drink. The three Turks stayed at the bar and watching their prey. Matt finally mentioned what happened in the restroom. "Don't worry, everything is under control. I didn't want those ass holes to ruin our dinner. When we leave, Alvarez's men will take us down the elevator and the car will be waiting."

They stayed, smoked and finished their drinks. After twenty minutes, they rose from their seats and walked toward the elevator and left the restaurant.

Once outside the Richmond Hotel, they followed their two guards and walked across the street to the water's edge. The night became cooler because of the grave yard fog coming off the Bosporus. They used it and the unlit walkway to their tactical advantage. When approached by the three Turks, continuing down the path setting a trap for their three Turkish friends was the goal. Before they could accost Matt, the three men lying in wait behind a large dumpster next to the walking path were surrounded by six of Alvarez's man brandishing AK-47s. The three Turks surrendered. Within seconds they were handcuffed with plastic ties and their mouths were taped shut with duct tape. The men were then pushed down to the ground and propped up on their knees.

Matt left Bi Ba, Frederic, and Gisele, ran over to Alvarez and yelled, "Give me your gun!"

He called over to the Turkish woman who was in the bar with Alvarez and said, "Be my interpreter. Tell them who I am. Give them my name."

Before she could finish the sentence, he slammed the gun against the closest man's leg and pulled the trigger. The 9 mm went straight into his thigh.

Papaz looked at the interpreter, "Tell him he has ten seconds to tell me who in the fuck he is and who sent him. Why are they following us?"

She related the message in Turkish and the wounded man shook his head in an up-and-down motion as if to say okay. Papaz pulled off the duct tape. The bleeding man said his name was Onot Ozkan the brother of Ozgur Ozkan. They were there to get revenge. Papaz had ruined his brother's military career and they were going to kill him as a payback. The two other men were cousins and they all were in the military. The three men's reputations had been destroyed by the lies Papaz told authorities about his brother and their careers in the military were all but over.

Papaz reflected for a second and shook his head in disbelief. He undid the belt from his slacks and put it around the wounded man's leg and pulled it as tight as he possibly could to act as a tourniquet.

He looked at the female interpreter and said, "Tell him I just gave him back his life. Tell him his brother lied and this will stop. Right here tonight or I will kill him and his pathetic brother and everyone in his family. Is that clear?"

Alvarez told the interpreter to have him tell Okan he is lucky this time. If I ever feel his breath on the back of my neck I will have all of you killed. He looked directly into the soldier's eyes and said, "Do you understand?"

Alvarez told one of his men to take the soldiers' identity cards, license, and everything including wallets. "That should scare the shit out of them. Let'em go. They'll find their way back. We don't have time for this shit anymore."

The group walked back to their waiting cars to be taken to the other side of the city.

Alvarez received a phone call. After disengaging the phone, he said their suitcases and all personal belongings could be shipped from the hotel to the airport by courier if they did not want to go back to the Four Seasons.

"We can do whatever you would like. It will not slow us down to have a courier drop off your bags. I have talked to the pilot, we can take off within fifteen minutes after arrival at the airport."

ISTANBUL

Bi Ba said, "I don't need to go back for any reason. Looking at the other three she said how about you? They all agreed to drive directly to the airport."

Matt and Bi Ba in route discussed whether to stay in their brownstone in Chelsea for a couple of days or fly directly home to Los Angeles. As they approached the airport Matt told Frederic and Gisele he wanted to somehow bring Ozkan and his cousins into their fold.

"We have time before we come back here so I want you to put your thinking cap on and figure a way we can get them to work with us. Create some job, I don't know, maybe even security. I would rather have them with us than against us. It is always better to have your enemy inside your tent pissing outside instead of him hating you and plotting some retribution against you from outside trying to piss into your tent."

Bi Ba said, "I can't believe you said that with a straight face. You sounded like your friend Kasogi, spouting off stuff about the desert. Maybe we've been in the Middle East too long. I'm just kidding, but is buying this hotel going to make a change in you? Are you going Armenian on me?"

They all laugh. The driver made a U-turn and told his passengers they would be at the airport in less than thirty minutes.

The traffic was light. At approximately 11:45pm, they arrived at the private aircraft satellite of Istanbul's International Airport. They waited in the lounge of Million Dollar Flying Service for less than ten minutes while the pilot resubmitted his flight plan. The copilot and the four crew members, three flight attendants and one business secretary, took their bags from the town car and stowed them into the aircraft. An area of the plane had been set up to act as an office with two computers each individualized to its own desk and a fax machine.

As soon as they were seated in the plane's lounge section Matt called over the secretary and asked, "Please make three copies of this forty-page document."

Bi Ba rolled her eyes and asked, "Are we going to be subjected to analyzing this Malgan Malgan guy?"

She started laughing and directed her comments to Frederic and Gisele as if Matt wasn't in the plane. "It isn't bad enough, Matt has a romantic interest in some Armenian dead guy. It is twice as bad he almost got killed over that guy's son. Now I think he's going to have the gall to ask us to read about him. I don't even know how to express how dumb that is."

She looked at the secretary and said, "I don't want to put you in an uncomfortable position but we don't need any additional copies of the document. I hope none of you mind, but it's late and I'm going to try to get some sleep." She kissed Matt on the cheek and said, "I know you can't help yourself. Have a good time with your cousin."

Frederic and Gisele decided they would watch a movie and wished both their friends a good night.

Part V -- Malgan Malgan

Chapter 20

Matt moved from the beige Napa leather stadium chair into the rear of the plane and adjusting the overhead lights, he pulled up a footstool and took off his shoes and socks. Still standing he untucked his blue plaid shirt from his pants, sat down with his legs extended comfortably and started reading the document: Malgan Malagn, whose real name was Haige Malganian.

Malgan was born October 26, 1904 in the eastern Turkish city of Harpoots. By all accounts, he was very verbally precocious. His parents considered him overly active or hyperkinetic, compared to his three siblings. Being the youngest, Malgan received the most attention, pampered by parental and grand parental stimulation, undisciplined and an American doctor from Massachusetts, Richard Jebejian, during his yearly visit to Turkish relatives diagnosed him as manic. Today he would be defined by the DSM 5 as high functioning with Asperger's disease. Jebejian prescribed lithium sent from Istanbul to counter the young boy's chemical imbalance. Research tells us, his mania was managed with drugs for the rest of his life.

By the age nine, he displayed signs of brilliance but his socially challenging mental disease plagued him. He had no need for friends but tolerated family and intellectually knew their importance. He had an investigative mind, always exploring engineering and mechanical inventions entirely by visual examination of pictures. He did not learn how to read until he was in his early thirties. Over his lifetime, a small circle of acquaintances were mostly held at arm's length. What he called his outer circle, people were in his life for expediency, simple embellishments for his business and charitable endeavors.

The young Malgan Malgan was raised in the impoverished city of Harpoots. It was trifurcated into segregated areas. An Armenian district, primarily Christian, mercantilism and education as important family traits. The second section was the Turkish section, exemplifying militarism, low-level labor skills, authoritarian compliance and Islamic teachings. The third section inhabited by Arabic speaking Assyrians agrarian in nature cloistered from European modernity exhibited large swaths of poverty.

No one in the Malganian family was formally educated. Baldon Malganian, Malgan's father, was highly skilled for someone from his socioeconomic strata. He was a mechanic, specializing in farm equipment, could not read nor write and due to exorbitant employment finder's fees, he was an indentured servant. Obtaining a job cost the older Malganian two years' salary in a single lump-sum payment and thirty-five percent of his yearly income for the remainder of his life. His wages were subsistence level for the family of six. They lived in a mud dwelling within the city's limits.

Shoci Malganian, Malgan's mother, was a church woman, whose only job outside God's cathedral walls was taking care of her family. The one room adobe house cordoned off by sheets housed four siblings with perimeter sleeping areas for their parents and Shoci's mother and father. In the inner portion of the wall less dirt floor structure was a stone fireplace acting as stove and heater. The low hanging thatched roof's hole acted as fireplace ventilation. Life was difficult for the Malganian family.

Research of similar area families shows average caloric intake was less than eleven hundred calories per person, per day. Child mortality rates were approximately fifty percent, Malgan had three siblings who died by age five. Because of a protein deficiency, both older brothers were mentally underdeveloped. They were viewed as dullards because they lacked intellectual acumen. One other, older brother died from tuberculosis at age twenty. In 1920's Harpoots, the average persons' and Malgan's lives were harsh and immobile.

Being a high intellect person, he was aware of his circumstances and expressed a desire to be different. He wanted to leave Harpoots and move to Istanbul or to the United States to be with his uncle. By eleven years old he worked as a garage/maintenance shop apprentice where his father worked. His grasp of mechanics was extraordinary and within five years he became lead mechanic for the small business. The master mechanic and shop owner had Malgam troubleshoot all the garage's difficult jobs. He was given his own shop area to develop new products and by eighteen years of age his income doubled his father's, surpassed only by the garage owner. Even though uneducated, he passed his time immersing himself into studying automated tractors. Tractor technology came to the Eastern region of Turkey in 1916 so it was in its infancy.

John Deere developed the first motorized tractor in 1901. By the time Malgan was eighteen years old and fully cognizant of its technology it was the early 1920s. He was the shop's lead mechanic and specialized in agricultural machinery. The problem of linkage was of paramount importance to farmers who were trying to modernize agricultural production methods. Malgan convinced the shop owner to add a gas station and parts department to their existing business encapsulating and monopolizing the tractor business.

In 1922 he convinced his employer to expand the shop and allow a John Deere dealership to be established in partnership with the Turkish mechanic shop. Malgan took a percentage of the profits in lieu of a salary which was unprecedented in Turkey. From 1922 until he migrated to the United States in 1930 he was solely responsible for overseeing the John Deere division of the company. The money saved from this business endeavor facilitated the United States trip with his older sister and two cousins. A successful American life passage started in 1931. He attributed it to his new family in Fresno, California.

Chapter 21

After Malgan Malgan came to the United States, he lived in Fresno, California, heart of the San Joaquin Valley. Staying with his two cousins, Elia and Aslan Aslan who owned an expansive 5,000-acre cantaloupe ranch on the American River banks, Malgan's value as a mechanic was immediately recognized. His managerial skills became apparent and within six months, he persuaded his two cousins to mechanize the enterprise with the latest technology. He did not have skills to present his financial analysis in writing so he verbalized the Aslan's financial opportunities versus the short run costs and won approval.

He was so embarrassed about being uneducated, even though he was articulate, he undertook the self-taught route learning mathematics through calculus and read all the classics in the coming years.

In farming's cyclical boom/bust nature, luckily the Aslan's financial reserves allowed solvency until their newly purchased technology garnered greater productivity. Their new tractor fleet mixed with the existing labor force increased the farm's gross margins by more than four hundred percent.

Malgan was responsible for introducing the latest John Deere models to San Joaquin Valley. He convinced them tractors and automated sprinkling system complemented irrigation ditches extending out from the American River. He set up a mechanic's, garage division of Aslan's businesses expanding Aslan Enterprises by adding retail services. Their business ultimately monopolized the Valley's tractor repair services.

In 1934 he developed and patented the three-point tractor hitch system, allowing farm implements to be attached to the tractor's back bumper. Plows or other farm implements the operator attached to the tractor gave the farmer additional choices for tilling the soil at different angles and different depths. He developed a drawbar allowing the tractor to drag or pull farm equipment. On numerous occasions over time Malgan and his foundation extended the patents and it is still in full force. The hitch or lever as it was called is still the industry standard. After his invention was patented, he sold the rights to John Deere Corporation for a gross sales percentage. His foundation still receives royalties. The Malgan Malgan Foundation developed a new drawbars generation and being produced by the Mahindra Tractor Corporation, now the largest producer of tractors in the world. The royalties from the two corporate giants constitute the largest bulk of income flowing into the Malgan Malgan Foundation which has assets of over $650 million.

By 1935 Malgan's expanding duties positioned him as the managing general partner of the Aslan cousins' farm. However, the same year, he was diagnosed with the mental disease of mania, but, his active mind used the more responsibilities and work to produce greater feelings of accomplishments.

He positioned their business into oil drilling efforts because the farm's marginal foothill lands could not be used for agriculture. Wells on the property produced less than one-hundred barrels a day per well. He developed pro rationing and fracking technology to increase their production leading to development of more than thirty drill bit patents. His primary patent a rotary drill bit derivative exclusive rights were sold to the California industrialist and aviator Howard Hughes. Hughes formed a new division of his father's industrial drilling business for the sole purpose of producing drilling bits for oil production. Hughes later merged with Baker to become Hughes Baker, largest worldwide producer of oil bits and coring bits. Malgan signed a consulting contract to work for the Hughes Corporation and ultimately, he developed directional drilling bits used for slant drilling. He helped Hughes innovate new, cheaper drilling technologies for underground mining as well.

Many technologies are used in Papaz mines in Zimbabwe and Kenya. The technology creates a more stable structure going through igneous rock formations which in turn creates less probability of the mines collapsing. Because the cleaner boring and coring methods used in the mining process the underground tunnels in the geological formations have smaller gas pockets and carbon dioxide venting becomes easier. There is no way of quantifying the number of people's lives saved but this technology makes mining safer.

There is a major connection or minimal degree of separation between you and Malgan because your mines in East Africa were first to use this technology. Your mine operators first purchased the technology for safety concerns, opting for safety over profits and is something your cousin would've done.

Malgan's rotary oil bits lowered the production costs over fifty percent. It revolutionized the industry and Malgan once again made lots of money, bought some land and mineral rights options in Bakersfield, heart of San Joaquin Valley. Malgan partnered with Arman Hammer and purchased a small stake in newly formed Occidental Petroleum. We know Mr. Agnon Kasogi of Egypt, one of your investment partners, was instrumental in helping Hammer negotiate with Qaddafi of Libya. Occidental Petroleum not only drilled for Libyan oil, they established refineries and Malgan was responsible for engineering the most sophisticated oil industry pipeline systems. As usual he made exorbitant profit amounts directed to his foundation.

Over time as your cousin accumulated wealth, he became more involved in the Armenian community. Instead of helping people migrate to the United States and provide them with housing and jobs he invested his time and monies in convalescent homes for the aged Armenian community. Kirk Krikorian one of his aviator friends who he met in Fresno was a prominent poker player, introduced him to the game, taught him how to fly jet aircraft and Malgan's farm had the Valley's first jet aircraft runway. The two men collaborated in building old age homes and medical facilities for the Armenian community. Krikorian played an instrumental role in Malgan's financial affairs from that point. Malgan invested with Krikorian in his fledgling Transamerica

Airlines which later became Western Airlines. He lent money to Krikorian to build the Hilton International and Gaming Hotel in Las Vegas, Nevada. He helped finance Krikorian's gambling empire and the purchase of the MGM movie studio. Both men were avid poker players and legend has it they would have home games in their respective houses in Fresno and Los Angeles with buy-ins of as much as one million dollars. The high-stake games brought in poker players from all over the world. This again is a small degree of separation from you. We know of your poker skills and some of the legendary games you played throughout the world. Also, Krikorian was involved in business ventures with Kasogi who is a known business partner of yours in the hotel business. Krikorian's MGM casinos run the gaming in the Four Seasons Hotel in Papagayo and Costa Rica where you are a minority partner.

Malgan in his later years allowed many of his enterprises to be overseen by Mr. Robert Manugian who became the acting CEO of his Corporation, Malgan Enterprises, and his foundation. Malgan stayed as chairman of the board of both entities, but his brilliance was now directed to Middle East politics. He became a technology and science advisor to Egyptian Anwar Sadat. Eventually, he helped Sadat manage his family's personal finances. During his life's political passage, he fathered two sons. Stanley Malgan born in the United States to one of his many female companions and a son in Turkey. We only have information about his American child. Both children were fathered in his sixtys. We theorized because of Malgan's advanced age for bearing children, his son Stanley was born with mental defects. We have no collaborative facts for the case of his Turkish son. Looking at Turkish psychological community literature, statistical analysis shows a correlation between advanced age and bearing offspring having mental disorders. The correlation is once a male reaches forty years there is a geometric relationship between father's age and infant mental illness. We surmise Stanley was one of these children. He was diagnosed as pathological at eight years because of his treatment of animals. He killed domestic pets on his father's farm by torturing them and then he set them ablaze. He was obsessed with fire, a pyromaniac. He also was diagnosed as sexually abusive and narcissistic. In his prepubescent years of ten to twelve he was arrested on two occasions for indecent exposure. His legal records were expunged because of his father's wealth but we have newspaper accounts of his aberrant behavior. It's not exactly clear what criminal activities he was involved in but he may have murdered three classmates at Fallridge a college preparatory school in Northern California. His reputation in San Francisco as a lawyer is one of being unscrupulous and heavy-handed. His wealth has created a hedonistic lifestyle of women, drugs and violence. The legal community fears him. He contested his father's trust the first day of Malgan's death. He receives a stipend from the foundation of $100,000 a month which he uses lavishly on his pleasures. It is rumored he buys the services of prostitutes both male and female. We believe it is better you do not pursue him. Stay arm's length from this man. He is a psychopath with extensive resources and enjoys inflicting pain.

Chapter 22

Matt was sedentary for almost five hours. While going over the materials he refused conversation, drink and food. He did not want to be disturbed. He made it abundantly clear he was tired of being harassed. After reading the document for hours he got up from the oversized chair and stretched. Everyone in the cabin was now asleep. He walked over to the restroom and washed his face and relieved himself. He walked to the plane's center aisle, stretched for a few minutes, did his Z-health exercises which took approximately five more minutes and resumed the same sitting position in his chair.

Papaz placed his feet on the footstool. He called one of the flight attendants and asked for his laptop.

"If it's not too much trouble I would really appreciate it." Ever trying to be polite he then said, "I can use one of the computers as he pointed to one of the desk set ups in the makeshift office, if it's too much trouble."

"It will be no trouble at all. We put most of your personal belongings in the front clothes locker closet, "the hostess said. "I'll be back in a second."

She walked to the front of the plane and got his Tumi over the shoulder strap case and presented it to him. He pulled out his Apple MacBook Air and a hard drive.

"Thank you very much," he said.

She asked if he needed anything else and he responded, "No thank you."

He retrieved a DVD from the research packet he had been given and placed it in the hard drive attached to his laptop. For over an hour he perused the researchers' photograph picture gallery compiled for him. The photograph collection and documents obtained mostly from public sources, i.e. newspapers and magazine articles. His Turkish team also contacted the Malgam Malgan foundation and obtain some stock photos and videos of Malgan that went back as far as the early 1910. The pictures ranged from birth to death. It was evident Malgan had a public face and notoriety over his life even though he did not covet it.

Papaz was fascinated by the metamorphosis over the years. He became more handsome and stately as he aged. This was not traditional for most Turkish or Middle Eastern men. Most of his peers dissipated in stature and became fat and dowdy with age. Malgan Malgan was 5'10" weighed approximately 160 pounds at his death. Papaz was amazed at the facts, he was almost the same physical size over the decades. Comparing pictures from the 1940s, 50s, 60s, 70s, and finally the 80s he looked almost the same. The face and body changes were incremental and almost perceptually impossible to see.

After reading about the man, Matt realized Malgan's mind matched his body. He lost no intellectual judgment or desire for growth in his advanced years. At death, he was still a person who casts a large shadow. In some of the videos it was interesting that he stood tall and walked with long steps. He did not stoop nor did he shuffle his feet as most elderly people did. He was peripatetic and ambled as if he were middle-aged. His shoulders were straight and his chin and was always pointed up. His posture was extraordinary. He had all his hair and did not become completely gray until his late seventies. His salt-and-pepper hair presented in his early forties stayed the same for more than three decades. It was almost surreal seeing the same human manifestation from mid-life into his elderly years.

Malgan's mind and physicality were not diminished by age. In a moment of reflection, Papaz recalled a conversation where he heard an apt phrase for his cousin, 'he must be well pickled, he never ages.' In Papaz's mind, a man's strength of character was measured by his soul and his accomplishments, not by physicality. True confidence comes from successful repetition and Malgan was never under prepared or over worked. A visionary who looked around corners where no one else's mind wondered, Malgan also had a tremendous work ethic.

After reading about his cousin, Matt knew this was a great man. What was most interesting to Papaz was all the document references about degrees of separation between himself and his cousin dealing with the world and its under-represented lower strata. It was as if Papaz were a modern Malgan.

All in darkness except for Papaz's cubby, the flight attendant who brought his laptop came to the back of the plane and asked him if he wanted anything to drink or eat. As she spoke she noticed the picture of Malgan on Papaz's computer. She asked, "Is that your father?" Looking at the full screen's black and white picture she continued, "He is a handsome man. You have the same eyes. Oh, my god, look at those old vintage cars. She caught herself and said, I don't mean to be so nosy."

Papaz smiled and said, "He was my cousin. I had some people do a work up on him because, I don't know it's, kind of a family genealogical thing. It's interesting. I wish I'd had the opportunity to know him. Thanks for pointing out the eyes. I was so absorbed in other things I really didn't pick-up on it, but you're right, I was so impressed by his accomplishments and having a chance to look at the surroundings I never took our physical similarities into consideration. I think you might be right about us looking like family. It's kind of frightening because our genes are really strong in my family." He chuckled and said, "We all look alike."

He asked if she had a second. "Sit down if you don't mind. I want to show you some incredible pictures."

He fumbled with his laptop, "If I can find them."

She smiled and said, "Sure I'd love to, I really don't have a lot to do right now."

He found a picture of Malgan in Egypt standing at the foot of the great Pyramids of Giza. "Now wait just one second," he said, as he went to iPhoto and pulled out a folder labeled Egypt. He found a picture of himself in front of the same pyramid.

He looked at her and said, "Is that scary? The only difference is I am a little more pretentious in my banana republic trekking gear."

He laughed as he flashed back to the black and white picture of Malgan wearing what appeared to be dark gray pleated pants, and a white short, sleeve shirt untucked and a pair of dress shoes.

"There is a phrase I'm running into all the time relative to my cousin. The phrase is, a simple degree of separation. It looks like he and I are clones."

He smiled and said, "Thanks for humoring me. I know it must be boring but thanks anyway."

She said. "It's not boring at all, Mr. Papaz, there's nothing more important than family and this is really interesting to me. Thank you for showing me your cousin, who by the way really looks like you but it is more than just the eyes."

Papaz replied, "Thanks again. I really wish I would've had an opportunity to know him. What's incredible is it seems our lives crossed paths somewhere. More than just the physical resemblance, oh well. Thanks again for humoring me."

Papaz decided to rest before they landed in New York. He stored his documents and detached the hard drive from MacBook Air and put everything into his Tumi bag and stowed it the overhead bin. He extended his chair into a reclining position, laid on his side and instantly fell asleep. He did not wake until he heard the landing gear lowering. He slept for over two and one half hours.

The flight attendant saw him move up on his arms to see his surrounding and said, "We'll be at JFK in less than forty minutes. You fell asleep like a rock. Pretty soon I will need to ask you to straighten up your seat and prepare to land. Can I get you anything?"

He nodded no. She smiled and walked away.

Bi Ba looked at him from across the plane and said, "How was your read?" She laughed, "Did I miss anything?"

Matt was still sleepy and did not want to deal with the sarcasm but replied, "You screwed up. Finding out about Malgan Malgan was better than sleep. The man was incredible. But like you always hear people say that's for me to know and you to find out." He sarcastically continued, "You'll never know."

She put her hands together as if she was praying and said in dead pan, "Please, please. I can't wait to find out about your late cousin," she started to laugh.

By the time, Frederic and Gisele chimed in. "Well let's hear it," Frederic said. "Was it worth not sleeping?"

Papaz said, "Okay, okay I'll fill you guys in later but he was an incredible man and there is, wow how do I say this, a connection between the two of us. It is more than just a statistical aberration."

Matt looked directly at Frederic, "As usual there is a caveat. There's even a kind of threat in the materials I want you to investigate. I think I mentioned it before but if I didn't, I'll make it quick. Malgan had an American son. His name is Stanley. He lives in San Francisco and is a lawyer by trade. There is a citation that's a clear warning to me, to us. I want you to look at. Basically, it says, don't investigate him. It's too dangerous! The researchers even put it in terms of don't have anyone else pursue him if it can come back to you. Stand arm's-length distance from this man. He is portrayed as pathological and a real sociopath. Here's what I want you to do. After you read the file and get a handle on this Stanley Malgan guy. Have Alvarez look into him. I don't want anything coming back to me. You know that means us."

Frederic responded, "I can't help saying this but why are people in your family so screwed up? Your cousin has at least two children we know. There could conceivably be more. They are both pieces of work. One is a sociopath. He pauses for a second, your researchers think he is so dangerous they ask you not to pursue him. The other thinks he is a modern-day Lawrence of Arabia or Yassar Arafat. They both sound like lunatics to me. Just as a point of interest, you haven't said a word about any Malgan Malgan problems. Is he normal or are you in some way protecting him?

Matt said, "I don't want to get into all of this right now because we're landing in a few minutes. If you look at the file, you'll see the researchers have their finger on why his offspring are crazy and he is not. Anyway, when you read the folder you'll get an understanding. I'm not kidding. analyze this guy"

Frederic said, "This is really messed up. I'll make some calls as soon as Gisele and I get home. We'll get on top of it."

He just shook his head and said, "Now I guess I better read the whole folder."

Bi Ba and Gisele chimed in and both acquiesced and said they better read the material as well.

Bi Ba said begrudgingly, "I guess you were right about asking for four copies of the stupid thing."

Matt said, "I'm not trying to make a big deal out of this but with our luck we can't rule anything out. The best part is I think you'll find him interesting. Maybe the worst part is I think I'm a lot like the guy. I'm sure you'll tell me what you think."

The plane landed. The four disembarked and went through the customs area of the JFK private planes satellite. A limousine was waiting for the two couples. Frederic and Gisele went back to his flat in Soho and Matt and Bi Ba went to their brownstone in Chelsea.

Frederic and Matt pulled out their iPhones in unison as if orchestrated and setting all electronics in their separate homes. Their doors would open, the lights go on, the coffee start brewing and all good things home would be waiting for the two couples at their respective dwellings.

Chapter 23

Matt and Bi Ba stayed in New York for five days to emotionally and physically cool down. His face was still swollen even though he was using the brine solution repeatedly during the day. Bi Ba decided to continue training at the Chelsea market Equinox gym. Matt hired a personal trainer for light workouts as well. His body was still sore but he wanted to engage in physical activity.

Bi Ba liked regimen admitting it for the first time, telling him as they made plans to go to the gym together, saying maybe she was a little more compulsive than she professed.

"It's also a form of psychological therapy," she said. "It takes my mind off everything."

Matt said, "I think I want to get back to the gym because I feel guilty. I haven't done a whole heck of a lot for the last three weeks. They walked to the Chelsea Market complex gym, only fifteen minutes from their brownstone. The two worked separately for an hour and one half. After cleanup, Bi Ba wanted to meet at the market juice bar before they walked home.

Walking back to their house, Matt called Frederic and pressed him on the Stanley Malgan investigation.

"I've been thinking," he told Frederic.

ISTANBUL

Frederic responded, "Can't wait to hear this one. Before you go off on some tangent and tell me what you want me to do." His voice deepened, "I have to tell you, you have too much free time on your hands. I'm sure all you've done is think about Malgansian and that's dangerous. Surely, the gym isn't enough. Promise me you won't go off halfcocked. Promise to talk to me before you decide anything. Okay, I got that off my chest, what do you want?"

Matt asked, "What have you heard about Malgan?"

Frederic responded, "It hasn't been twenty-four hours yet. I've made some calls. Gisele made some calls. We should hear something soon. Hopefully we'll have some preliminary Intel this afternoon. If not, we'll get something for sure by tomorrow. Slow down. I know you are pissed. That's not a good place to make any decisions. There's got to be more to this call than just asking me where we are on Malgan. What else do you have to tell me?" Frederic knew his friend well.

Matt continued, "I want to work through some intermediaries and have him represent us in some fictitious business that can't get back to us. I don't care how we do it. Even if it means we must buy a small business just to suck him in. I want him to represent us. Let him think we are an easy mark for either over billing us or even taking control of the company. Let's see how he operates. I want him close if we should deal with him. I have a feeling he will look at us as what I call the ATM client if we seem weak. If he is as greedy as the research said, he can't help but try to screw us over. You know, he will be so outrageously litigious just to bill hours he'll look at us as a cash machine."

Frederic interjected a thought. "You don't have to tell me we don't want things to come back at us. What is this, a play out of Sun Su's book the Art of War? Keep your enemy close?" Frederic cracked up, "Don't tell me you're reading again, that can be dangerous." He laughed a belly laugh. "All right, all right I'll get on it. We must be very careful. If he finds out you are a cousin, he will probably think you're going to contest the trust and you have eyes on Malgan's money. That could be dangerous, if what your Turkish friends have found out about him is not an embellishment. We will slow play him into representing us in some fashion or another. Just let me think about the best way to do it. Now that you have that out of your system, how about dinner for the four of us tonight? We will walk over to your place."

Matt said, "Bi Ba is here with me right now. We are at 15th on our way home from the gym. Give me a second."

He asked, "Do you want to go out with Frederic and Gisele?"

She said, "Sure"

Matt resumed, "Why don't you guys come by around 7:30 or 8:00pm?"

Frederic said, "I have something else to discuss with you. I guess you didn't spot our security team or you would've said something. Alvarez said they were good. Anyway, he doesn't think there's a problem but just to be safe there'll be two guys following you while you are in New York. There will be two guys following us as well.

His people and Gisele and I feel we left our problems in Istanbul but until we find out more about this Stanley Malgan, we can't be too careful."

Matt said, "Yeah I agree. I know you're right but every time I'm sure about something things always go upside down. The slope can be slippery and I don't want this to creep into something big. What's the military call it, military creep or something. Let's just make sure we don't end up someplace we don't want to be. Hopefully this will be different."

Frederic said, "We'll see you guys around 7:30. We'll talk about both of Malgan's kids and where we are with the hotel later tonight."

After dinner with their friends Matt and Bi Ba decided four nights were enough in New York City. They would use a new charter company, Jet Set Charter and arranged for a Dassault Falcon 7X for luxury passage back to Los Angeles. The sixteen-passenger aircraft with a range of 5,950 miles would be more than adequate. It would not have to refuel. The plane would fly at an altitude range between 33,000 - 45,000 feet. It's cruising speed of 570 mph bringing them into Los Angeles in five hours depending upon the weather conditions. They would leisurely leave JFK around 10 o'clock in the morning and reach the small private Van Nuys Airport, by 12:00pm.

Chapter 24

From Van Nuys Airport, Jet Set's hanger where the plane landed, the drive to their home in Bel Air took less than twenty minutes. The 405 freeway was uncrowded for 12 o'clock in the afternoon and the surface streets from Sunset Boulevard to Bellagio Drive were traffic free. As the car pulled up in front of the Villa Bi Ba said, "It's going to be nice to be home. We can just hang out until you feel better. There's nothing pressing."

They exited the car and walk through the grotto to the house front door. The villa's electronics activated during the flight over Nevada. Facial recognition software opened the large house's glass double doors.

Matt said, "Even though the plane was comfortable I got really cramped up. So, I think I am going upstairs and change. Then I'll go down to the gym. You need me to carry anything for you?"

She said, "No thanks. I'm just going to get the mail and I'll meet you by the pool when you finish working out."

He said, "All I'm going to do is some stretching and my Z-health exercises. When I get done I'll go sit in the Jacuzzi."

The Jacuzzi was part of the infinity pool overlooking the Bel-Air Country Club golf course. "I'll meet you outside."

Bi Ba brought the mail and a DHL package, labeled from Istanbul to a table was next to the swimming pool and waited for Matt.

As soon as he arrived she said, "I brought you a box cutter. I think it's your backgammon set."

Matt cut open the package and pulled the set from the bubble wrap encircling it. He unlatched the clasp holding the two board sides together and opened it. He grabbed the wooden and ebony chips he had picked in the little shop near the Four Seasons Hotel. Under the velvet bag holding the black and brown chips and dice was a small envelope. He opened it. There was a handwritten cursive note inside.

The header said, "Cousin: you told me you would be receiving information about my father and brother before you left Turkey. I understand you left under special circumstances and I apologize for your treatment. It is regrettable you were treated as my ally and therefore their enemy. When you are presented knowledge of my family it is now important that I see it. I now have questions about my brother. My contacts in America have expressed concern about him. Any information your researchers have unearthed relative to his activities and to my father are of great importance." It was signed, Alwan Al Bactar.

Matt was again impressed by his ability to articulate so well in English. He was well spoken on the beach in

Bodrum and abundantly clear in the message attached to the backgammon set. Matt read the note to Bi Ba.

She looked down the hill onto the golf course and the Pacific Ocean positioned west of their home. She turned around and looked at Matt.

"This crap never stops, does it? A couple of things really strike me. He's got contacts in the United States and they know where we live. And, she raised her voice not in anger but in distress, you can bet your life on it they'll contact us. He didn't leave an address or any way we can get the materials to him. It's strange. I know he doesn't communicate in any form of electronic technology. So, he is inferring he'll give us an address some time in the future?" She paused, "Which I don't foresee. Or is he going to have somebody pick it up?"

Matt shook his head. "I sure as hell don't know! Let's give this stuff to Frederic as soon as possible and let him and his people work it out. My first intuition is we give Al Bactar everything we got as soon as he contacts us. I have a suspicion it's not up to us what he does with it."

Bi Ba said, "I'll take a picture of it. She pulled her iPhone out of the back pocket of her jeans. She held out her hand for Matt to give her the note and she put it on the table. She took three pictures and emailed them to Frederic without any explanation. She did not want to bias his thinking by trying to explain anything.

"The note itself will speak for itself," she said. She got a response within ten minutes.

"I'll call back in a few minutes. I want to pass this along to Gisele and get her thinking on it. It seems either his people will contact you or maybe he'll be crazy enough to come himself. The Malgan brothers are real pieces of work. Every day it is something new. I will call as soon as Gisele gets back to me."

Chapter 25

Everything at the Papaz house was sedentary for the next five weeks. Bi Ba and Matt resumed their daily routines. Finalizing the Sultanahmet Four Seasons Hotel purchase required close contact with Frederic. Matt also worked with Sully and his research team on the hotel's museum conceptualization. Bi Ba concentrated her efforts working with one charity, The Village Nation.

Since Matt received the backgammon set, over forty days passed without hearing from Alwan Al Bactar. Frederic and Alvarez were collecting Intel on Stanley Malgan, investigating businesses justifying engagement of his services.

Both Matt and Bi Ba were comfortable with their new premise protection security team, allowing two guards to live in the villa's casitas. Bi Ba expected the other shoe to drop in Steven Malgan and/or Alwan Al Bactar relationships. Her phraseology was 'bad news or bad actors always come at the least opportune time' when talking to Matt about the inevitability.

Sully's team finalized their research on Malgan Malgan and chose a new candidate for analysis. They submitted the name to Papaz with an academic intent letter postulating why he was their choice. Tayyip Erdogan, Turkey Prime Minister was to be the next person of interest or influence depicted on the hotel walls. Papaz responded by email telling the team to put their maximum effort into profiling the politician as soon as possible. Sully answered affirming their efforts on Erdogan, emailing the following text.

"Our problem is too much information on the Prime Minister. His long public history requires condensing to make it readable, cutting down propaganda and political hyperbole, creating manageable levels. His very controversial long memory and uses executive power to send enemies to jail. What makes him intolerable is his very pompous and self-righteous attitude. Many of his opposition believe his Islamic extremism is tempered only by Turkey's secular past. His pathway would make a fundamentalist state governed by Shi'a law. He has the intuitions of a rat, no compromise ability and when pushed into a corner strikes viciously. Most of his followers are uneducated in Western ways, especially in central and eastern parts of the country.

He is autocratic and the young people in Turkey tire of his ways. There is much political unrest in Turkey today and he tried making solutions with an iron fist. He attacked the judiciary, the press and tried putting restrictions on social media. A covenant since Mustafa Kemel Ataturk, the first Turkey president, mandated a secular state with rights for all religions. Erdogan tried returning to the religious ways of centuries ago. He was very progressive and liberal in business but not religion. Under his direction, Turkey advanced economically so quickly the entrepreneurial and middle-class considered it appropriate for entrance into the European Union. But his conservative Muslim religious and social agenda associate controversy and paradox terms with him.

We found a link between Erdogan and Malgan Malgan and of course that makes one degree of separation between Erdogan and you. You will be especially interested in your life's trajectories. He too stayed in room #207. As Istanbul mayor running for a parliamentary seat in 1999, he stayed in the Four Seasons Hotel. He used it as his campaign headquarters and gave his acceptance speech there after winning the election as an Islamic Welfare Party candidate. He delivered his speech from the old jail patio.

At the place, Matt and Bi Ba took their pictures, there is a similar picture of Erodgan and his wife in the same position leaning against the banister in front of the jail."

Sully included the picture in the e-mail and continued, "He stayed in the same suite as you. He met Malgan as a young Muslim political leader at University. Malgan sponsored him opening Armenian community doors. At the time, he acknowledged religious diversity and wasn't such an Islamic zealot while he went to university and studying business.

You dealt with many of his contemporaries. Agnon Kasogi, one of your many business partners, financially sponsored some of his early ventures. Hopefully I'll be able to send a full report next week. Your friend and humble employee, Sully."

Two weeks passed quickly while Matt and Bi Ba became more comfortable with their daily activities. Part of the routine was going to the gym. They both frequented Spectrum Club at the Howard Hughes, Culver

City Promenade. This was another one degree of separation between Malgan, Hughes, and Papaz. Papaz after his daily workout walked to Starbucks, had a cup of tea and caught up on his email. At an outside table looking at his iPad he noticed a message from Sully with the Subject: Tayyip Erdogan. It was an extensive file. Matt knew it was the research paper he expected. He immediately went to Gmail opening his email.

The first section of the text was Erdogan's early life history. With a couple of hours before he had to go home, Matt decided to look at the document.

The prologue started off with: as with many Turks, it was a hard life for the young boy. Born in Kasimpara, an impoverished neighborhood of Istanbul, he lived with his first cousin because his mother and father could not afford to keep him. His parents returned to Rize, Georgia, where his father was a farm worker. He was not reunited with his parents until the age of eight when they came back to Istanbul. To differentiate himself from the other young men living primarily on the streets, he put all of his efforts into school and football. To augment the family's income, he worked as a street vendor selling lemonade and sesame seed pastries to passing cars. His mother and father were devoutly Muslim and he was subjected to rigorous religious training. His extremely dominant father berated his son verbally and abused him physically. As previously stated, his only outlet was school and sports where he joined every organization for an excuse not to go home and deal with his parents. He went to the primary school Imam Halip. He became class president, affording him a scholarship to secondary school. He worked hard and graduated with distinction from Eyup High School followed by continuation of his business studies at the Marmara University where he became class president and captain of the football team. In 1977, he graduated with the equivalent of a Master's degree in economics. His father always wanted him educated, but not westernized. Invited to play professional football with the local professional team, his father intervened severely beating him and forbidding his participation as folly. Even though, bigger than his father, he never lifted a hand, defenselessly accepting the beating, internalizing his father's hatred established his behavior towards others for the rest of his life.

His treatment of others became devious and insipid, saying what was politically correct then viciously transferring his anger in extraordinary ways. He was capricious and irrational in his hate for people who opposed his ideas. Erdogan learned religiosity captured his venom. Lacking self-confidence and coveting his parent's love he became a hateful young man. Outwardly, he was polished and socially correct at all times. He read the people's tides and said what they wanted to hear, but at the same time imposed his Islamic agenda."

Bi Ba arrived at the table for coffee and finding Matt totally engrossed in the document suggested, "Let's go on to the house where we both may work on our projects."

Matt agreed but kept on reading as she drove.

Chapter 26

"In 1974 Malgan Malgan was finalizing financial support relationships between a nongovernment organization and moderate thinking imams who were accepting the Armenian minority, he met Erdogan at the Ortakoy Mosque, Istanbul. Erdogan, a political organizer for the mosque and its strong university student following, was eloquent and articulate not a firebrand speaker for the cause. At that time, he was a staunch supporter of religious diversity and embraced the Armenian Apostolic Church as having an equitable religious community position in the country's capital. He was outwardly a secular state supporter, but inwardly favored Islamic fundamentalism and Shi'a law. His real interest was power in the new secular Istanbul and Imam Guncel, head of the third-largest mosque in metropolitan Istanbul was Erdogan's mentor and sponsor. Guncel was alleged to be moderate and educated in Great Britain before World War II.

Well respected and a voice of the new Turkey, Erdogan was considered a leading disciple and the under twenty-five age group community face of the mosque. Polished and moderate Erdogan was considered as a model for Turkey's religious states new secularism.

In reality, he held firm beliefs in conservative Sunni Muslim doctrine. His Islamic philosophies hidden until his political resources were large enough to prevail over European and Ataturk disciples' secular movements. His teachings and philosophies were obliged to be politically correct and westernized externally but held fundamental Islamic views internally. He conjectured it would be just a matter of time before he climbed the political ladder and autocratically imposed his conservative religious philosophies upon the community.

In 1974 when he met Malgan Malgan at an Ortakoy mosque religious conference, Malgan was so impressed by the young well-spoken respectful student he financially sponsored him by paying his tuition and giving him money to support his parents. Malgan also took Erdogan to Egypt to meet Anwar Sadat. Charming his Egyptian host, Erdogan was given direct access to Imam Nasar of Mohammed Ali mosque, largest Cairo mosque. The two men started a cross national relationship lasting more than twenty years until Nasar's death. Nasar was more conservative and fundamental than most imams of the post Abdullah Nasser period in secular Egypt. Discovered after his death, clandestinely he worked with and sponsored the Muslim Brotherhood. Teaching trickery and subterfuge, later became Erdogan's hallmark traits, both men were outwardly oriented towards the West moderate religious thinking but inwardly were unwavering fundamentalist faith. To Erdogan's credit, over his long career he politically adapted the art of compromise but only as a pragmatic necessity to keep power, not as a belief.

He took a Keynesian Western financial agenda, long-run macroeconomic wealth building view as his major economic development platform, understanding the need to balance entrepreneurial skills with government regulation and subsidy. He relied on a semblance of the Communistic Chinese entrepreneurial model but was pragmatic and willing to break all communist state rules to foster economic growth. Erdogan kept power through pragmatism not dogma. His only determinant was retaining the Prime Ministership and 15th century Islam, politically challenged him not to show bias regarding religious philosophy. If he were honest, he would have called from the heavens telling people he wanted to be the Caliph of the Turkish state.

As you will see, his policies and personality were responsible for Istanbul resurgence and illustrates his power collecting brilliance and cunning. For the most part, he hid his Islamic fanatical views like a wizard.

Over time as Malgan understood more about his sage's political ambitions and religious philosophies, he separated himself politically and financially from Erdogan. In 1984 just before Malgan's passing Erdogan was elected to Istanbul's Beyoglu District city chair position. He received a note of congratulations from his old sponsor using it as a platform continuing his friendship duplicity towards the Armenian community. In his first politically elected position, he was extremely successful exposing and then pushing for liberal financial positions. His judgment was being the district chair and delivering voters benefits allowed him more expression in his social platforms and started revealing more change toward a conservative religious direction. The oxymoronic liberal economic policy blending and conservative religious philosophy was acceptable to his district constituency.

By 1991 he became the party chair of the Islamic Welfare Party for all Turkey. He now became more brazen in religious philosophies but his successful economics made some of his Islamic views more tolerable. His understanding compromise importance and making concessions, verbally pushing his religion limits but politically voted moderately. He always concealed his true Shi'a law convictions and never had a political position strong enough to impose his will upon the community. With his highly successful economic platform this masterful politician withheld his religious agenda until Turkey was ready for sectarian changes.

On March 27, 1994, he won mayoral election for the city of Istanbul. The metropolitan area had a population of over thirteen million making it one of the largest cities in the world. Many of the opposition suspected he would impose Shi'a law but being pragmatic and not wanting to lose political power he decided not to fight urban center wars he could not win. The secular law tradition in Turkey and movement towards Western culture and modernity were too strong even for Erdogan. He used his energy and political capital tackling the city's most pressing fiscal and infrastructure's overwhelming issues, water shortages, pollution and traffic, not its social problems. The water shortage problem was solved by laying hundreds of kilometers of new pipelines. The garbage problem was eliminated with construction of the most modern state-of-the-art recycling facility in all Europe. Pollution was dealt with by the using more natural gas subsidized by the city. Short run tax increases to modernize the city's infrastructure led to its resurgence. He tackled traffic problems by building more bridges, viaducts and highways paid by a user's gasoline tax. In his first term 1994 to 1998, the city's ten percent economic growth was the highest of any major metropolitan area in the world. The police budget doubled in less than the half decade he was in office. The city's financial footing became so positive it produced a surplus used to pay down the city's bond indebtedness.

A simple one-degree of separation. In the 1974 meeting in Cairo he met Agnon Kasogi, guest of Malgan Malgan. Kasogi brought to the meeting his partner and brother-in-law, Sherif Al Nasser. You are in partnerships with both men in the hotel business. Erdogan has maintained communication with both men even until this day. Al Nasser, founder, and owner of Stella Beer Egypt, was persuaded to bring his brewing company to Istanbul in 1995. His corporation received tax credits, called revenue sharing incentives, amounting to millions of dollars. The subsidy was an incentive developed by Erodgan. It was an integral part of the city's campaign to bring in foreign investment.

Chapter 27

In 1999 the Islamic Welfare Party was alleged unconstitutional and was shut down by Turkish Constitutional courts on grounds it threatened the laicistic[2] order of the Turkish Penal Code. Their bombast and contemptuous disregard for sectarianism and religious distance from the state heightened their public displays in Taksim Square demonstrations. Erdogan became a constant speaker in the square trying to get public support to reinstate his religious party. His opposition to religious freedom and diversity came to the surface. He felt his party had made inroads against secularism[3] because of its economic transformation of Istanbul. He miscalculated his power and national determination not to accept intolerance for other people's beliefs. He was arrested for reciting a poem, The Siirt[4], in public which under Turkish law was regarded as an incitement to commit an offense and incitement to restrict religious freedom or racial hatred towards others. The poem included a venomous verse, the mosques are our barracks, the minarets our bayonets, and our faithful are soldiers against nonbelievers. With his conviction, Erdogan was forced to give up his political position as Mayor of Istanbul. He spent four months of a ten-month incarceration sentence. He completed the terms of his sentence in late 1999.

By 2001 he reestablished himself and gathered a trans-Turkish following in the conservative pockets of Istanbul, Ankara and the Eastern and Northern parts of Turkey. He established a new political party with the same platform as the Islamic Welfare Party, now called the Justice and Development Party. In 2002 Erodgan's party won a national election in a landslide but because he personally was restricted from political office because of his former indictment and arrest it was a shallow victory. The sub-chair of the Justice and Development Party, Abdullah Gul, became the Prime Minister. He held the office for less than one year. After a Supreme Election Board ruling allowing Erdogan to run for political office, Gul disbanded his government and called for new parliamentary elections. The Justice and Development Party won by even a larger margin, sixty-four percent of the electorate, and the legislative body named Tayyip Erdogan the new Prime Minister in February 2003.

In his new position as the country's leader he incrementally tried pushing Turkey into a more sectarian state restricting the rights of women, imposing de facto Shi'a law when applicable, and championing the cause of homophobia. He attacked the military and judicial hierarchy trying to replace its highest-ranking members with his own sectarian people. On the social front his policies were reactionary. On the financial and economic front, he followed the teachings of Vartan Tashjian, an Armenian professor at Marmara University, who was Turkey's leading Keynesian advocate. Turkey's economy under Erdogan's guidance with the use of massive fiscal policy infusions as his primary tool in fighting deflation increased the manufacturing base and the country's exports by more than ten percent in his first two years in office. It was an economic revival moving Turkey from a net importer to a net exporter. An increasing GDP caused a wealth redistribution fostering a young professional class beginning. With educational opportunity expansions, economic manufacturing subsidies, export related industries and entrepreneur's tax incentives, Turkey had one of the fastest-growing economies in the world.

Between 1990s and early 2000's there were signs of a deviation in society. The first flank was Turkey became more religiously extreme and fundamental, the second most religious Western countries followed the United States with its Christian majority. No other country in Western Europe was as religiously conservative as Turkey. The second flank of bifurcation was growing professional class in the major cities who were noncommittal to religion or were agnostic.

Economic growth fostered by oligopolistic mixed economy outperformed all Europe's other economies brought with it a burgeoning young professional class savoring the tastes of modernity and material wealth. This class of people were hedonistic at their core and the antithesis of fundamentalist Islamists. Hence, a separated society. The young and the educated wanted to be in the Twenty-first century but the old and religious, represented politically by Erdogan, were more comfortable with Sixth Century Koranic law and the tenants of Mohammed. Because of the mullah's fervent religious nature, unable to make an ideological compromise and the growing undisciplined professional middle class not tethered to any ideology except money, a tension of political discourse took hold in Turkey.

Erdogan was not the titular head of his party, he was the mainstay of its ideology. He kept pushing for further Islamic control over society, knowing zealotry always wins over hedonism. In private discussions, he called his goal of Islamic rule, insidious creep. As with all research, things are dynamic. Erdogan was now facing greater challenges from the young professional class which became more mobilized through social media. The Justice and Development Party has not made the new world adjustments to Facebook and Twitter.

Chapter 28

Erdogan expressed a very liberal position of the 1915 Armenian genocide because of his early years' tutelage under Malgan Malgan. As stated earlier, Malgan pulled away his financial support from the Young Turk but they maintained a personal relationship until Malgan's death. Erdogan said he would personally acknowledge the massacres of 1,500,000 Armenians in the early 20th century after a thorough investigation by a joint Turkish/Armenian commission consisting of historians, archaeologists, political scientist, and other scholars of reputed stature. If a finding was agreed upon by the academic community, he would call for a reconciliation commission led by his own Justice and Development Party. His personal condolences statement at a joint conference between the two nation states of Turkey and Armenia was regarded as a brave political announcement. One that could have had negative political consequences but he felt the hidden bones of 1915 had to be addressed.

Political analysts suggested his Turkish position softening towards the Armenians was a move to buy acceptance into the European Union, but our research shows his views towards the Armenians developed through relationship with Malgan. Malgan crossed the line from Armenian to Muslim and then to agnostic but was still supportive of his heritage even though its roots were Christian. Erdogan learned from his master, principles can cross ethnic and religious lines especially on issues of great import. He did not feel hypocritical or inconsistent in his thinking about being a Turk and expressing regrets for the massacre of more than one million people because of their political beliefs. He once said he respected American President Bill Clinton for his conviction not his consistency when he praised the abortion rights. Erdogan fervently disagreed with abortion rights, while totally opposed to the death penalty. He said in the world of educated men, you do not have to be consistent to be correct. My position on the Armenian massacres might not be consistent with what many other Turks would like to hear but I think we must address history objectively.

A new degree of separation. You are of Armenian heritage but our research does not make us aware of any involvement in organizations or philanthropic endeavors on your part towards your people. This seems very inconsistent with your charitable giving and participation helping the disenfranchised and minorities suffering at the hands of a tyrannical majority. We surmise your present museum interest may lead to some expression of Armenian community support. The Turkish/Armenian dialogue is a most contentious issue and your support for the Armenians can be constructive. For the most part religious and ethnic differences in urban areas have been ameliorated to an acceptance point by the younger Armenian community population, however in older Turkish heartland community's hatred dies hard. In the central portion of our nation research suggests hatred is not ethnic but religious in nature. If and when the inter lands move towards modernization expanding education and knowledge it should lessen religion's stupidity and intolerance burden. After extensive research, we have found no public declarations attributed to you on the Armenian genocide. It is our belief you will meld towards Erdogan's position. It is our feeling your degree of separation will lessen and will become more consistent with his goals of reconciliation. Your museum in the Four Seasons Hotel declares your Armenian community affirmation. You will move from a neutral position to a positive position in regards to your own people being integrated into Turkish society on an equal basis. We take moral issue neutrality opposition to your museum will be a support statement for your own heritage.

Papaz did not understand the true intent of the writer. The academic directed his proclamation and tacitly instructing Papaz what course of action he should take. This certainly was not a scholarly treatment of Tayyip Erdogan. It was a subjective value judgment of someone's agenda. Sully told him his research team would be nontraditional in their subject matter approach, but this seemed too personal. There was another problem drawing Papaz's attention. He and Sully had not set up any preconceived parameters for the research but it was apparent Papaz was a subject of the investigation. The team had probed into his history and personal life. He knew Frederic developed a hardcover perfect profile for Papaz and all of his associates.

Admittedly the scrutiny of all the major security agencies throughout the world could not crack his false identity but paying for someone who could inadvertently disrupt his cover seemed disconcerting. He knew he was safe and his and Bi Ba's false personas would remain intact. Frederic's false identities were bulletproof and impervious to investigation. He was positive the identities of his group; Bi Ba, Frederic, Guzman, Bill, Malique and the mercenaries, Vega head of the Tijuana cartel and Kasogi were so authentic and backed by historical data that they were bulletproof as well. Even though he and Bi Ba were safe and their business entity operations and foundations were beyond reproach, he still felt violated. To be investigated by his own academic team in such an open and arrogant manner felt like a betrayal. His gut sentiment said he was intellectually filleted by his own people. He was no more than common gossip. He would talk to Frederic for assurance his identity and history were safe from scrutiny.

Russell C. Arslan

Part VI – Los Angeles

Chapter 29

After making a phone call to Frederic and being assured of their safety, Matt returned his attention to the document.

Erdogan's coalition government policies were a direct reflection of his personal conservative ideology. He was a powerfully persuasive man whose human rights position reflected his fundamental beliefs. The opposition party depicted him as Judgmental and unwavering. Turkey's desired integration into the European Union put enough pressure on the Justice and Development Party moving it to a conciliatory position. It was forced to recognize the Kurdish problem. The Kurdish minority was vilified, discriminated upon, incarcerated and not given opportunities to assimilate into Turkish society. It appeared obligatory for Turkey to seed autonomy into its North East Kurdish population before gaining entrance into the European Union.

Erdogan's reading of the political winds told him he must negotiate entrance into the E.U. to maintain his power base. In the ebbs and flows of Turkey's desires to negotiate/not negotiate integration he expanded and contracted the Kurdish people's freedoms. True to his Sunni Islamic core he showed his true colors once again when Turkish discussions stalled with E.U. negotiators.

He suppressed the freedom of speech by purging the press and even cut off public assistance to the predominantly Kurdish small towns and villages in the North East. On two occasions, he shut down the social media titans, Twitter and Facebook, as a reaction to public demonstrations against his hard-liner position on the Kurds. The judiciary put an injunction upon his sites closures and the social media outlets immediately reopened but did not stop him from doing it again. All of this was in response to the Kurdish population wanting opportunities to seize autonomy and asking for political process participation.

In juxtaposition to the Kurd's freedom restrictions, every time the E.U. negotiations resumed, he reached out to the PKK, the Kurdish Workers Party, offering political participation and multiplicity of other concessions. In trying to solve the issue his government said they would allow the Kurdish language to be used in the broadcasting media. The government would also be willing to open up and have political dialogue with any and all opposition parties. The AKP (Justice and Development Party) made concessions renaming many Kurdish cities and villages that had their names changed to Turkish. Erdogan even called for reconciliation meetings and some form of retribution to Kurds who had their properties taken away by the right of eminent domain. While trying to win entrance into the E.U., he granted concessions. When entrance discussions fell apart he took a hardline position and restricted Kurdish freedoms.

He was known as a political bully who was schizoid in nature. He made concessions but it was not his true character to deviate from sixth century Islamic ideology. His xenophobic stance on the Kurdish issue, his hatred for the LGBT community (lesbians, gays, bisexuals and transgender), and his misogynistic views of women were part of his mindset towards minorities. If a cause was more politically important to his survival or keeping his personal power, he accommodated or acquiesced to the demands of the more powerful group. Erdogan's history showed only a momentary step back. Do not underestimate his chameleon behavior. After defeat he expanded his political horizons until he felt his power consolidated enough recover his old ways and slowly move toward a more conservative fundamentalist governance.

Very much like Putin of Russia, he cannot sustain long periods of change without going back to his fundamental religiously inert character. He will always gravitate to an equilibrium of conservatism and try to follow the righteous tenets of Mohamed. We have a saying in Turkey, he can't help himself. He does not have an elastic mind.

When analyzing his Kurdish position, on face it seems to change like the winds. The pressure to give religious and ethnic tolerance acceptance is short run for Erdogan and is a form of acquiescence to the emerging autocratic class he has championed. In Turkey, we have a saying about people like Erdogan, they lie, they cheat, and they steal to make a contract that they will then do anything to break. He politically gravitates toward allowing Kurds into Turkish society as a way of advancing into the European Union. Once Turkey is a member of the European organization, he will try to reestablish a repressive law system again subjugating the Kurds to Turkish rule.

The new laws, customs and traditions supposedly liberalizing Turkey's Kurdish stance is a charade. Any concessions made by his party seem equitable but they will only be more sophisticated hurdles for the Kurds because he will make sure they foster subtle discrimination in even harsher terms than before.

Erdogan does not want the Kurds to have equal status with Turks. He would be vehemently opposed to a minority marrying into his family. The only minority marrying one of his daughters more reprehensible then the Kurds would be someone whose sexual persuasion was homosexual. Kurds to him are like blacks to some conservative Americans. In many ways, his Justice and Development Party is very much like the right wing of the conservative Republican Party in the United States. The class of people like Erdogan and many of your Republican counterparts may have talking points sounding politically correct but once in power they view minorities as unworthy and unequal.

We perceive a large degree of separation between you and Erdogan. His loyalties and his integrity to any doctrines are shallow at best. You are a man of commitment to ideals and have an undying loyalty to friends. He has only one conviction and that is to his own power. He is comfortable in the house of the Koran and is extreme in the teachings of Mohammed. The certainty of a Muslim life is soothing to him but is the antithesis of his ambition for power. In his life, there is always a constant tension displaying itself in fits and starts. Ambition versus the teaching of Koran and the leading of a simple humble life. After much investigation, we conclude the two of you are separated on the important values of honor and fraternity.

Papaz was again put off by the tacit familiarity the researcher had with his history. The comparisons with Erdogan made him feel his life was being investigated. It was too late to tell the researchers that delving into his past was out of bounds so he had to rationally minimize the threat. He had to take Frederic at his word that his identity and his life's work were placed in a lockbox that could not be opened.

Chapter 30

RESEARCHERS' NOTES: it is evident Tayyip Erdogan has a long memory. He is narcissistic to a point of protecting his image by any means necessary. We think being shown in a positive public posture is of paramount importance to him because of his many insecurities. He has a history of reprisals against his antagonist; the least being moral suasion and the most being capital punishment. That being said, you must dampen your public proclamation of Erdogan in your Museum's gallery of influential people. You must portray him in a positive light. If not the retributions placed upon you personally and professionally will be greater than any price you are willing to pay. If he or his inner circle members are offended by the Museum's depiction of him, then the full weight of the government will fall upon your house. Law enforcement's reactions to a negative portrayal of Erdogan, may it come from executive order or existing criminal code, will be quick and severe. The penalty for defamation of his character, libel or slander, will range from closing down your hotel and taking away your business license to taking away your visa.

The government has the ability to ex-appropriate all of your bank accounts and freeze your assets. Any and all of the above penalties will come down by judicial review of a referee who has been appointed by Erdogan himself. There is no precedent for you to be incarcerated but there are heavy fines associated with libel and slander. The fines can be as much as $100,000 American dollars per count. If there is a revocation of your visa you will be declared a persona non-grata and your future rights to visit Turkey will be under judicial review. The government has the right to sell your hotel and give you what the court deems as fair market value. That could be as little as 10% of the hotel's sales price.

It is obvious we feel the penalties for depicting a sitting prime minister, as strong as Tayyip Erdogan, are draconian. It is our belief that it is imprudent to be objective about Erdogan while he is a sitting Prime Minister. We have written a secondary position paper as to his history. We suggest if he is still in office when the gallery is opened that you use this highly subjective edited version of his life. It is our desire to distance ourselves from any possible capricious political retributions from Erdogan and his Justice and Development Party cronies. Again, the documentation of materials reflecting Erdogan's history must be edited such that he be seen in a positive light. THIS DOCUMENT must be viewed as a for your eyes-only document. You must protect our anonymity. The potential wrath from the Erdogan's government opposition to your gallery is too high a price for us to pay for researching the truth. This is Turkey. No matter how one perceives our shifts towards Europe and modernity we are still governed by a Middle Eastern strongman with a long memory and a short temper.

Russell C. Arslan

Chapter 31

Matt couldn't believe the researcher's notes section of the file. He asked Bi Ba if she would tell him her thoughts.

"I would really like you to read this thing and tell me what you think."

As was his way, he did not want to express his opinion first because it might bias her interpretation.

Bi Ba agreed to read it, "Give me a little time. I want to look at the whole document. I'll make sure I pay special attention to the researcher's notes. I really can't read your face right now but it looks like something is bothering you?"

He replied, "If you don't mind, just read it without me influencing you. Then we will talk. There is something that's not right, I wait till you get done."

"Okay," she said, "it shouldn't take me that long. Maybe an hour or so. You really look like you are on edge. Did you relate any of this to Frederic?"

"Yeah," he said, "as I read the document I called and e-mailed him. It was like a running commentary. I pushed Frederic on some things for his opinion. I probably should have asked him to read it first and then we could talk about it. As usual, I just jumped into it. It is a lot to digest. Thanks sweetheart. This is real important to me."

"Send the file to me," she said. "I'll go up to my office and get my laptop. Back in a minute."

When she came down from her office the first thing she said was, "I was reflecting back to Turkey, that stuff with Ozkan really ticked me off. We should watch our backs when we go there to finalize the sale of the hotel. Stuff always has a way of happening. If there's anything in this document that could give us trouble, we should just walk away from the whole thing right now. What is your phrase? Your first loss is your best loss. Sweetheart, if you think they're going to be any problems, just terminate the project. I'll go look at it right now." She stopped for a second. "If my input can make any of this clearer or make it safer then whatever I have to do I'll do it."

"I have not said this before but there is no need for this Armenian thing to be displayed in the hotel. As far as I'm concerned if you put in the gallery or not I am just an observer. It your project. If you do it or if you don't I really don't care. Other than your personal feelings I have nothing invested. My instinct tells me that none of the guests at the hotel will think it's important one way or another. Frankly there are better ways to express your concerns about the Armenians. When Sully's guys finish their research, it might be a proper time to put this in perspective and see if you really want to do it. We should let his people finish before you make any decision. Worst case is they are doing this work for your consumption only. Maybe you're reading it as the final outcome. If this project is going to be bothersome then, why do it?"

As she walked past him going out to the pool she continued, "We can look at this thing as a way for you to have subsidized some good academic types in Turkey. I am sure you can use them in the future. Kind of like a jobs program. With all the money, you spend what's one more thing. I want to make sure it's enjoyable and safe, that's my only concern."

She laughed, "You have all these little projects and you spend money on them because you can. You deserve to indulge yourself as long as it doesn't put us in danger. Let me get to this document and we'll talk."

She walked through the house's large living area, opened the sliding glass doors and looked at the golf course below. It was almost sunset and the soft breeze off the Pacific was coming up Roscomare Canyon cooling off the heat of the day. Bi Ba walked over to her favorite rattan sofa with large soft oversized cushions and stretched out with her feet hanging over the arms of the brown and white piece of furniture. In a lounging position, she quietly read for almost an hour and then all of a sudden, she popped straight up into a sitting position.

She did not utter a word but looked directly at Matt who was sitting at a table between her and the infinity pool reading the newspaper. Her eyes enlarged and became peeled as she read the researcher's notes section of the document. After digesting the last paragraph of the document, she closed the PDF file and pulling down the upper half of her laptop. As she began to talk Matt walked over to sit next to her.

"Well what did you think," he said. Matt, "those guys are really scared. They must've said they were afraid ten different ways. That bit about anonymity for them and you facing the possible loss of your investments and being kicked out of Turkey was pretty strong. There is no other way to read it. These guys believe Erdogan isn't someone to mess with. He is a bully and they are really frightened. What really interests me is they were so truthful about not liking him. He must be threatening to their secular way of life. He sounds like he is polarizing and a hateful political figure. He reminds me of some of the conservative Republicans in Congress. The researchers certainly were put off by his fundamentalism. Erdogan sounds like a real smart guy but on social and religious issues he is backward as hell. This is just me expressing my opinion but I don't think you should put him into your gallery. That is if you're going to have one. It's a no-win situation. If you mention his name you have to dumb down what a jerk he is. He is so controversial and religion is such a contentious subject in Turkey you can't be honest. You will be forced to paint a dishonest picture based on lies just to protect yourself. Why have a gallery honoring influential people if you can't be truthful? The way they make it sound, if you mention his name, you might as well just have him write his own bio. I'm not a fan of his. I'm being as truthful as I can when I say you don't get anything out of using him in your gallery. I guess the big question is why you want a galleria anyway?"

"You don't have to do this. All this document tells me is you don't need this in your hotel. Matt, the Four

Seasons is a great hotel. You don't need this Armenian/Turkish gallery. All you will do is offend people. You can't win and you aren't really an Armenian anyway. You are American Armenian or you are a person of the world. You don't need to build up some false ethnic pride because of something you think you are lacking."

Bi Ba paused for a second, "After reading the whole document let me be as truthful as I can. I think you'd be foolish to use him in your gallery of influential people. And, I am kind of pushing towards why have a galleria at all? It's not necessary. Like I said earlier, let the researchers do their work. We will see where it takes us. It is interesting to see all of the degrees of separation between you and some of the hotel's guests. Why don't we just leave it at that and say it was an interesting project. I'm not really sure if there are any points of intersection that mean a darn thing except coincidence between you and Malgan and Erdogan. I'm sure it will be the same for the other people your researchers present. A good writer can put anything together and make it sound logical. For the most part they are no more than word merchants. Maybe that's what these guys are. You are paying them a lot of money and I'm sure they want to impress you. They even expressed early on that they might fudge a little bit on the truth. This sure as hell isn't an academic paper. Why don't you look at their work as being enjoyable and don't believe it in a literal sense? Accept it for its entertainment value. Let them finish and we will digest all of it when it's done."

Chapter 32

During the month and a half that pass between the Erdogan file and the next inductee's file, Matt and Bi Ba continued passing their time in an unfamiliar zone of stress free activities. They continued working on their separate projects. Bi Ba the Village Nation and Matt his business endeavors. Twice a week they visited cultural attractions in Southern California. They went to the Getty Museums (the Malibu Villa and the main museum in West Los Angeles), the MOCA and the Natural History Museum adjacent to the University of Southern California where they saw the space shuttle. They spent three days visiting California's missions in Santa Barbara, Capistrano, and San Diego. They visited the Hearst Castle, the Wine Country in Central California and ventured into Death Valley. The couple had cultural specific things to do almost every day.

Frederic's and Gisele's teams continued surveillance of Steven Malgan and Alwan Al Bactar. There was no new activity on their part relating to either Bi Ba or Matt. Malgan was still practicing law in San Francisco and trying to accumulate businesses in a nefarious way. He had no sense of being surveilled by Frederic. Al Bactar was into the wind. His proclamation of someone getting to Papaz in the United States for more information about his father was just that, a proclamation. Neither he nor his men ventured out of the Middle East for a meeting with Papaz.

Everything was too simple in the Papaz's and Lamaze's household. Life was easy and not fretful; an unusual existence for the couple. Bi Ba summed up the month before the new file was to arrive.

Discussing the vagaries of easy street she said, "Being safe is not all that is blown up to be. I am actually bored not looking over my shoulder and feeling another shoe is going to drop. Having a normal life is somehow," she was looking for the right word, "perversely mundane. There must be something wrong with me. We have peace and quiet and all the money in the world to do whatever we want. We are not physically screwed up or wounded from some unbelievable circumstance we have been through and had no control over. We are pretty much healthy and physically fit for the first time in a long while. I've got you. I hope you know how important that is to me. I mean, I've got everything. But all this is somehow boring. How messed up am I?"

"We are leading a life that anyone would die for and somehow it's not enough!" Matt said.

"Yeah, it's all too perfect. When things are too good I'm really skeptical." She nodded her head in agreement.

"You're right. Let's appreciate this as long as we can even if it means it isn't that stimulating. It's kind of boring not being adventurous and not having something to lose. I feel I'm doing everything kind of like a walk-through. I'm just biding my time."

Bi Ba responded, "Well, at least it is not dangerous. That is something good. Isn't it?"

Matt said, "You're right. I think I'll call Frederic and check up on things."

As if to say he was hoping either Malgan or Al Bactor would somehow appear and bring some semblance of life into their existence.

"You know sweetheart," he continued, "for the first time I understand what somebody means when they say they are retired with a whole lot of time and more money at the disposal than what they can use and their bored as hell. I am on the cusp of looking for something else to do. I should call Sully and see when we are going to be getting our new research. If the new work is anything like the research on our first two guy it will be pretty exciting."

Bi Ba questioned him on the Museum. "Have you decided about it. The hotel should close escrow soon. I know there's almost nothing to do in terms of remodeling or marketing. All of that is tied to your franchise agreement with the Four Seasons. They are going to do day-to-day operations so what else is left for you before you take over the hotel. It's no more than a business transaction as far as I can see."

He responded, "Yeah, there's nothing major for us to worry about. It's just small stuff, no real money or real time on my part. My decision for the gallery is not etched in stone but for the most part I think I'm going to pass. I will probably opt out but there are more inductees and that could change things. I doubt it but since we paid a lot of money so far let's not shut the door on the museum totally. The chance is very small, maybe five percent, I will do it."

Bi Ba said, "Money should not have anything to do with your decision. I look forward to seeing what else our team will come up with too. Maybe we can use the researcher's points of interest not necessarily discussing personalities who have stayed there. Something that does not step on anyone's toes. Whatever the case is if you set up some type of gallery we have to make sure it will not come back to haunt us. You know I am opposed to this."

Matt responded, "I promise I won't do anything that will endanger us. You know I wouldn't do anything without your input. Like I said, I don't think this is going to happen. We might not even have the wall space for the display. Let's see what our guys come up with. You're right about the money but you've got to admit it's been pretty interesting up to this point."

Bi Ba said, "Interesting! What the hell are you talking about? Interesting is not the word I would use. How about the word dangerous? I hope you haven't forgotten how Ozkan almost killed you, and Al Bactar said, if you take this to the wrong place it could mean your life, and of course how about that psychopath cousin of yours. I've heard of having a short memory but this is ridiculous. Don't for one second think this could not be dangerous. I don't care how you think you are going to present these inductees; I think it's left better alone. Having your team continue looking for interesting people tied to the hotel is fine for entertainment purposes. Like you said we've already paid for most of the project. But don't think for a minute that means you must use it. Matt, I know you think I'm being aggressive and not willing to compromise but I don't see any upside in this. For once, let's take the easy path. I know we both need something. We are bored but not this, please."

Chapter 33

As Matt drove downhill from his house, the iphone in his left jeans pocket made a bell sound telling him he had received an email. His intuition told him it was from Sully.

It took another five minutes before arriving at a red light on Sunset Boulevard where he stopped. He undid the seatbelt and pulling the phone from his pocket he saw the green icon on the face of the phone a typed paragraph heading with the sentence, 'New Candidate for Gallery.'

He saw the light start turning yellow for the cross traffic and put the phone into the car's cup holder console, buckled his safety belt, proceeded through the green light and instead of taking Sunset Boulevard to the freeway he decided to drive a mile to Westwood Village. He drove past the UCLA campus and in front of Pete's Coffee parked his car. After getting out of his newly purchased Lexus 550 hybrid SUV, he walked into the coffee shop, ordered a tea with milk and proceeded to find a seat at the counter overlooking the street. Sitting high on the window stool he pulled the iPhone from his pocket and went directly to his Gmail. As he opened the file, the first paragraph grabbed his attention and enraged him.

It started saying: "after much deliberation and investigation we unanimously decided the next candidate for induction into the Four Seasons Hall of Influence is Mr. Mathew Papaz."

Papaz just sat there on his stool staring into space getting angrier and angrier. Thoughts of an academic team investigating his past and activities were racing through his head. The single worst thing was the fact he had not set up research parameters protecting himself. He was furious for not properly instructing the team against delving into his and especially the Papaz Group's information. The small iPhone screen size and the coffee shop noise added to his frustration. Before he finished reading the first paragraph, his stress level surged to an intolerable level. He clicked the phone getting out of the file and placed it back into his pocket.

Walking out of the coffee shop to his car, he decided to travel back up the hill to his house. Once there, he could read the entire document before making any irrational decisions on how to deal with being investigated. Thoughts were racing through his head as he traveled up Bellagio Drive towards his house. After getting to the top of the hill he turned right on Roscomare Road and drove another 100 yards and turned into his driveway.

His rage built. He felt violated but more importantly he felt naked as to how much the team had found out about him and his group's activities. He had conflicting thoughts. Did they or didn't they uncover his past? Did they know or not know of his criminal activities? Every conceivable thought from being incarcerated to not worrying about the team's research because of Frederic's past mystification were swirling in his head. He got out of his car, walked into the house and called up to Bi Ba.

"I got the file," he said soberly. "I need to talk about it."

He tried to make his yelling as neutral as possible not upset her. He hoped he did not fall short of his goal.

Bi Ba yelled down from the master bedroom, "I'll come down in a minute. I have to finish cleaning. It'll just take a minute."

He didn't want to frighten her or put undue pressure on her. He was frustrated and needed to discuss it with someone. Before he could settle himself at the breakfast table, he picked up his laptop from the kitchen counter top.

Bi Ba called back down, "I just got done working out. You don't sound okay. What's going on? I'm coming down right now. Hold on."

He couldn't maintain his feelings and as soon as she sat down he said, "I'm literally sitting here with a loss for words. I haven't read all the document yet but," he was quiet for a second collecting his thoughts, "the new inductee for the hotel is me. Can you fucking believe it? Those sons of a bitches decided to investigate us, I mean me! I don't know what they found out but this can't be a good thing. I have only looked at the first paragraph and I am beside myself. I am really pissed. More than anything else I am pissed for not having set the ground rules. Like I said, basically all I have done is look at the forward."

She cut him off and said, "Slow down, slow down. I think you're overreacting. Frederic said, we are bulletproof, so don't worry. He developed a past history for you that holds water. It cannot be broken into. Sweetie, don't be too upset by this whole thing. Let me run back to my office and get my laptop. Send me the file. I'll see if I can remember how to get my computer to read it out load. I think I just highlight what I want the artificial intelligence to read and say, 'read it'. I'll try to figure it out so I can catch up to you and we can listen to it together."

He responded, "I think you're right about reading it together. All you do is highlight it and say 'read it,' an icon pops up and you click on it. Sorry if I sound so upset. I'll cool down."

Chapter 34

Bi Ba set up her computer on the granite middle island kitchen counter top to read the transcript. She clicked the document reader icon and started listening to the prologue. She was not as disturbed by the Papaz description as he was. It identified him as a hugely successful American/Armenian entrepreneur whose businesses and philanthropic activities benefited Turkey. It wasn't anything she felt was offensive or threatening. She was sure she could bring him down from this anger.

He felt incredulously violated but she knew it wasn't warranted. Delving into his past was only one part of his anger. The little voice in her head said there was much more to it. In retrospect, it could be delayed action syndrome. He wasn't in any physical danger and the chances of the academics finding out about his history was miniscule. Papaz was overreacting because of the savage beating by Ozkan. He had always trusted Frederic's skills to create a false identification that was beyond law enforcement and national security agencies ability to find out about his activities the last six years.

She thought he felt vulnerable because of the beating. He wasn't completely well emotionally. She knew he must be reassured he was safe and was protected by his friends.

"Matt, you need to cool down. I know I have not read the full document but you're overreacting. I'll be upstairs in the shower, then I'm going to get something out of my car and we can start all over again. When I'm upstairs if you want to continue looking at the materials, fine. When I get back we can go over the stuff together. She left the kitchen and went upstairs to take a shower".

The shower and dressing took less than fifteen minutes. She walked to her car parked in their circular driveway and retrieved her iPhone. Returning to the kitchen, she walked through the grotto to the house's twelve-foot glass front doors. Standing on the flagstone step ready to open the door she noticed Papaz was still sitting in the kitchen with his laptop.

She opened the door and called his name. He was so engrossed in the document he did not hear her. She knew if she made any loud noise, she would frighten him out of his hazy consciousness. In his present state, she did not know how he would react, so she intentionally cleared her throat to get his attention.

He spun around quickly and acknowledged her. It was as if she somehow shattered the trance he was in and broke his concentration.

Matt blinked his eyes and spun around, "I didn't hear. You startled me."

He gathered himself and continued, "Since we talked, I feel a little bit better. I am still really pissed. I know I shouldn't feel this way. I'm probably irrational but those guys were so presumptuous. Digging into my past is really up setting. I'm sure I'll get over it but I can't believe it."

"I don't think it's really that bad," she said. "To tell you the truth, they really put you in a good light."

Bi Ba tried to bring levity to the conversation and continued, "They must like the money. You are paying them enough to make you sound great. With their brain power, they could probably make anybody look good. I'm just kidding. The picture they have of you was totally contrived by Frederic. They are right on in terms of what a good person you are and your feelings towards people that are less fortunate. Sweetheart, I know you are pissed but why? Saying they could have unearthed something accidentally is very thin as far as I'm concerned. They have no clue about your past. If major government agencies can't unveil your history, then these Turkish academics sure as hell shouldn't be a problem. They only know your six-year window since you have been with Guzman. They know what you've done for the last half decade but it is an abridged version. I'm assuming they know exactly what Frederic has created for public consumption. What they came up with speaks well of you and your accomplishments. If the FBI and the NSA haven't cracked your false identity, then don't put much stock into these Turkish guys causing you any trouble."

"Let me get something to drink and then we will analyze the whole document paragraph by paragraph. Do you want anything?"

"Yeah, please," Matt said.

She walked over to the refrigerator and came back with two Diet Coke's. "Okay, let's tear this down sentence by sentence and see if you are in any danger. For that matter we should see if anybody else is in danger. Let's try to look at third-party connections that might open us up to the world. No matter how small anything seems we shouldn't take it lightly. Why don't you text Frederic and tell him what we are up to? I don't really think we need his help but just in case we need some damage control. The sooner he's involved the better you will feel. Have him talk to Gisele. Let's tear this thing apart. If anything doesn't make sense we will figure out a way to deal with it. Matt, I am confident there is nothing in this document that can come back on you. I have not read past the first section but my gut tells me you are safe."

She took the seat across the table from him and they synchronize their laptops to the document. She activated the 'read it' software. It started to read each of the forty-two pages out loud. Every word was dissected and every meaning was taken to its last iteration.

Bi Ba was more analytical and objective than Matt. He read too much into the researcher's interpretation of his past. He tied clusters of events together in ways as to leave room for re-examination and misinterpretation of his intentions. He was so smart he had the ability to connect dots to nonexistent events and create problems. He over thought the document and inferred correlations not there. His mind focused on the negative. After approximately an hour Bi Ba pulled her chair away from the table and breathed out a sigh.

"What are you doing? You sound totally paranoid!"

She had never seen him like this before. Every minute he was becoming exponentially more negative. He was tying threads of information together to paint a picture that left him vulnerable to audits, to grand jury investigations of his business practices and even to indicting him on counts of murder and mayhem relative to unsolved crimes.

She said, "We must stop for a while. You're out-of-control. I don't know how I'm going to get you to understand but you are so far off the mark you are scaring me."

Bi Ba left.

Matt was alone for more than two hours. He decided to walk down the dirt trail from their backyard to the Bel Air Country Club golf course below. He walked for almost forty-five minutes and then sat under an oak tree on the fairway leading to the sixteenth hole. The light breeze buffeting his face started to cool him down. While stretched out on the grass contemplating his future, he felt such despair and a sense of self-pity, he wondered about his existence. He had to pull himself together and get on with his life. It was the first time in more than three months he allowed himself to recognize the damage Ozkan had done, both physically and emotionally. He had not been able to talk about his grief with Bi Ba because he was ashamed of being weak. She was the only person who truly understand him but he couldn't express his feelings to her. He was in great emotional pain and didn't want to socialize it onto her.

If he revealed how vulnerable he was, he thought she would somehow transfer the guilt and responsibility for his beating to herself. He kept his pain inside and trying to isolate himself. It seemed to work until Sully's team started unearthing his history. Feeling naked and not having a place to hide was too much for him. He had to make choice. Be weak and fall victim to the paranoia set in motion by Ozkan or as Bi Ba label it, man up. He knew he needed to pull himself up from the floor and be a man about it.

Matt decided to take the latter of the two choices and got up to walk back to the house.

Bi Ba was sitting at the table looking at the document. She looked up as he ascended from the golf course.

Before she could say a word, he said, "You were right to call me out. I was acting like a wimp and allowed every negative thought I've had the last three months to take over. Obviously, it hasn't been good for me. I just passed that on to you. Sorry sweetheart. I guess I didn't know how badly that son of a bitch beat me. I'm ready to get back to work."

She said, "We don't have to discuss this anymore unless you want to. You just fell on your face and didn't know how to deal with it. You'll be all right. You can't let that son of a bitch have this much power over you."

Matt agreed and tried to make light of the situation. "Well," he was quiet for a couple of seconds, "at least I found out one thing."

With a shit eating grin on his face he said, "I sure as hell can take a punch. There are supposed to be lessons in life and I guess that's what I learned from that Turkish ass hole. Thanks sweetheart, you always bring me back to my center. You have a way of getting me to understand things when they are hard for me. Enough of me feeling sorry for myself. Let's get back to where we left off".

He sat back down at the table. They decided to read the section called Partners Capital Solutions, one of his early hedge funds name. It made specific reference as to how he accumulated money at an early age allowing him to start buying properties in Southern California. Frederic had falsified documents and created a paper trail for the LLC which was highly profitable in the volatile California real estate market. In the early 1990s. Papaz's fictitious corporation was aggressively accumulating investors and pooling their money to buy properties. He was portrayed as extremely good at his craft and an ethical salesperson. The LLC was highly leveraged, Papaz had no money of his own in any of the deals and he charged very high promotional rates and management fees. None of these business practices were illegal but there was a high-risk rate associated with these business practice types. High risk, high reward. The investment fund was successful and moved from apartments and commercial real estate in Los Angeles and Phoenix, Arizona to the international market where his new offerings (Partners Capital Solution Equity Funds 1, 2, 3, and 4) were also highly successful. The funds had an incredible six years run accumulating assets of more than two and one half billion dollars. PCS branched off into mining precious and rare earth metals, five-star hotels, farms, large property swaths in East Africa and South America. In the document was a list of assets in the public records with the name of his investors. Frederic also created falsified deeds of trust, tax reports, investor perspective, death certificates and any public acknowledgments that would create a business persona for Papaz and his group.

In actuality Papaz' vast fortune was created through intricate business deals with the Tijuana Cartel and its ex-leader Jose Guzman. Frederic's elaborate investment scheme was no more than a front to launder the drug cartels annual hundreds of millions of dollars. Cash that had to be legalized. On paper Matthew Papaz was an American success story. The Turkish academics accepted every piece of information in the web of lies created by Frederic. Their research presented Papaz in a very positive light. He was viewed as an Armenian son of Turkey whose philanthropy was a godsend for the poor and disadvantaged.

"Let's tie this thing up." she said. "We've been at this for almost five hours. We're not going to get anything more out of it."

He agreed. "Yeah, my legs are starting to bother me a little. Let's finish up and go for a walk. How does that sound?"

Bi Ba said, "Okay that sounds good."

Papaz got up while they continued talking. "You were right. I really overreacted. But Frederic was Frederic. Why am I not surprised he did such an incredible job. No loose ends. I look like a self-made guy who has not lost sight of being humble and doing all the right things."

"You came off clean and there was no mention of any of our people"

"I was really paranoid. That's for sure. Obviously for no reason. I saw problems around every corner and that's never been my nature. I can't believe you put up with me for the last three months. Sorry sweetheart."

As he continued talking they started walking through the house out to the car. He was still in mid-sentence, "I'll call Sully and tell him he and his men did a great job but it is totally out of the question thinking about me as a personality on the wall of the Four Seasons. Not only is it not my nature to be the center of attention but I can't imagine being so egotistical that I would portray myself in any light on any of my properties."

She gave him a look, he responded by saying, "I certainly won't sound harsh about it. I won't let him know my disappointment in his team thinking it was even a possibility for me to be a candidate for the museum."

Bi Ba said, "I don't think you should tell him we're not going to have the museum. His team has done a heck of a lot of work and done an incredible job. It would be a real disappointment for them to call off their research now. Even though they still get paid that would put a damper on what they have accomplished. I am sure this has been the most fun they've had ever in academics."

Matt said, "You're right. I'll have them come up with three or four more candidates. The way they tied these people into degrees of separation with me is entertaining and maybe there's enough truth to get some future benefits. It can't hurt, let me rephrase. It shouldn't be a problem letting them finish up the project. I can't help but laugh. Nothing goes smoothly for us. Even though I got the shit beat out of me and have been depressed for three months Turkey will be a good ride."

Matt started laughing again and Bi Ba did as well. She said, "I think trouble always follows us and we can't lose our sense of humor over the ass holes."

They had been standing in the driveway next to his SUV for almost five minutes while they finished their conversation. He opened her door and walked around to the other side of the car.

Once he got inside he said, "Let's get out of here. How would you like to go down to Santa Monica and walk by the beach? Maybe we'll go eat at the Ivy?"

Bi Ba said, "Sure."

ISTANBUL

Chapter 35

The next candidate file, Turkan Dink 1938-2009, was sent to Matt three weeks after he communicated with Sully rejecting the use of his name as an inductee for the Hotel Hall of Influence.

In 1952 post-World War II, this new candidate restored a portion of the old Sultanahmet jail to be used as a school for ages seven to eighteen girls. The Istanbul municipality granted her construction permission for the new all-girls school as a symbolic way to show the cities' desire to modernize and integrate into European society. Dink championed causes of impoverished females during the post Mustafa Kemal Ataturk period.

The Turkey founding father died in 1938 and the inertia for social reforms slowed considerably during World War II. In early 1950s Dink, leader in the Turkish feminist movement, became a medical doctor opening numerous clinics throughout Turkey for the poor and underprivileged. She sponsored women's educational reform, led in human rights expansion for all Turkish people even the hated and vilified Kurds. Her forward thinking was instrumental helping people with leprosy who were feared and despised by the Turkish population. Dink collected monies setting up intercity housing and jobs for lepers enabling them to get off the streets. She established three leper colonies in central Turkey.

In 1985 she became a cabinet member of the Motherland Party under the Prime Minister Turgut Ozal. She was the first woman without portfolio to be the head of the Ministry of Education (1985-1988). After her three-year stint in government she worked with major international NGOs dealing with the plight of females. She was responsible for bringing the organization Doctors without Borders into Turkey to work with young women born with the medical malady, cleft palate. She also collaborated with Oxfam, again helping females with more general medical conditions and educating females as to birth control. She was an antagonist of female circumcision and worked with the Motherland Party passing laws stopping its practice in the early 1990's.

In the later years of her life (2003-2009) she moved to Great Britain, Manchester England, to be closer to her adoptive cousins and became a fundraiser for the Turkish Red Cross.

Her relationship with Matt is blurry at best. She lived in and used the old jail as a residence and educational facility. Suite #207 was a storage facility of maintenance equipment for her school. Education and medicine are common threads between the two, but her degree of separation from him was infinite. Papaz and Dink had many of the same philosophies. They both personally engaged in assorted activities benefiting the disenfranchised and poor but neither Dink nor Papaz, nor their acquaintances, nor their employees, nor their family members ever crossed paths.

Turkan Dink, born in Ethiopia to father, Yekunoamlak, and mother, Sitsi, one of two girls separated two years. Her older sister Fowsia was lighter skinned and more prized by the family. Anaya was Turkan Dinks' Nubian given name. Born Ethiopian, but Nubian by culture, she was given only one name. Her father was an animist purported to have supernatural powers. He was seen as a witch doctor or shaman.

Yekunoamlak was 6'10" tall, very thin by western standards and very light skinned. He looked like a Ditka warrior except for his piercing blue eyes. By age fifteen, he had a following as village healer just outside the capital, Addis Ababa. When he married at eighteen, his bride's dowry allowed him to leave his family's farm and practice medicine on his own.

As was the case with most Ethiopian men, he had many children outside wedlock but he had two children with his wife Sitsi. At age twenty-three he and his wife journeyed to the land of his heritage, the Sudan. The family took passage with a camel caravan bound for Khartoum. In route the caravan was attacked by a group of Sunni slave traders and Fowsia, the older and fairer of the two daughters, was kidnapped. Anaya, her mother, and, her father continued on the two-month journey and arrived at Abu Sim, a small village, on the outskirts of Khartoum where Anaya was sold to a cousin who took her to the city of Omdurman in central Sudan.

For six years Anaya lived with her cousin Ahemed Dejene, his wife and two daughters. She was abused by him, a spice merchant and flesh seller who sold her to another merchant who had a stall in the Khan el-Khalili, the Grand Bazaar of Cairo, where she worked packaging spices until she was old enough to be sold in the adult sex trade.

She lived in the back of Dejene's mud house near the bazaar under living conditions with no water, no electricity and slept on the dirt floor without blankets. She had one change of clothes and she did not have access to people her own age. Within two years she started displaying her father's healing powers and learned enough Arabic to advance from packaging spices to working in the kiosk front selling Ahemed healing products. Her knack for languages was such that she could speak seven different languages fluently by the age thirteen, two different dialects of Nubian, one derived from the Noba or the nomadic people with ancestral beginning in the old Kush civilization and the other from the Nilo or sub-Saharan farmers in central Sudan. She also spoke Arabic, Hebrew, learned as a child in Ethiopia, Ethiopian, English and some French used in the marketplace.

At age fourteen her cousin decided to cash in on her value and sold her to an old Ottoman family who brought her to Istanbul where she was given the new name of Turkan Dink.

Dink was their family surname and because of her unique qualities, not only as a healer but also because of her physical appearance, they brought her into the fold and treated her as a family member not a commodity to be sold at auction. Ata Dink and his wife appreciated her and her powers to such an extent they sent the child prodigy to private English school where she graduated with a secondary degree in less than one and half years by taking comprehensive examinations. She applied to medical school and was admitted to the University of Istanbul at age seventeen.

Turkan Dink graduated with a medical sciences degree with special emphasis in infectious diseases at age twenty. From the time, she arrived in Istanbul and lived in the house of Dink she practiced nontraditional medicine and was a healer of the poor and disadvantaged. Her great demand in the poorer large city areas evolved from nontraditional medical skills of placing hands, herbal medicines and the ability to speak in tongues. After two more years in post medical school her services for traditional medicine were highly sought after in the Jewish and the Christian communities. She was considered secular and her demand as a western physician exceeded the amount of time she had to practice. She was the first non-European female doctor in the great city and her medical skills became legendary.

Dink had folklore popularity not only because of her medical skills but also because she was physically striking and of Amazon proportions. She was 6'1" tall, her skin color was of deep black Nubian ebony, broad shoulders with the muscularity of a swimmer, her eyes were hazel green because of her Ethiopian heritage, her face had high cheekbones reminiscent of Eritreans, and she had a long strikingly beautiful neck that held her head firm. She processed the power of beauty and an eclectic array of cures which made the demand for her skills epic in proportion to other physicians in the city. On a daily bases her clinic served more than 200 people. To the poor

"Anaya" only had one name, which added to her mystery and allure. She became their champion and opened up a school at the old Sultanahmet jail in 1952. The secular rich and powerful became aware of her popularity and sponsored and subsidized the construction of a large clinic and the expansion of her school on the grounds of the old jail. The clinic's specific purpose was to provide medical aid for the large burgeoning ghettos of Istanbul. As the clinics income and contributions from the wealthy increased she trained and paid for other women to go to medical school to become nurses and doctors with the guarantee of working in their own clinics throughout Turkey. It took less than a decade for the mortality rates of women to start to go up. Because of her advocacy to criminalize female circumcision and medical attention for women that had the procedure, fertility rates started to increase throughout the country. Her school's academic performance was so high, thirty percent of its students went on to university, where as in Istanbul's matriculated public schools less than five percent progressed to university.

    At age thirty-three her success imparted the ability to direct some time towards fighting a new disease. Turkey was plagued with leprosy. She turned her resources toward setting up clinics in Istanbul and Ankara. Her clinics were the first in Turkey to use the broad-based antibiotic penicillin. In the heartland, North Eastern Turkey, she set up leper's colonies both housing and employing people with the disfiguring and debilitating disease. Women living on the isolated properties were taught carpet weaving skills and their wares sold throughout Europe. Men worked on the colony's land, planting and harvesting poppies the producing medical opiates. Turkey became the largest world producer of medical opiates. Her leper clinics were the first in Turkey to decimate the Polio vaccine which enabled the Euro/Asian nation to eradicate the disease for all intent and purpose by 1990.

Chapter 36

As the standing Minister of Education, 1953-1958, Turkan Dink spearheaded mandatory education for girls. There were no religious exceptions for universal education. Under her direction, the ministry created new national secular curriculums for all public schools. Nationally directed teaching with mandatory secular textbooks, new syllabuses and course outlines of all subjects. Education not only became mandatory for all Turkish children it became standardized and separated from sectarian Shiite or Sunni teachings.

Private schools for Islamic, Jewish and Christian faiths required licenses and standardized test accredited educations were required for all children. As minister, she was instrumental in developing a new nationwide curriculum mirroring the English education model. All classes were standardized Oxford units applied to primary and secondary schools. Under her mandates schools could no longer teach religious classes. All classes had to be taught in Turkish. Students were required to take an additional language over and above the mandatory English that was taught in all grades from primary through secondary school. The country was immersed in English energizing its economy and bringing it closer to Europe. She imposed longer and more days of education. More mathematics and science classes were taught. Students wore uniforms. Any signs of heterogeneity or students wanting to express individualism in dress was prohibited. Dink was utilitarian in her approach to children. Muslim girls were asked to discard their burkas and traditional garb for uniforms but it was not mandatory. Stiff penalties were codified for sexual harassment and discrimination against females in public schools.

Dink established tuition free trade schools for post-secondary students with state paid books and fees. University enrollment under her master plan increased from three percent of the graduating secondary school seniors to more than fifteen percent in the ensuing decade. The federal education budget during her three-year tenure increased an unheard-of seventy-five percent, from four percent to seven percent of all expenditures.

Ministry construction project corruption was slashed by disallowing single bidding. She created earthquake standards for construction on educational properties of all new buildings and pushed for earthquake reinforcement of existing buildings and facilities.

She increased teachers' pay over 300% during her Ministry tenure. Her medical background directed all schools have a nurse on-site. Students absent from school more than one week because of illness were required to consult a medical official. Dirk required singing Turkey's national anthem (Istiklal Masi) starting the school day. She was very proud of her adopted country and felt nationalism was important for Turkey's younger generations to move towards a more secular and western lifestyle. She wanted to use education not only as an informative instrument increasing literacy of the population but wanted to use it as a socialization approach bringing Turkey's youths into the 20th century.

Wandering and always looking for new challenges, her ministry stay was longer than anticipated and moved to another socially responsible endeavor using her considerable political sway she created nonprofit women trade schools to learn secretarial and nursing skills. She acquired foreign capital for construction of fourteen campuses and used her political powers persuading the Turkish government's operations of day-to-day school subsidies. Tuition was free for all students regardless of income or religious faiths. The all-girls schools segregated a purely secular nature. At Turkan Dink's death in 2009 Istanbul's Learning Institution's name was changed to The Turkan Dink Learning Institute.

Chapter 37

History: being a human rights advocate and having great empathy for female circumcision or female genital cutting victims and working against its practices in Turkey were major causes Anaya fought all of her life. She lived in abject poverty in Ethiopia, the Sudan and in Egypt before her passage to Turkey. She was subjected to physical, sexual, and psychological abuse. Her early life hardships were immeasurable and she spent years in virtual semi-isolation. She was sold to a cousin in the Sudan who was a masochistic predator with two daughters of the same fold.

As per Sudanese Muslim tradition she was to be circumcised at age thirteen. The barbaric medical procedure created everlasting scars. The medical tools and dirty environment used in her operation caused health and emotional problems framing her adult personality. The day of her circumcision came as a surprise to Anaya. She was not forewarned. Her two older female cousins who were abusive in nature were commanded by their father to take her to the butcher shop in the small village's marketplace to be circumcised.

At 6 o'clock in the morning, fifteen minutes after sunrise, she was pulled off the floor by her cousins. They dragged her across the back room of the mud house into the street. Anaya had no idea what was to befall her. As was a common occurrence the two sisters beat her while they pulled her by her tightly curled black hair. They dragged her up the dirt road to the marketplace. She was yelling and screaming but no one came to her aid. The streets were crowded with people because prayers had just ended and the doors of the city's only mosque were opened but no one lifted a finger to help the young girl. Once inside the marketplace Anaya was taken to the stall of Mohammed the butcher. The smell of the hanging camels who were being blood let, piles of rotten renderings on the floor, and goats and sheep ready for slaughter were horrifying to Anaya. A large man wearing a bloodied bib with a knife in hand was waiting for the little girl. The sight of him caused her to vomit. He grabbed her by the scruff of her neck because her clothes had literally been torn off by the cousins as they dragged her to the marketplace. He instructed the two girls to lift her on to a large wooden butcher block and hold her down. The animus of the two older lighter skinned girls towards their beautiful darker skinned cousin was evident as they both spit into her face. The butcher had to the cousins ripped off her remaining clothing. He walked over to a table on the other side of room to pick up a razor, another tool of his trade. She was firmly held down by her two cousins and continue to scream to no avail. Anaya was so frightened she continued to regurgitate the food she had in her stomach and almost choked from her own vomit. She passed out before the butcher returned from across the room.

Tradition in the Sudan's Muslim community created strict protocols for circumcision which in most cases were not a point in the maturation ceremony for young women. At the ages of six to thirteen girls were cut by a local spiritual person usually a butcher or a barber. In other African or Middle Eastern nations girls were circumcised either at birth or up to the age of five years was not the case in the Sudan. Depending upon the country, ethnic background, and religious customs interpretation there are three major circumcision types. In type I, all or part of a woman's clitoris and clitoral hood is removed. In type II, the clitoris and hood and the labia are removed. In type III, which was violently perpetrated upon Anaya, and considered the most severe of the procedures, all the clitoris and the inner and outer labia are removed. Diabolically the procedure is extended to close the vagina by sewing it shut except for a small hole to allow for the passage of urine and menstrual fluids. The vagina is to only be opened by removing the course threads used for stitching it together. The only instance for removal was intercourse and childbearing after marriage. This procedure, type III, a practice infrequently used in the Sudan is done with the use of knives, razor blades, or glass cutters instead of scalpels. Because of the hatred of her keepers Anaya was subjected to the most reprehensible form of circumcision. There was no use of antiseptics or antibiotics or anesthesia. Later in life when she publicly discussed her personal ordeal of circumcision she said it was "painful and dirty". A truth that stuck with her the rest of her living days.

After her circumcision, Anaya was dragged by her cousins out of the butcher shop to the dirt road at the front of the marketplace. The two young women were screaming obscenities and pulling her by her hair as a way of displaying their treasure. She was battered and nude which extracted the highest degree of contempt from the townspeople who were milling in the streets. The butcher had used a dull knife as requested by Anaya's owner/cousin, Ahemed Dejene, to cause great physical pain. After the mutilation, Mohammed, the butcher, feed her body parts to the dogs sitting in his kiosk to add to her degradation. In the butcher shop, she had been given a linen type shirt for the upper half of her body. She was naked from her waist down but the massive bleeding from the operation obfuscated her genital region. As she was being pulled down the street it was obvious to the villagers the girl had been unceremoniously cut as a punishment for her dark skin and embarrassment to her cousin. Once the two girls had brought Anaya back to their home she was forced to dress herself and go back to the marketplace and resume work in her uncle's stall. She was not allowed to clean herself and because of the filthy conditions in the butcher shop and being dragged through the dirt streets she became acutely infected causing sepsis[5] which would have lifelong medical implications.

The negative health effects from non-medical circumcision depends upon the individual practitioner and the environment in which the procedure was conducted. Over eighty percent of the women of Anaya's generation suffered negative medical consequences from the procedure. The chronic side effects are: recurrent infection, severe pain, cysts, infertility, complication during childbearing, fatal bleeding during the operation (five percent), and death (two percent). There is no way to evaluate the emotional deficit placed upon woman from the operation itself. By any standards, the conditions in which most of the circumcisions were performed were barbaric and led to personal indignities and humiliation. In many cases women suffered from physical disfiguration as well as massive scarring. Most all of the above applies to Turkan Dink.

The social implications of genital cutting, type III are rooted in gender inequality. The Muslim tradition of females as being chattels has been a custom from the mid-650s A.D. to the present. Closing off a woman's clitoris by sewing it up with heavy gauged woolen thread after circumcision is indicative of a male chauvinistic society whose ideas about purity, modesty, and the male's ability to control women's sexuality are improper and immoral in the twenty-first century.

By the time,Anaya was sold to Ata Dink, the Ottoman trader, she had re-acquired her physical vitality but she was so emotionally damage she barely uttered a word. Dink's wife Doha, had not been subjugated to circumcision. Once she was made aware of Anaya's condition she took her to Marmara General Hospital, a secular institution, where the stitches were removed. Doha was so put off by the procedure and the horrible mutilation of this now lovely young woman that she and her husband paid for reconstructive surgery to help promote a cleaner and more hygienic genital area that would give Anaya, now Turkan Dink, and lesser chance of chronic infection and relieve some of her chronic pain. Ata and Doha Dink who did not have children of their own wanted their adopted daughter physically brought back to a normal life as best as medically possible.

Turkan now had a true family. She blossomed like an orchid and her exceptionalism was evident. Because of her many medical procedures to address the pain of her circumcision her interest in traditional medical practices grew to obsession level. She wanted to be Turkey's first female medical doctor educated in Turkey. Her ability to heal people would now take on a more scientific path. Doha was progressive because of her English education. She made sure that Turkan would have access to the best schools in Istanbul. Because of Turkan's disposition towards medicine her academics were directed to her entrance into medical school. She would be allowed to practice nontraditional medicine and work in Dink's spice stalls while in school. Work was not for money. Her parents wanted her to understand the importance of discipline and productivity.

It is apparent why Turkan Dink had such strong feelings for human rights, particularly female circumcision. She would emulate her adopted mother's progressive political ideals of suffrage and equality. She engaged in providing Istanbul with education institutions and medical clinics as an extension of her troubled life. To her very core, she did not want any other young girls to have to suffer the indignities of her miserable childhood. The scars of circumcision even with all her accomplishments never lessened. She made it her mission help the less fortunate. It is our academic consensus that she picked up the cause of lepers because of her humiliation and disfigurement that accompanied her circumcision. She felt disfigured her whole life even after reconstruction surgery which made her exterior whole. Her work with lepers was extraordinary because of the social taboos associated with the disease and the illiterate response of Turkey's citizenry who felt the disease was communicable. The isolation of the leper community did not resonate well with Turkan Dink. She felt empathy for those people that the Turkish society had discarded.

RESEARCHER'S NOTES: we find that Ms. Turkan Dink is the most noteworthy candidate of the 153 possible inductees we have had the pleasure of investigating. Of all of the people we have looked at we consider her contributions to Turkey as having the greatest positive consequences on our population. She is held to be the champion of the poor, disenfranchised, and of course the leader of women's rights movement in Turkey. She was not Armenian and her civic efforts were not substantially directed to this ethnic minority but the overspill of her programs, especially human rights, uplifted their position in Turkish society. Her efforts to help females break away from the degradation and the discrimination of the past are extraordinary. Her work with children and the creation of a network of schools to meet the educational needs were the forerunners of Turkey's educational Master Plan. Through her efforts, the poor and the impoverished received needed medical attention. This was the impetus for Turkey's national healthcare program that exists today. Her empathy for lepers and her funding for cures for the hideous disease speak to her heartfelt desire to help the poor and underprivileged. You did not have the pleasure to cross her path but many of your own civic projects parallel her's. Turkan Dink was a great woman, a great citizen, and most importantly a great inspiration to young Turkish women. Head analyst, Aga Asil

Chapter 38

Papaz put down his laptop and got up from his desk. He had just finished reading the document sent from Aga Asil. He walked down the hallway that led to his office and then took the spiral staircase to the first floor of the villa. He found Bi Ba sitting in the kitchen.

"You have to read the document Sully sent us! This woman, Turkan Dink, is the most inspirational person I have ever read about. You won't believe how courageous she was and how much she did for Turkey. I had never heard of her before and now I'm overwhelmed by her accomplishments. She's one of the most forward thinking people you could imagine."

Bi Ba replied, "I haven't seen you this upbeat about any of the research. Does this mean you want to establish the museum?"

"No," he said. "That's not it at all. She was just amazing. Right now, all I really want to do is have Frederic look into the charities she established and see if we can be part of them. To get back to your question as far as I am concerned the museum is dead. You just need to read this document. The woman was incredible. I'll email it to you. There is something he sent me but it's not of much interest. I'll just send you the file."

Bi Ba replied, "I've got nothing set up for this afternoon. As soon as I get back from my training I'd love to look at it. It sounds really intriguing. You are never so overstated on anything. I have to get going, I'll see you later," as she picked up her gym bag sitting on the floor next to her. "After I get back I'll look at it."

She got up and kissed him lightly on the lips. She held his face in both of her hands and continued, "Stuff like this is the reason t I love you."

When she got back from the gym Papaz was gone. He left a note saying he had gone out to do some errands and would be back shortly. Bi Ba had cleaned up at the gym and was looking forward to reading the file. She went upstairs to her office and sat at her desk.

She immediately opened her laptop while she fidgeted in her chair until she was completely comfortable. She clicked onto the icon Gmail to retrieve the file from Papaz. It took almost two hours for her to read the file in its entirety. She intentionally read it at a very slow pace. Bi Ba felt that there were two major ways of approaching reading. The first way was to read for comprehension and retention, as was the case of the document on Turkan Dink. The second approach was reading for recognition which was slightly more than skimming through materials looking for information to acknowledge a schema that she already had a grasp of. The Dink file would take time to absorb. Bi Ba was a note taker. She felt note taking complemented her reading. It was another method of learning. The synergism of reading and writing made for greater comprehension. After viewing the total document, she reconciled her notes by honing them down to make for a more concise understanding of the material.

She placed the pages of her handwritten notes into a document scanner transcribing her writings into text. She pushed the green start button and waited for less than two minutes before her three-page note collection dropped into the printer's tray. She pulled them out and walked out of her office down the hallway to the central staircase of the villa and walked downstairs to the living room.

In a loud voice, she called out for Papaz. He had earlier come into the house and intentionally didn't want to disturb her. He was now sitting outside by the swimming pool, relaxing.

When he heard her voice, he replied, "I'm by the pool. You want me to come up, thinking that she was in her office."

She said, "I'll be out there in the second."

When Bi Ba arrived at poolside she had a glass of lemonade in each hand and a bag of almonds clinched in her teeth. The notes she had compiled were in her jeans back pocket. She handed Matt his drink and pulled the bag of nuts out of her mouth and sat down.

"Matt, you were so right about her. From those photographs, she must've been one of the most beautiful women in Turkey. When they talked about her Nubian heritage and how beautiful she was I kind of pictured her looking differently. God, she was beautiful. Being black didn't describe how dark she was but with those green eyes she just looked incredible. Very imposing to say the least. Just her looks must've made her formidable. What she lived through and the stuff she accomplished was unbelievable. What an incredible woman."

Bi Ba related a couple of Turkan's accomplishments as if Matt had no knowledge of the Turkish woman. Bi Ba discussed her as if she was a historical jewel and wanted to share her findings with Matt.

Her enthusiasm for the Turkish woman who started her country's feminist movement was boundless. Matt could not get a word in edge wise. As she spoke she crossed out the bullet points on her amalgamated notes as if she were giving a presentation. When she finally finished, she put the three pieces of paper down on the ground and took a deep sip of her lemonade.

Although, Matt was astounded by her passion, he finally spoke. "I haven't seen you so sure about anybody like this before. You are almost coming unglued. You are right, she was something! I knew you would identify with her. You are a lot alike, she was a different kind of tough than us. We are sometimes formidable because of circumstances. We have the luxury of always being able to come back to our modern life which is a pretty safe and affluent compared to hers. Conviction for us is merely a hobby or it's a defensive measure against outside influences. For her, wow, I can't believe what a hard life she had and what she must have gone through. She lived with pain and indignities we have no comprehension of and look what she did with them. Somehow, she made them a positive and used them as an incentive to help others. The hardship she lived through I can't even imagine. She somehow made pain her ally and used it to bring about change for others. What an incredible woman."

Bi Ba found yourself saying, "Matt, I hope you won't think I am shallow for what I'm going to say. Why didn't Sully's researchers, especially this guy Aga Asil, say a word about her personal life? They didn't say anything about her adult lifestyle other than her accomplishments. I have no clue if she was married? Maybe she couldn't find anybody to keep up with her or meet her standards? Can you imagine what a tough act she must've been? They didn't mention any children. It could have been the circumcision, hell it could've been an aversion towards men after all she went through. If she did have children. They are adults by now. I couldn't help but think what lives or careers her kids would have. I would love to see who they are and what they're doing."

"I may be way off base but Turkish men are funny about female homosexuality. I wonder if she was gay and that's why they left out her personal life. They respected her but not saying anything about her personal life is really strange. It was as if after her childhood all she did was work. She was great! I'd like to find out more about her. Do you think we can have our people consider any of this? It would really be interesting to see who she really was. It doesn't make a difference to me and it won't affect how I view her accomplishments but I would sure like to know as much as possible about her personal life. All I can say is she was really terrific."

Matt agreed with her about pursuing further investigation of Tukan's personal life. He said, "I'm going to pass this along to Frederic and Gisele. If anyone in the world would appreciate this woman it sure would be Gisele. They have to read the document. I am sure they will feel the same way we do. Frederic can pass on our concerns to the right people and have them look into her personal history. That should be easy but I would like to go little further than you on this. How do you feel about placing some money with her charity? We will have to do our homework but if her schools and clinics aren't corrupt and do more than just window dressing then I want us to get involved. What you think?"

Bi Ba responded, "I would love that. Maybe you can see if we can funnel some of our money through our clinics in Kenya and through our foundation? If her charities are run by the right people and help, then I would like to participate. But, and this is important to me, I'd like for us to be anonymous."

She smiled, "You being Armenian and all."

They were in total agreement about Turkan Dink and how they wanted to ensure her legacy.

ISTANBUL

Part VII -- Steven Malgan

Chapter 39

Five days passed and Frederic had not corresponded with Matt which was highly unusual. He was supposed to get back to his friend on the progress he had made on the Turkan Dink investigation.

Bi Ba said, "It's strange not hearing from Frederic. He is usually really good at keeping us in the loop. He's never gone more than three days without some contact. I hope nothing is wrong. I know we've been gone."

She and Matt had visited Carlsbad and the Del Mar racetrack and were out of Los Angeles for four days. Alvarez's men who were still surveilling the couple had been in communication with Frederic the whole time they were gone.

Matt said, "I'll call him right now. It's not too late."

Frederic answered the phone. "Matt, how was your trip? Alvarez gave me a running commentary on your activities every day. I felt pretty comfortable with your safety so I thought I would contact you after you got back. I was going to call but this is even better. Let me be upfront. We have a problem. I didn't want to bring it up until after you were home. As long as you were safe it made sense for me not to interrupt you."

Matt had Frederic on speakerphone. Bi Ba said, "What the heck are you talking about? Problems? Not big enough to worry you but something we should talk about? What does that mean? We know we have had security ever since the Malgan thing. It's been a couple months. Does this have anything to do with Matt's cousin?"

Frederick replied, "Yeah, it does. We have a problem with this guy, Steven Malgan, he could be dangerous. Somehow, he found out we've been looking into the Malgan Trust as well as his law firm and business practices. I have no idea how he could have found out we are investigating him. We used outside contractors, everything electronic had a NSA signature. Nothing should have come back to us and it did. He is aggressive and within a couple of weeks we expect him to come after you. If his past record is anything like what he will do, then he will come after you with multiple lawsuits. He is extremely litigious. That is his play book. First law suites then physical threats."

"His team has openly been looking into some of our companies that we set up to investigate him. We can't figure out how he could have tied you to any of our sting operation about representing you but he did. All we can see is that some of his clerks out of his San Francisco office are combing through the County Hall of Records documents on our fictitious corporations. Somehow, someway, they figured the corporations were a set up to pry into Malgan's operation. On two different occasions, we have followed one of his clerks to the records office in San Francisco where he fraudulently placed amendments to your business license application for your LLC. Once we created our cover story we falsified a lot of documents to keep you at a distance. Malgan's people somehow identified you and asked for copies of anything related to your corporations. Not all documents were scanned into the offices' electronic files so we don't know exactly what materials were pulled up. All we know is that they somehow they tied those LLCs to you and expanded their investigation from our sting to you going after his father's trust."

"He has formidable resources and will apply a full-court press into digging into your complete history. He won't be able to crack your cover. If the Turks couldn't then his people sure as hell won't be able to find out your real identity."

He paused for a second, "But we have to be vigilant. What is disconcerting is how litigious he is. He will not only come after you but he will come after Bi Ba and any partners you have. His mode of operation, and he uses it as a template for legal bullying, is to go after your partners to apply as much pressure upon them as possible. They will ultimately apply pressure upon you to relent on your position and give in to his demands. His clerks all come from the University of California's Hastings Law School. It is Cal's stepsister or second tiered law school. Bolt is there more prestigious law school with students of higher standing. It is unusual for university to have two law schools but Malgan uses it to his advantage. He only employs clerks who have made the law review at the lesser of the two schools. They all want to prove they should have been admitted to Bolt. They all have a chip on their shoulder which is evident in their aggressiveness in pushing past legal boundaries. It sounds like it is simple collegiate competition but it is not. The Hasting's students are compensating for lack of recognition. This is an incredible motivating factor because it makes them hungry and passionate. More importantly it gives them a competitive edge. We have to expect they will stretch the law and with the liberal San Francisco courts who have a bias against people with wealth, it puts us at a great disadvantage. The courts in San Francisco in general are antibusiness. This just means a legal mess which Malgan plays. Delay after delay and all the god damn legal maneuvering you can imagine. His ultimate goal is to keep you in court as long as possible and extract a measure of competitive edge. Looking at his record most of his lawsuits are frivolous but they cost his opponents a great deal of money. He buries them with expenses. He pays his clerks $110 an hour and his adversaries have to pay up to $500 an hour to law firms to represent their positions. He papers his opponents into submission."

"Now here is where it becomes dicey. If he can't get his way in the courts either because he's wrong or his opponents have deep pockets and they can afford the cost of litigation, then he becomes violent. Here is where it gets bad. You know this already; California has the largest Armenian population in the United States. Most of them are in Glendale right over the hill from you. The estimates are 300,000. I don't have to tell you this, but there are a hell of a lot of them that are Russian and are involved in gangs. He has already contacted a mobster called Hurat Markalyan. I have sent pictures of him and his associates to Alvarez's men. We are going to beef up your security. Matt, he wants to make this a long war not only on the legal side but his gangsters will do everything they can to try to intimidate you. He does everything by the same playbook. He has not killed anyone yet but intimidation is his style and people have been hurt. He is small potatoes compared to what you have been through but we can never underestimate any adversaries."

"Let me throw a couple other things at you. Alvarez and I have two different approaches on how to handle the situation. He flat out wants to kill the psychopath. It may come to that. If he thinks you are after his meal ticket, his uncle's trust, and gets out of control we might have to kill him. He will do anything to protect his income from the foundation. Alvarez thinks he is certainly capable of killing anyone who would cut off his funds. My line of thought is to try to figure out how we can walk away from all of this without any violence. We don't need this shit and all Malgan ultimately wants is his money. There's got to be a way to co-opt him. Simply buy him off as a worst-case scenario. I think we keep all the options on the table and try to settle this peaceably. Alvarez wants to end this before it begins. His exact words were, let's just kill the son of a bitch."

"José Alvarez is on his way to LA as we speak. Gisele and I will be on a plane later tonight. She is flying in from Paris and I will meet her at JFK. We have chartered a plane and will be coming directly to LA. We should get there sometime early tomorrow morning and the five of us can figure out how to deal with this ass hole."

Bi Ba said, "I know it's not your fault but how did things fall through the cracks?"

Frederic thought for a second and responded, "Maybe that just tells us we are dealing with an extraordinary adversary and we have to be very careful. Whatever it is we will see you tomorrow morning and do what we always do. Maybe Alvarez is right. On reflection, it doesn't sound so crazy just to kill that son of a bitch and not have to worry about dealing with all this. Anyway, we will talk tomorrow."

Chapter 40

"Well it's started." Matt scornfully said to Bi Ba after one of Frederic's lawyers phoned. "We are being sued by some Montage homeowners."

Matt and Bi Ba and a partner, Alice Golden, purchased the Montage Beverly Hills Hotel and its condominium residences less than a year earlier. Steven Malgan's law firm sent investigators to approach the owners of all of 65 units and said they would represent them on a contingency because of the hotel's noncompliance to California OSHA rules dealing with disabilities. In California, real estate contractors or developers post indemnities or warranties having a 10-year duration for any wear and tear over and above normal usage situations, *i.e., cracks in the walls due to shrinkage caused by noncompliant materials or structural malfeasance.* In the event of a property sale, these warranties are passed on with the new owner absorbing the liabilities.

In this case Matt and his partner, Alice Golden, were now legally responsible for the warranties. Malgan's law firm sent a battery of investigators to solicit business, telling homeowners their property was flawed and could get corrections and compensations for damages, if they signed up with the law firm's class action suit. The law firm would represent the owners on contingency, when, not if, the suite was won, Matt would have to comply with the safety ordinances.

In this case, the granite top kitchen islands were not in compliance with Cal OSHA's codes because they were one-third of an inch lower than the regulation thirty-six inches. This suit alleged it posed a health risk. Frivolous as it sounded the state of California takes safety regulations on real estate very seriously and prosecutes to the fullest extent of the law. The remedy for the plaintiff in most cases is the cost of bringing the malady up to code. Awarding the plaintiff three times the cost of the physical damages and the possible granting of punitive damages on a case to case basis decided by a judge or arbitrator.

Matt knew the lawsuit was trivial but as Frederic had pointed out it could be a litigation nightmare, not only consuming time, but affecting his reputation.

Typifying this class-action type were the untold depositions larger in scope than the actual violation. Depositions used as a vehicle by the injured party for delving into areas far afield from the actual violations. California's deep antipathy towards property owners could drift from code adherence evidence moving into areas dealing with personal and financial information reflecting negatively on the defendant. It was a tactic to personalize the legal theories or strategies used by the plaintiff to win a decision and at the same time threaten the defendant with public exposure. Whether it was true or untrue. The threat of putting depositions in the public domain was tantamount to blackmail. Matt wasn't worried about the situation as it related to him but it could open his partner, Alice Golden, to public scrutiny.

Malgan's tactics and aggressive strategies were simple. He filed the lawsuit contending a pattern of illegal transgressions existed and to prove a pattern he asked the court for the right to look at all the opponent's business and personal practices to show proof. He would tell the courts he wanted to prove premeditation and malice of forethought. It was no more than blackmail but in most instances, it proved productive to the extent people acquiesced to his legal demands. Most people did not want to be open to the public light even if they didn't have anything to hide.

Malgan's young associates and clerks pressed for internal business documents, falsified information and made allegations trying to set into motion IRS audits. They delved into defendants' personal activities and questioned them about their sexual preferences, their fidelity and their health. All these maneuvers were frontal assault forms to discredit their opponents. Malgan's team engaged a negative social media campaign blitz to besmirch their opponent. If their pray was a celebrity, a person or figure of public notoriety or a politician, they would slander or libel them knowing the interpretation of the Constitution didn't protect public figures.

Papaz was only concerned about Malgan's bulldog attack methods as they related to Alice Golden. He had been through legal inquisitions before but he didn't know how she would withstand the ultra-combative illegal practices of the San Francisco lawyer.

"Bi Ba," he said, "can you call Alice and tell her we would like to have lunch? Let her know part of lunch is business because we have a problem and she should hear it from us first. Man, this guy is such an ass hole. Frederic was right about how he was going to play this."

Bi Ba said, "We don't need another headache. This guy really is a maniac. We can take care of ourselves but for sure Alice doesn't need this crap. I'll call her right now. I haven't talked to her since we got home from Carlsbad. I'm sure she'll love to have lunch. Knowing her, she won't blink an eye over this thing but you're right we should tell her as soon as possible." Papaz said, "After Paris and the Claymore thing I have nothing but total respect for her."

Ten months earlier in Paris while Papaz was participating in a social media and cyber world conference, they had invited Alice and her friend William Pele to come for a European weekend where the four of them shared time after the seminar where Papaz presented a paper.

As with all things Papaz, the two men were kidnapped by terrorists and subjected to torture. Neither man was seriously hurt. Both men were held captive for less than a day but the way Alice Golden reacted to the incident was extraordinary. Her calm response to the situation showed Matt and Bi Ba she had been through many wars. They felt she had a great deal to show the couple in regards to dealing with adversity.

Matt said, "It's more than just Paris. She never really pushed us to see what happened during that whole incident. I'll never forget Alice stepping up to the plate, protecting you and never asking any questions about why we were in such a predicament. Of course, the way she handled our problem at the Montage ultimately led to her being one of their partners. She put one-hundred million dollars into the partnership and never asked why we were in trouble. All she wanted was to help. She always had our backs. The only thing that ever really bothered her was when her friend Pele was hurt in Paris. Even then she didn't say much but that's her way. She is terrific. If there is any trouble, she is the first to help. You are the daughter she never had. She would do whatever we ask, but she doesn't need the crap Malgan is going to throw at her."

Frederic called Matt, "I just received an email. Shit, I can't believe this. It has happened already! I can't talk much right now but expect a lot more lawsuits. The Montague is the first of many. Your friend Alice is the first outside person he will go after. I know you guys are close so you should tell her as soon as possible."

Matt said, "We're having lunch with her later today and will fill her in on everything."

Frederic continued, "I'll contact all our other partners and tell them we have a problem. I'll tell them we'll shoulder all the cost and limit their exposure. It's a good thing most of them are outside the United States and can't be subpoenaed. We will pay any legal cost and I will verbally indemnify them. Every one of our partners will understand. Oh yeah, one last thing then I have to get off the phone. I talked to Guzman as soon as our lawyers got served the papers on the lawsuit. He said we should give Malgan a good reason to back off, like not taking his life.

If he doesn't give credible assurances and stand down, then Guzman wants us to kill him. He told me he would call you sometime today. He said you and Bi Ba shouldn't personalize this. Don't do anything stupid like going after Malgan yourselves. Talk to you later."

Frederic hung up.

Chapter 41

"Tell her we'll pick her up. That'll be easier because I have to talk to Howard Levine." Levine was the general manager of the Montague Hotel. "What time sounds good to you?"

Bi Ba asked, "I'll tell her 1:30pm. Will that give you enough time to speak to Howard?"

Matt replied, "Let's play it by ear. If there's no traffic and I can get a moment with him before lunch, then fine. If not then maybe you could take Alice shopping, of course we will pay for it, and I will meet you guys afterwards. It shouldn't take more than a half-hour."

Bi Ba responded, "I will call the Beverly Wilshire and make reservations for outside by the rail at the Boulevard Café. It's always fun to sit outside and look at the people."

Bi Ba made her call and Alice said she would be ready and waiting for them in the lobby at 1:00pm.

"I'll come downstairs. Call when you're pulling into valet parking."

Driving down the hill from their house toward Sunset Boulevard Matt mentioned to Bi Ba that he didn't understand how Malgan's investigators could have access to the owners of the condominiums.

"They must've gone to one of the homeowners' association meetings or one of the owners represented their interests."

"I looked at all of the agendas of the HOA meetings for the last three months and there is no mention of an outside vendor."

"I'll have Frederic looking at the video tapes to see if anyone talked to any owners. Frederic's lawyers said almost everyone signed up for the class-action suit. I think he gave me the number of 61 out of 65 people are going to sue us. On their part, there is no risk and no money out of pocket, because it's on a contingency basis. I guess most of them figure seventy percent of something without any risk or expenses is a pretty good deal."

By the time, they reached the hotel, it was ten minutes after one. After pulling into valet parking they left the car. Bi Ba walked over to the lobby while Matt called Levine to tell him he would drop by his office around 3:30pm, after he finished lunch.

Matt caught up with the two women and the three of them proceeded through the hotel to the gardens. As they walked across the greens of the hotel Alice commented on the white antique roses in front of the culinary school/restaurant contiguous to Beverly Drive. They turned left and walked a half block to Wilshire Boulevard and then turned right and walked a full block to the Beverly Wilshire Hotel. It took less than ten minutes to reach the café and be seated. Alice Golden had walked at a brisk pace for a woman of her age. She uncharacteristically had a long gate and her posture propelled her chin straightforward. She was square at the shoulders and walked with the surety of a thirty-year-old. Alice was wearing a yellow short-sleeved, round neck tee-shirt, a pair of jeans purchased at AG down the street from the hotel and a pair of Ugg's white tennis shoes.

Alice dressed much the same as Bi Ba who was almost forty years her junior. They did not look like the proverbial sisters but their age differential looked marginal. Both Bi Ba and Matt were wearing T-shirts, jeans, and tennis shoes. Neither had on jewelry except for their watches. The three walking towards the restaurant looked Beverly Hills casual. They chatted about social things. There was no hint of seriousness or discussion of business matters.

Once they were seated Alice said, "Okay what's going on at the hotel? Some other owners are avoiding me like I have the plague. A couple of them won't even look me in the eye, let alone speak to me."

She grabbed Bi Ba's forearm and started to laugh, "Well, they can't force me out like last time. We own the place!"

Matt said, "The way you are being treated is because of us. That's one reason we needed to talk to you."

Forever the charmer, he also said, "But the main reason is we wanted to see you. We haven't seen you in a while and you know how important you are to us."

Bi Ba interceded, "That is way too syrupy for me."

She started explaining the situation as a waiter appeared with some menus for the table.

"We are involved with a guy named Steven Malgan. He's a second cousin of Matt's."

She explained the purchase of the Istanbul hotel and the attendant Museum. She told Alice of Malgan Malgan and his two sons.

"This guy Steven Malgan is a psychopath as far as we can determine. He feels we are after the family trust and he will go to any lengths to protect his position. We feel we may have put you in danger because he goes after anyone and everyone close to us. That means you. The guy is crazy and this is very personal to him."

Alice smiled and said, "I guess I'm in the crosshairs again. I am not only a friend but I'm a business partner."

Matt interrupted, "He uses the tactic of coming after people we know or do business with to put enough pressure on them until we feel obligated to back off. He tied both of us to the hotel and filed some OSHA violations in a class-action suit against us. Alice, here's the big problem. He will deposition us to get into our personal finances and our personal lives putting pressure on us. Us means you and Bi Ba and me. He will go public with your personal life and use it as a pressure point to exact some type of guilt from us to comply to his demands.

Alice stopped listening and started to talk. "Hold on. He can come after me all he wants. I am transparent and at my age any recognition can't be bad." and she smiled. "What's he going to do? The worst thing he can say about me is," she reflected for a second, "He can say I had an affair when I was younger. Or that I was some type of whore. Maybe he'll try to paint a case that I defrauded some investors brought along with me on some of my projects? In this town, it only makes my legacy riskier.

Matt, that's not a threat. That's an opportunity. I appreciate both of you trying to look out for me but I'll be fine."

Bi Ba jumped into the conversation. "Alice, everything we know about him suggests he is dangerous. You don't need that. So, we are going to provide twenty-four-hour security for you and you can't say no. Right now, all we are concerned about is your protection and how did these people get to the owners here at the hotel."

Matt said, "We are worried they will use the same tactics and try to look at all your business activities over the years. We don't want to put you in a bad position."

Alice said, "I do appreciate the security. I will not lie to you and tell you I don't want it. I can never be too safe especially at my age."

Both Matt and Bi Ba hoped at her age they would be in such good shape.

"The business stuff, my assets are not in jeopardy. The only real investment I have unprotected is our partnership at the hotel. All my other investments are with major financial institutions. I don't have passwords. All of my transactions are done in person and there are explicit directions that I have to be involved in everything I do. No one has power of attorney and no one has direct access to any of my wealth without my direct permission in front of at least two people and a notary public."

Matt told her of all Malgan's team going into the hall of records and falsifying documents. He told her of their IRS whistle blowing and calling for audits of alleged tax violations.

Alice's response was of great interest to the couple. "I learned some important things a long time ago when my grandfather was brought up before the Committee on Un-American Activities. They devastated him because he didn't have records or proof of his activities. They built him up as a straw man who collaborated with communists. The committee falsified records of him funding left-leaning organizations. He was acquitted but in the aftermath of the hearings he was vilified and later blackballed in Hollywood. Because of that I felt compelled to maintain a paper trail that could not be adulterated. I needed a paper trail always in my control. No one would do to me what McCarthy did to my grandfather. For that purpose, it cost me about one percent of my net worth for the lockbox all my business and personal transactions stay. I have done this for the last 50 years. The only thing that has changed is the technology. I have originals of everything I have ever done and proof of document existence and authenticity by impeccable sources. Someday if you are interested I can give the details of how the process works. You once told me in regards to something else that you were bulletproof. Well, I am truly bulletproof."

"If those guys come after me I will bury them in court. Now as far as the physical threat is concerned that is another matter. If you tell me I am safe that is all I need to hear. In reality there's not much this guy can do to me. How much is the stipend or retainer or allowance or whatever you call the money he receives from the trust?"

Matt said, "It is $100,000 a month."

"Well," she said, "worst case is we pay them $1 million a year. Between the two of us that is easily doable. We won't even miss it. If that doesn't work out I know you have people to handle the situation. Not a big deal. Let me be honest, I'm really not concerned by any of this and nothing more needs be said."

They ordered lunch from the newly created molecular gastronomy menu created by Chef René Lachman whose infusion methods with liquid nitrogen were cutting edge in Beverly Hills. They ate and people watched for almost two hours. When they finished eating Matt and Alice sparred over who would pay the three-hundred-dollar bill. It was their way of showing respect for one another. Matt let Alice have her way with the proviso that when she and Bi Ba went shopping, she would let Bi Ba pay for anything they purchased.

Matt said, "I must go back to the hotel for a few minutes and talk to Howard Levine. Bi Ba and I have already talked about it. You and she are going to go over to Saks or Barney's or any place you would like and she's going to pay for whatever you guys buy. You can't say no because we want you to pick out something for San Diego. We're taking you and William Pele to the Aviara Resort in Carlsbad. I am going to reserve some rooms. I still feel like crap about what happened to him in Paris. I won't take no for an answer. Call him and set up a time next month. You guys work out the dates and we'll be available. I don't want to but I'll send a plane for his transportation if he has any problems making arrangements. I know he has access to CBS's plane but just in case. I know this is going to sound stupid but I feel like I owe him big time."

Alice didn't object. She knew her friend would like the opportunity to see Matt and Bi Ba again.

Chapter 42

Back at the hotel, Matt said to Howard Levine, "Howard, we have a problem. We are being sued by sixty-one of the condo owners for Cal-OSHA violations. It's a class-action suit."

He explained the granite top problems and potential health risks as they were laid out in the lawsuit.

"You will be subpoenaed. I will have our lawyers contact you later today and walk you through it." Matt reflected for a moment, "There are more serious problems. The firm representing the owners is called Steven Malgan and Associates. We cannot figure out how their investigators contacted our homeowners. We checked all the meetings of the HOA and even looked at videotapes of the procedures and we saw no evidence of their communicating owners here at the hotel. We have not seen any contact evidence between Malgan's people and our residents. Do you have any ideas?"

Levine shook his head and said, "I have no clue."

Howard Levine was thirty-eight years old and graduated from the University of Las Vegas' prestige hotel management program. Prior to coming over to the Four Seasons Montage he worked in small boutique hotels in New York City. His position at the Montage, a five-star Michelin hotel with a residential complex, was a coveted job. His salary was $130,000 a year plus bonuses. Timid in appearance he was formidable in performance. Levine was five feet, eight inches tall and overweight at 210 pounds. His black hair was thinning and to compensate he combed it over to the side making him look much older and less self-assured. His face was round but not youthful. He had dull dark brown eyes and a mustache that favored the face of an old Middle Eastern merchant. It was thin and cut halfway up his lip. Simply put his looks were deceiving. He looked as if he were weak but he was decisive and articulate about his visions for the hotel. He was an extraordinary number cruncher whose financials were of the first order.

Matt queried him for a second time about Malgan's associates. Howard is there something I don't know about happening here at the hotel?

Levine fumbled for words. "Sorry, Mr. Papaz, I thought we had handled what I considered to be a problem that might be related to this. About three months ago, a man by the name…of," he clicked his notes icon on his iPad. He reviewed his notes and then said, "His name was Hurat Markalyan. He approached, Mavis Lewis, my secretary and asked her to set up an appointment. It was nothing out of the ordinary. He came to the hotel in person, not a phone call or email, and wanted to set up an appointment for the next week. It is usually not our policy to do business with outside vendors but Mavis said she had a feeling he might be able to provide us a service. I told her to schedule a meeting but appraise Markalyan I only had a fifteen-minute window. She scheduled the meeting and neither one of us had a second thought about it."

Levine got up and walked over to his desk. The two men had been sitting on a couch in his office. He opened the top drawer and pulled out one of Markalyan's business cards. He handed it to Matt. The card identified Markalyan as an insurance salesperson for the Farmers Property Management Group. Matt looked at the card's red logo which was an identical replication of the multinational Farmers Insurance Company.

Matt said, "Obviously, it was a fake business card. In truth, I don't fault you for not picking it up. I would never have noticed it, Howard. What do you recall about the meeting?"

He looked at his iPad again and said, "It was on May 3rd. My notes say he was aggressive and asked for information about our residents and how he could sell them insurance. I wrote he wasn't very professional and wasn't very prepared. We never called him back and passed it off as bad judgments in making the meeting. In hindsight, maybe he was checking us out."

Mr. Papaz he said, "Since then, our meeting procedures for outside vendors has gone back to the position of we don't do business with people we don't know."

Howard Levine continued speaking, "About two weeks after the meeting we saw Markalyan on one occasion in the lobby of the hotel. Then we saw a flood of dark looking ethnic men of an intimidating nature in the lobby and in the restaurants. We talked to security, I think you know Latish Paul, we asked her to handle it. I can get her over here if you'd like to talk to her."

Papaz said, "Maybe later."

Levine continued, "As soon as we pressed the dark skinned looking men in the lobby, I don't want to sound like I'm profiling but, the Middle Eastern looking men, they vanished. We never put any of this together. My job is such that I have problems every day and this was just out of the ordinary, nothing major."

"Maybe there is something else, I don't know. We were approached by three young men calling themselves Associates of some law firm in San Francisco about the building meeting code."

Still standing at the desk he pulled out three business cards and all three associates worked for Malgan.

"They said the previous hotel owner, prior to you, had shown a shoddy work pattern not compliant with code. They wanted to investigate. I thought it was a scam to solicit our business. I told them I wanted to look into it. I told them we usually dealt with these things internally and I would contact them. I called one of the companies we deal with, Harrison & Son. They are architectural contractors and planners. I'll email you the report. In essence they said we were clean of any code violations. They said I could get insurance that would warranty any problems with being up to code. I told him I had only heard about this type of insurance for homes and then asked them if they knew any companies that would warrantee a project as large as ours. He said he would call but up to this point I have not heard back from him. I really think I took all of the appropriate business procedures into consideration when dealing with these problems. I can show you my personal notes. Like I said, I'll send you the emails. This kind of stuff happens every day around here. I didn't pass it on to you because I felt not only did I address the problems but it isn't my job to go to you with day to day operational things. I only try to bring situations to your attention that deal with policy.

Papaz said, "Howard I would've probably done the exact same things you did but not as effectively. Send me the emails. You know I don't ever micromanage so you're not bringing this to my attention falls in line with my philosophies of management. To be honest, we pay you a lot of money to handle the stuff and keep me out of the loop. I trust your judgment and decision-making. We are fine on this but we still have to deal with this lawsuit. I need to know how Malgan got hold of our owners. He filled Levine in on some of Malgan's maneuvers and warned him of an eminent subpoena. He's not a good guy and his people will come after you. You're not paid for this kind of stuff, it's not your job, so we will shoulder any legal liabilities you may incur if it comes to that. You can use our lawyers but if you feel you have more confidence in someone else I will pay for it."

Papaz finished saying, "Malgan's people are hired guns. He is all that is bad about the legal profession. We feel he has you in his sights. Our investigators are looking into this. They want to make sure it stays a legal problem and doesn't move into any other realm."

Levine questioned the word realm.

Papaz told him of Malgan's intimidation and violence proclivities but that he would be protected.

"I want you to alert security. If they see any of Markalyan's people I want them dealt with and the police called. There is something else. Have security look at all of the tapes in the common area of the hotel and try to identify Markalyan's colleagues. I am over cautious but I don't want this to get out of hand. As far as your safety is concerned we will let security at the hotel stay in place but once you leave the hotel I will pay for some bodyguards until this is straightened up."

Papaz started to get up to leave the office and continued, "You did a good job. If you're subpoenaed just tell the truth. Don't embellish, don't lie and don't try to protect me or the hotel. Just tell the truth. Contrary to what people say the truth can't come back and bite you on the ass. Lies are how you get in trouble. Our lawyers will get hold of you and a team of bodyguards will introduce themselves to you before you go home today. You did a good job. Sorry you are involved in this mess."

ISTANBUL

Chapter 43

Matt called Bi Ba as soon as he walked out of Howard Levine's office and asked where she wanted to meet.

She said, "We're down the street at boutique Faconnable. It's an old established French haberdashery purchased by Nordstrom's department store last year. Why don't you come over here? They have some real neat things you might be interested in."

The boutique was only a few blocks from the hotel. He told her he would be there in less than ten minutes.

On his way, he received a call from Frederic. "Where are you? I am with Gisele and Alvarez. We literally just got here, making reference to the fact that they were in Beverly Hills. We have to talk."

Matt said he was walking over to meet Bi Ba and Alice Golden down the street from the hotel. He gave him the name of the store and asked if they were close.

Frederic said, "Yeah, we are. We'll meet you over there. I think you need to hear what I have to say. We are right in front of David Yarman's on Rodeo Drive a couple blocks from Wilshire. We should be there in a couple of minutes."

Within five minutes Frederic, Gisele, and Alvarez walked into Faconnable and spotted the two women. The two pods of friends got a glimpse of each other from across the store. Bi Ba and Alice were carrying arm loads of clothing to the register and the three visitors were carrying a serious determination to discuss Steven Malgan. They merged in the center of the men's department.

Bi Ba shook her head and said, "The expressions on your faces looks like business."

Alice extended her hand out to Frederic and said, "Frederic Vallans, correct?" She then turned to Gisele. "Gisele Lapiner is that correct?"

Finally, she extended her hand to José Alvarez. "I only remember you as José. It's nice to see all of you again."

Frederic spoke for the three visitors. "I wish we were here for pleasure but it's business. I don't mean to sound like the world is ending or we face the next major extinction but things are escalating with this guy Malgan. After you purchase this stuff we should get out of here."

Bi Ba said, "Matt is on his way here. He called from the hotel."

Frederic responded, "Yeah I know. I just spoke to him. By the time, he gets here you should be done. We should go someplace private."

As soon as Matt walked into the boutique Frederic approached him and said, "I know this will sound dramatic but all hell can break out at any moment. Let's go over to the hotel and talk."

Upon exiting the store the six friends were flanked by security guards who walk them over to the Montague. At the hotel, Howard Levine was waiting. Looking directly at Matt Papaz he said, "I called at least three times. Are you all right?"

Papaz pulled his cell phone out of the back pocket of his jeans and said, "I'm really sorry. It was on vibrate and I didn't notice anything."

Levine said, "We have a problem. The Armenians are back. They threatened some of our residents in the parking garage. None of them were hurt but they were seriously intimidated. I called the police. I guess you guys missed them because you came in from Beverly Drive. The police are on the other side of the hotel on Canon. They are interviewing some of the residents that were confronted in the garage and asked for our video tapes. I know it's that guy Markalyan. The Armenians were here. They bullied Mr. and Mrs. Tapper in #1602, and Ms. Williamson in #1901 and the nicest Thelma Daughtry in #2003. It was no coincidence. They are three of the four owners who had not signed on to the class action suit."

Matt said, "Let us handle this. We don't want to take a chance of doing anything illegal. Where is Ms. Paul?"

Levine said, "She is probably with the police."

Matt replied, "Get her over here when she's done. I would like to talk to her. We'll need more security for the hotel. I don't want to frighten you but your personal security might be in jeopardy. Like I said earlier, don't leave the hotel until you talk to our people!"

Frederic spoke, "This is the reason we came here. We had some information that the Armenian Mongrels, they are one of Glendale's most notorious gangs, were on their way to Beverly Hills. We thought they were coming after you." looking directly at Matt. "Let's go upstairs and finish our conversation up there. This place is too public. Howard, when you finish with the police you will need to hear what we must say. You need to be part of our conversation. Come up to our suite."

The six walked over to the residential bank of elevators. They were followed by the bodyguard team who had walked them to the hotel.

One bodyguard approached Frederic and spoke softly, "Sir we can put men on Mr. Papaz's floor. Do you want us to place any security on Ms. Golden's floor?"

"No, that would tip off our hand. What you can do is have someone go up to each of the rooms and make sure they're okay."

"Alice," he said, "Let me have your key card. What suite are you in?" He handed the card to the guard.

The six were only standing at the elevators for five minutes before Frederic's security team came down and told him both suites were secure.

"Everything is fine. We scanned the rooms for electronics and they both were clean." the head of the security detail said.

Frederic said, "Since everything appears to be all right we should go up to Matt's and Bi Ba's. We need to discuss the Armenians. They proceeded to the 11th floor.

Once everyone was seated Frederic said, "I'm going to let Gisele and José talk to you guys. They have a better handle on some of this than I do."

He looked towards Gisele and she said, "We were at a loss as to how Malgan's law firm contacted all of the owners to be part of the class action suit. So, we did a search of each occupant to see if we could cross reference anything with Malgan. Nothing came up but we found the gentleman in Suite #1202, Dennie Morris is the second cousin of one of your former owners. The guy that lived here before. His name is Roland Williams, who is paying the mortgage for Morris through some accounts they are trying to hide."

"After finding this out we looked at all the common spaces video in the hotel residency parts and found Dennie was having meetings almost every night with 8 to 10 home owners and three associates of Malgan's law firm. It's not that important but the Associates names are Russell Wilson, Paul Shaffer, and Able Myers. They were given access to the residency part of the complex by way of the service elevator. They entered the hotel from the underground garage. Mr. Morris had given them a key and they clandestinely entered the hotel the night of each meeting. Suffice it to say they did a heck of a selling job on the class action suit, sixty-one out of sixty-five owners. Alice I am assuming I am right by saying you were not invited to any of the meetings."

She responded, "No I wasn't. I really didn't know Dannie except to say hello to him in the hallway but his cousin, that Williams person, is one of the most despicable man I've ever met. I had hate in my heart ever since he said the homeowner's association needed a Jew lawyer to deal with Matt and Bi Ba when he took the lead in trying to get them evicted from the hotel last year. He's no more than a cowardly anti-Semite. If anybody would be behind trying to get rid of us by a class-action suit it would be him."

Gisele responded, "Our problem is we can't find a link between him and Malgan. We know they are collectively behind coming after the two of you since Alice Golden owned forty-nine percent of the hotel. As for their relationship with the Armenian Mongrels I will let José speak to that."

Papaz spoke up, "José, before you say anything I want to put in my two cents. I was starting to be embarrassed by being an Armenian before all this happened and you have to know how I feel now. I am truly sorry I got everybody involved in this. Alice, I'll tell you all of this later but this began by me buying a hotel in Istanbul and wanting to pay homage to my heritage. When I was a kid I swore, I wasn't Armenian. I even took on the moniker of a person of the world. I think I liked it better that way. After buying that hotel it sounded impressive to be an Armenian. Anyhow, I am now embarrassed by the American side of my heritage. Sorry José, why don't you fill us in."

Before he could say anything, Frederic said, "I just got a text from security downstairs. Let me pass something by you guys before José talks about the Armenian gangs. Alice, your unit is the only one on the floor correct? What is the other square footage up there used for?"

She said, "I don't really know it's cordoned off by drywall. It's owned by the hotel."

Papaz said, "When Levine gets up here I'll ask. He should know."

Looking at Alice Frederic continued, "You're not going to be staying in your place for a while. We're going

ISTANBUL

to set up some type of sting to get the Armenians. We'll have one of our people pose as you to hopefully encourage these gangsters to try to intimidate or physically come after you. Matt, Bi Ba we'll do the same for you. We will work it out to make it look like you are staying here rather than at your house in Bel Air. We will have two people posing as you staying in your unit. You are the only ones on your floor, right? If we place guards on each floor it will tip off our hand. Let's present a situation for the Armenians to come after you. If we do it right, we can tie these gangsters to Malgan. Guzman said that because you are virtually segregated from the rest of the homeowners by being on your own floors the Armenians will come after you one way or another. They're violent but unsophisticated. Setting up a sting operation shouldn't be too hard. Once we put everything into place I will fill you in on particulars. José, it's your turn. What do you have for us?"

"Let me call one of our men from downstairs. His name is Richard Avazian. He is much more familiar with the Armenians than me. He used to head the LAPD's Armenian and gypsy task force."

Chapter 44

Avazian wasn't anything the group had expected. He was rail thin with spindly legs and a big belly. His hair was a thinning black and white pepper color. It was dirty and uncombed. He wore trendy red rimed 4X glasses that extenuated his large nose. His clothing was an amalgam of unmatched purple pants, a green plaid wrinkled long sleeved shirt, and high topped Nike black basketball shoes. Many of his colleagues felt his dress eccentricity was a way of deflecting his homeliness. He looked a mess. Ordinary men sometimes surprise you by doing extraordinary things. Normal people like Avazian can do uncommon things like head a task force.

When Avazian spoke, he was all business, "I am Armenian not Russian Armenian. My name ends in i-a-n. I am not like those dirt bag Russian Armenians whose names end in y-a-n. They are dangerous and will never be part of the American fabric."

"Now that I exposed my prejudice I will fill everyone in on why we're here. We got some information from one of our sources in the LAPD that the Armenian Mongrels were setting up some type of protection scheme in Beverly Hills. Our preliminary information showed Markalyan was going to use strong arm tactics to shake down some rich people at the Montage Hotel. West Los

Angeles is far a field for him so this raised red flags. The Mongrels' primary turf is usually Glendale or Hollywood. The police didn't come up with any names because a lot of their Intel was in an Armenian dialect that their interpreter had problems understanding. At the same time one of our federal sources said another Armenian named Andranik Aloyan, head of the Armenian Animals was stealing financial information from some Montage Hotel permanent residents. Markalyan is very violent and his tactics are always physical intimidation. Whereas Aloyan is more financial racketeering involved, mostly preying upon the elderly. Both coming to Beverly Hills meant only one thing to us. We figured it was a play by Malgan to come after somebody. Historically the Animals and Mongrels are competing gangs so there must be lots of money for them to abide by some peace agreement and work together. Both guys are extremely violent but Markalyan has a reputation of being a hothead and leaving many bodies in his wake. He is the more dangerous of the two."

"Personality profiles show them as what we call low thinkers. They are violent, irrational and act without regards to authority. Both think from the back of the brain, near the medulla oblongata. You know, the reptilian evolutionary part of the old brain. They are not like us. We use the more modern part of our brain's cerebral cortex, the frontal lobe. Markalyan and Aloyan are like animals. They calculate the distance they need to leap to pounce upon the prey and kill it very efficiently. They never calculate the consequences of the kill because they are primal in their thinking and have no concept of guilt, evil or crossing the line. On the contrary, we are limited in our options by our guilt which is a more modern concept in the evolution of man. Suffice it to say, they are very dangerous."

"This morning after talking to Jose and receiving his information, we immediately sent two mercenary teams here to Beverly Hills. You already met one team. They escorted you from the clothing store to the hotel. The other team is working with hotel security and the police. You are safe but the gangs are relentless and are in play. We are putting some measures into effect that will apply pressure on Malgan trying to get him to back off. He is crazy but not stupid. He knows if he is tied to any of their illegal activities it can reflect back to him. Our analysis shows there will be a problem for Malgan because once these guys smell money they won't back off. Markalyan and Aloyan are cousins and come from Yerevan in Armenia. They are Russian Armenians and that doesn't bode well for the situation. Russian Armenians are extremely violent and irrational. Malgan made an agreement to give both gangs all the class-action suit information so they could virtually strip these rich American assholes of all their money when this operation was over."

"We know Malgan is after you, but has determined he can scam all the homeowners, getting a percentage of the money the Armenians take from them. We figure Markalyan will go after them for protection money. He likes physically pressuring people and sadistically uses violence to extract as much money as possible."

"Aloyan is more like a gypsy or Roma in Eastern Europe. He's a scam artist and perceives himself as a mobster. He and his gang are more into racketeering. They target the elderly. Initially, he only worked in the Glendale Armenian community. This new opportunity is big for them. As I said earlier, they are not extremely bright so they prayed upon the poor and the relatively uninformed. The Montage might be a stretch for them. That's why Malgan elicited the support of Markalyan. He believes rich people always yield to violence. Most of Aloyan's activities are low-end but he has the ability to steal financial information. His gang steals credit cards either scanning them in restaurants and gas stations or pickpocketing. They're capable of kidnapping older people and draining their bank accounts. Aloyan has the ability to manufacture counterfeit credit cards. Because some of his men are new immigrants from Eastern Europe he is moving into extortion and fire arms. All of these activities are low-tech but he is very successful."

"That's the primary picture of the two gangs. Our operation will protect you and we'll deal with the problems these gangs present! First as Frederic mentioned, we will have people who double for you. They will stay in your condos and role-play as if they are you. The three of you, as he talked to Matt, Bi Ba, and Alice, will be portrayed as vulnerable. Your doubles will be put in positions of being by themselves in unguarded areas of the hotel and on Beverly Hills streets. We will schedule that on a daily basis your stand-ins will be open to either intimidation or kidnapping. Alice, your double will go for walks every day. She will take the elevator to the garage, walk up the driveway to the street and from there proceed to Santa Monica Boulevard Park. Our men will be placed in strategic areas. Once your double is attacked, we will apprehend the Armenians. Pure and simple entrapment. They are so greedy they won't be able to leave you alone. We think the Armenians will try to draw your double into a van. The way the Mongrels do business is to get a person inside one of these vans and beat them to an inch of their life. From that point they've had the ability to get whatever they want."

"Matt, Bi Ba your doubles will stay in your condo not your house. We are going to put the two of you up in Santa Monica Loews Hotel. Just in case, we have security at your home so they don't vandalize it or burn it down. Matt, I promise a better outcome than what happened before."

The Papaz's villa was attacked by 18th Street Pico Union gang and major damage inflicted eleven months earlier.

"As soon as the Mongols or Animals come after your doubles we will have our security team, LAPD and the Feds apprehend them in the act."

Alice said, "José, can I say something?"

"Sure," he said. "Am I to take it that I leave my home and a double is used to trap the Armenians as they try to kidnap me and take my assets?"

"Yeah Alice. The same for Matt and Bi Ba. If this doesn't work and they somehow figure out where you are and come after you, we just kill them. Our first choice is to have the LAPD catch them red-handed and press charges so we track it to Malgan. Either scenario, catch them or kill them is fine. We just have one objective to end this situation."

Chapter 45

After packing some clothes for their Loews Hotel stay, Matt, Bi Ba, and Alice left the hotel guarded by Alvarez's group. Simplifying security, the three stayed at the same hotel,

Frederic and Gisele went to the Beverly Wilshire making it their new home until the danger passed. Alvarez and Avazian decided to walk down the stairwell to the lobby from the 11th floor doing reconnaissance for the operation. They looked for blind spots, areas where hotel cameras didn't provide adequate coverage. Alvarez was surprised by Avazian's candor and deep hatred for the Russian Armenians.

He said, "The Russians are an embarrassment to our people. They are barbaric relics of the past. My hatred comes from all the people they killed on the streets of Glendale. They're like Ottoman rulers. Hate runs deep in the Armenian community poorer sections because of their barbaric ways. Every one of us in Hollywood or Glendale has lost someone to these gangsters. We are under their control just like the Mexicans are subject to the laws of the Pico Union gangs. The only difference is the 18th Street Gang is not so arbitrary. Part of the Armenian Russians' power comes from the fact that no one in their fiefdom knows the rules, but are expected to bow to their demands. Uncertainty is a powerful weapon."

"The Mongrels under the command of Markalyan have been known to kill for sport. Part of their new member initiation is to have a recruit rape a family member to show gang loyalty. There are occasions when potential members were forced to rape their own sisters and at least one occasion where a recruit raped his own mother. If they fail to follow the pledging initiation, they face death. Most Armenians think there is no way out, especially for children in Glendale's poorer sections. It's the gang's way or death to anyone deviating from their authority. The Russian Armenian's control of illegal activities in Glendale and Hollywood is total. It makes life hell for the real Armenians. If I sound irrational it is only because I have seen more than you. The only way to deal with these people is to kill them."

Avazian pulled his cell from the pocket of his purple pants and called the head of the LAPD's Armenian task force.

"Arat" he said, "I need a favor. I know it's a joint operation between you and us but I need some time with the Russians when we get our hands on them. I need to interrogate them alone. Let us run point and apprehend them and we will hand them over to you. When we finish, they are yours. I promise I won't kill anyone but that's all I can promise."

He got off the phone.

Alvarez looked at him, "I like the way you think"

Avazian replied, "I am paid handsomely by you guys. I will get whatever you want. I feel very lucky working with you because I will enjoy every bit of hurting these bastards and getting them off the streets. What makes my skin crawl, and I am not religious, is these pieces of garbage wear silver and gold crosses and have tattoos of crosses, Christ and the Virgin Mary all over their bodies. Shit, they can't even spell the word Christ. They are evil. They are a lot like the Boko Haram in East Africa. It is a badge of honor to rape a rival gang's woman and impregnate her as if that dilutes the enemy's gene pool. They are animals. If I could spay, the Russians I would. I must sound ghetto but José you have not had to deal with these animals your whole life."

"As for Malgan, I'm not personally familiar with him. Some of the police on the task force say he is sadistic. He is hands on when it comes to hurting women. With men, not so much. If there is a chance of physical harm coming his way, he is out of there. He is a God damned coward. He is the kind of guy who likes to watch people get tortured. I picture him masturbating over someone else's pain. I am sure he can't get it up with a real woman. The only thing that excites him is some sadistic expression of someone's misfortune. José, I am sorry. My going off this way has to be boring as hell."

Alvarez started laughing, "I can't imagine how much you would unload on me if we were friends. Just kidding. There are certain things push me up the wall. So, I know exactly how you feel. Even the mention of someone's name can set me off. When I am off tilt it's a long day for me and anyone near me because it takes a long time to cool down. It is all right if you are not professional about how you deal with an adversary. Great passion allows you to have the advantage in dealing with threats. If you're not passionate it could be fatal. I never believed in the BS that you have to be professional and objective. Every time I let my guard down by doing the politically correct things around bad guys, bad things happened to me and the people I care about."

He put his arm around Avazian's shoulder and said, "We are pretty much alike. It's a good thing."

Chapter 46

Papaz's house in Bel Air was secure. Alice, Matt and Bi Ba were sequestered in Santa Monica. The sting was proceeding.

The doubles Avazian arranged were ready to play their easy mark roles. Routines were scripted placing first Alice, then Bi Ba and Matt in vulnerable positions at the Beverly Hills Montage Hotel. All the doubles were sized to fit. Masquerading as Matt, Bi Ba and Alice, they learned how their counterparts walked and replicated physical traits such as the principles' posture or gait as closely as possible. Facial masks fashioned with a three-dimensional printer, rendered the trio undetectable by the human eye.

Avazian knew the Armenians' greed would activate the sting in short order. As with all low thinkers, the Armenian's desire for blood and treasure was impulsive and demanded short run action.

The first morning of "Operation Malgan" Alice's double prepared to leave the hotel by 9:30am going for a walk on Little Santa Monica Blvd. and Crescent Height's greenway. Laurie Zafert, a twenty-eight-year-old, five feet two inches tall ex-Marine weighing one hundred-five pounds was Alice's double. She wore her mask and walking outfit making an exact double of Alice Golden.

The costume she put on each morning took over twenty-five minutes' preparation and was worn all day. She put on a pair of Lulu Lemon black jogging pants, an athletic bra to suppress the size of her breasts, a white high necked T-shirt and loose sweater. A pair of black Nike running shoes were deemed appropriated for the green. Once dressed she placed the full-face mask over her head and pulled the T-shirt over the long neck rubber extension leading from the chin of the mask. She placed a gray wig on her head, affixed it tightly with a rubberized adhesive glue, looking into the bathroom mirror with a video of Alice projected from an iPad sitting on the granite countertop she practiced Alice's stride and posture one last time. Just before leaving the condominium she strapped on a shoulder holster for a 9 mm Glock over her right shoulder and put on a black hoodie and zipped it up to the neck.

Zafert followed the course plotted by Avazian, her handler. The day before the operation, she did a dry run doing her own surveillance, trying to get a feel for the walk and be more comfortable with it. She knew how long it would take from the elevator of Alice's unit down to the hotel's underground parking structure. From the parking structure, up to the street and time and distances for all points to and from the park to the hotel. Zafert had knowledge of the Mongrels most likely position with the greatest possibility to take her. She knew exactly where her cohorts would be stationed. The excursion from the hotel and back took exactly one hour and forty minutes. She was back to the condominium at exactly 11:10am. After entering the master bathroom, it was made to appear she took a steam bath and a long shower. All of this was part of the sting operation because she had intentionally left the condominium door unlocked to allow for Markalyan's men to have free entrance. The more options the Armenians would have to engage her the faster the sting operation would be completed. There were two security guards in the condominium always for Zafert's protection, if the Armenians came trying to kidnap or intimidate her.

Nothing was left to chance. All scenarios allowing the Armenians to confront her were intentionally opened. The slow thinking Armenians were measuring the distance for the kill. That was evident because time was lapsing. Once they decided to act the problems of not understanding their new environment would be their downfall. Beverly Hills was not Glendale and Alice, Matt and Bi Ba were not the Armenian's ordinary pray. A sting operation could only be as successful as dragging the fly into the spider's web. Avazian's team had created situations where Alice's double looked vulnerable not only in the hotel but on the streets of Beverly Hills.

Zafert followed her routine exactly for three days without Avazian's men sighting the Armenians. The morning walk, leaving the condominium unit open, now was augmented by an early dinner walk.

At 5:30pm Zafert left the twelfth-floor condominium went through the lobby, exited on Canon Drive and proceeded to dinner. Avazian made a 6 o'clock standing reservation sitting at a front table outside La Florino, an Italian restaurant.

Zafert wore a different outfit of jeans, a light cotton long sleeve turtleneck sweater and a baseball cap. She carried a lightweight jacket cradled in her arms, giving her the ability to have her Glock, a teaser and a knife at the ready. She ate by herself until 6:45pm, then walked back to the hotel.

On the fourth day, the Armenians were spotted on Canon Drive sipping coffee outside the Brazilian Café, Bamba. They did not approach her but were in constant communication with Markalyan. The conversation was picked up by the LAPD under a court-ordered wiretap.

Markalyan's lieutenant placed a seventeen second call saying, "We just saw the bitch. It looks like she goes to the same place to eat every night."

Markalyan responded, "Get her tomorrow!"

The lieutenant shot back, "It should be easy. We'll work out the details."

Markalyan replied again, "We'll talk. Get out of there and come to the store."

He was making reference to his office. The seventeen seconds were clearly not legal proof of intent to kidnap. There was no explicit terrorism threat or kidnapping. At best, it would only be circumstantial evidence that would be allowed in court but it was all the LAPD and Avazian needed to set the trap for the Armenians the next night.

On the fifth night Zafert intentionally took a different route to La Florino. The change in plans was to throw off the Armenians, make them improvise and take away any advantages they thought they had.

When Avazian put the correction into place, he told the LAPD's task force, "Low thinkers don't adapt to change well. I will make sure they have to grab their victim coming from the wrong side of the street. That will take away any advantage they have when they try to pull her into the van."

The only place a van could pull over and the gangsters could apprehend Zafert and get her off the street was the entrance to an underground parking structure mid-block on the west side of Canon Drive. Avazian's men were at the egress and ingress of the structure and dispersed inside and outside giving them the ability to intervene when Zafert was taken off the street. Once she was inside the van it would take less than 10 seconds to free her from the Armenians.

The next day Zafert as planned walked over to the Santa Monica green at the prescribed time of 9:30am. After doing the circuit around the green she went back to the hotel and followed her regimen of staying inside with the door open until 5:30pm when she exited Alice's condominium and proceeded out to dinner. Her route that night went through the hotel to Canon Drive and stayed on the west side of the street for one block until she passed Dalton Way. From there she crossed the street to the east side of Canon, walked to the Nightingale Boutique looking at clothing and exited within 10 minutes. After leaving the boutique she continued on Canon Drive for one more block to Brighton Way, crossed Canon's west side and entered the restaurant. She was seated outside and had her dinner.

Instead of walking on the west side of Canon, crossing the parking garage entrance between Brighton and Dalton, going directly back to the hotel she again changed her direction and cross the street to walk back on the east side of Canon. By crossing the street, the Armenians were now parked thirty feet from their prey in the garage entrance. They were low thinkers not fast thinking, could not improvise so they could only hope she would follow the original plan going to and from the restaurant the next night. They phoned Markalyan who called off the operation.

Markalyan modified the number of men for the next night's kidnapping from four to six. The two new men dressed in suits sitting in the lobby downstairs from her unit followed Zafert out of the hotel to La Florino acting as command and control, passing information to their four partners in the van about when and where Alice's double could be picked up.

Initially the Econoline van parked in the underground lot driveway where they would give the pick-up directive as she approached the restaurant if she walked on the west side of Canon. If she made it to the restaurant, command and control would make a determination of where the van should wait for her after dinner depending on which side of the street she walked.

Zafert left the hotel walking towards the restaurant on the west side of Canon. As she approached the black Ford Econoline a call was placed, two man darted out the sliding door on its right side and pulled her into the back seat. Four of Avazian's people were on the street five paces from the van standing in front of a small café as if entering the establishment. Three more men were across the street and six men were in the underground garage near the cashier's box fifty feet from where the driveway hit the street.

In less than ten seconds four men had commandeered the driver and pulled him out at gunpoint. They entered the back and side door of the van extricating Zafert without harm. The rest of Avazian's men blanketed the Armenians carting them to a waiting Cadillac Escalade to be interrogated. They were taken to a vacant storefront in Westwood three miles away. The LAPD agreed to watch the operation with knowledge that the six Armenians would be theirs within a few hours. Per his agreement with the LAPD task force Avazian had two hours to extract information on the Markalyan complicity in the kidnapping, all his racketeering practices and his relationship with Malgan.

Chapter 47

The six Armenians were taken to 1161 Westwood Boulevard, a vacant retail building between Westwood and Santa Monica. The building had been unoccupied for almost a year. Its dirty windows were covered with brown butcher paper. There was graffiti on the outside of the building extending across the glass windows and door in the shop front. A Coldwell Banker for lease sign was left on the building to make it look more innocuous.

The previous renter was a copying and printing company. As with many unsuccessful businesses in Southern California who had to file bankruptcy, the Speedy Printing Company left the premises a mess. Paper and debris littered the floors. Any fixtures or machines with value were stripped from the building. The retail space laid idle and unattended because its elderly owner felt it was too much trouble, too little money, to try to lease it.

Avazian learned about the property, leased it for a safe house and starting and ending point for his black ops. The only tenant improvements, if one could call them that, were done to the back room. It was sound proofed and a heavy gauge plastic covering was placed on the floor. The ceiling's three overhanging fluorescent lights were fixed but still flickered and threw off a loud buzzing sound. In the middle of the twenty-four by sixteen feet room, six metal chairs were brought in from the front shop area while the Armenians were in route from Beverly Hills.

The Armenians were brought into the back room via the alley. Once inside of the building they were taken one by one, stripped bare and tied to metal chairs with plastic hand and leg cuffs. A plastic mouthpiece looking like a drain plug was placed in each man's mouth. Up to this point there was no physical abuse of the captives other than being subdued and placed in their chairs.

After the last man was firmly secured Avazian said in Armenian, "Look at me you pieces of shit. Its me, Dickron Avazian."

Dickron was Armenian for Richard. "You are going to find out what it feels like being at the other side of the table."

He looked at the third Russian from his left and said, "Adan do you remember me? I was the guy you went after when I was the head of The Knight of Vartan. You fuck, do you remember what you did to my sister? After you gang raped her she fell apart and committed suicide. You fuck. Now it's my turn."

Avazian walked out of the room and picked up a ten-inch metal pipe resting on the floor. He looked directly at Adan Tashjyan and pushed the pipe into his stomach.

Tashjyan shouted at him, "Yeah I remember you. But I remember how we all fucked your sister. She liked it. She was a juicy piece of ass. Too bad she died before we could fuck her again."

Avazian's sister had been picked out to be raped because Avazian informed on the Mongrel's activities in Glendale. It had been six years and at this moment all Avazian wanted to do was kill the Russian animals. Now he had his chance to extract some revenge with an implied consent from the LAPD.

What he would do next to Tashjyan would make death a preferable option. He pulled the pipe from the Russian's stomach and shoved it into his scrotum.

"I will only say this once. Who set this up?"

Tashjyan spit in his face. He pulled the pipe up with tremendous force and slammed it into the Russian's ball sack. Then he jabbed the open end of the pipe into his captive's flaccid penis severing it from its stem.

"You weren't going to tell me shit you fuck," Avazian yelled at the naked slumping figure of his bloodied adversary. He then looked at the other five Russians and plunged the end of the pipe into the right eye of Tashjyan. Blood started to spurt from his eye socket and flowed down his neck to his belly and eventually met the tide of crimson liquid that flowed down from Tashjan's groin to the plastic covering on the floor.

Tashjyan was still alive but barely breathing. Avazian yelled for one of his men to bring him the bottle of the sulfuric acid and a pair of yellow rubber gloves that were sitting on one of the abandoned copying machine in the front room of the print shop. When Avazian's man came back into the room handing him the bottle and the gloves. He then slowly put the gloves on and opened the cloudy bottle of sulfuric acid, poured it onto the blood drenched genital area of Tashjyan cauterizing the wound.

The smell of sulfur and dissolving flesh permeated the room.

Avazian yelled, "You piece of shit."

The dimly lit room was quiet with fear. Avazian stood in front of the remaining five Armenians and said coldly, "Every one of you knows me. Every one of you have either hurt my family or my friends. I have waited for what seems like half my life for this. I will ask once. Just once. If you don't satisfy me with your answers I will do worse to you than I did to that fuck."

He walked over to the first chair. Sitting in front of him was Avet Bosajyan. He grabbed him by his long black hair with such force he almost pulled him out of his seat, yanked the plug out of his mouth and Bosajyan started to scream, asking for mercy.

"Please don't kill me. I will tell you anything you want to know."

"That's too easy," Avazian shouted striking Bosajyan in the mouth with the lead pipe. Blood spewed from his mouth as he spit-out what remained of his upper and lower front teeth.

"We were sent here by Markalyan he mumbled. He is at the office, a storefront in Glendale. I don't know who hired us. He threw up as his head draped forward towards the floor."

"Is that everything," Avazian yelled?

Bosajyan tried to lift his head as he started screaming, "Please don't kill me. Please don't kill me."

Avazian struck him in the temple causing him to black out and walked to the next chair pressing the Russian for information. The scene played out four more times; questions, beatings, questions, beatings until all six of the Russians were bloody masses near death. Before the agreed-upon two hours had played itself out he had all of the information needed. He called the LAPD who were in the process of apprehending Markalyan with the help of the Glendale Police Department.

While the LAPD and the GPD were rounding up Markalyan and the higher-level members of the Mongrels the Federal Marshalls and the FBI were in the process of arresting Aloyan and seventeen of his men for racketeering, mail fraud, tax evasion and arms dealing. Within four hours an arrest warrant was issued for Steven Malgan by the San Francisco Police Department.

Chapter 48

Frederic called Papaz who was having dinner with Bi Ba and Alice at Loews Hotel Santa Monica.

"It's over! Markalyan and Aloyan and their men have been apprehended."

He told Papaz as much as he knew. Alvarez was his contact and was in constant communication with Avazian but he had no part in the operation. He was the information conduit for Frederic as related to both Armenian gangs. The information flowed slowly because so many law enforcement agencies working together to remove the two Armenian gangs from the streets.

Frederic finished discussing the Armenians by saying, "Everything should be tied up by tomorrow morning. Do you guys think you want to meet later tonight or do you want to meet tomorrow morning?"

Papaz leaned forward towards Bi Ba who was sitting across the table asking her and Alice if they were interested in seeing him later tonight.

Bi Ba said, "Tell him no for me, breakfast tomorrow morning is fine."

Papaz said, "We are tired but breakfast sounds good."

Frederic told him, "Gisele and I will pick you up tomorrow morning. Why don't we go to Manhattan Beach and have breakfast? We can walk down to the pier and go to the Strand and then walk to Hermosa Beach.

We'll pick you up, how about 9:30 in the lobby? Change that, if you don't mind we will pick you up outside at valet parking. Talk to you tomorrow unless I hear anything else from Alvarez."

Papaz wanted to continue the conversation. "Good work. Hopefully this thing is really over. I'm going to call Jose. I want to hear some of the account first hand. I think I'm going to call Avazian later. I'm sure he has an interesting take on where we go from here. I want to feel you out on something before we get off the phone. You don't have to say anything until tomorrow morning."

Frederic said, "Sure."

"Okay then, what do you think of our friend, Avazian? I want him to be part of our team in some capacity?"

Frederic replied, "Just off the top of my head it sounds reasonable. My gut reaction is I like his work. Maybe he will be able to help us keep tabs on your cousin Al Bactar. Let's see if his skills and contacts have a long enough reach to follow him all the way to Turkey and the Middle East. I will talk to Gisele. She has much better knowledge of Europe and what's going on in the Arab world. I would like to get her input. Do me a favor? When you talk to Avazian hold off on asking him if he wants to work for us. It sounds right to me but we are in no hurry. Like I said, I want Gisele in on this."

Gisele whispered in Frederic's ear. "Tell Bi Ba and Alice I am glad this thing is over. It looks like we're done with these ass holes and believe it or not we didn't have to lift a finger. I wish it were like this every time we got involved in something."

Frederic passed on the message and finished the conversation with, "Talk to you guys later. If something comes up I'll call, if not we will see you at 9:30am."

Papaz told the two women, "The Armenians have been rounded up. Frederic really didn't say much more than we will get a full briefing later and that we are going to meet him and Gisele tomorrow morning. He will fill us in then. They'll pick us up downstairs at 9:30am."

Bi Ba asked about Malgan.

Papaz said, "I have no clue. He didn't mention anything about him. The mission was about Markalyan and Aloyan. I am certain when I talk to Alvarez or Avazian, they will have more information. We should know either later tonight or tomorrow."

He changed the subject. "There is something I want to talk to the two of you about. I only want your first impressions. What do you think about Richard Avazian?"

Alice had a strange look on her face. "You want my impression? He was real funny looking. No, I'm just kidding. Looks aside I would hire him if I had any problems that were in his province or purview. What amazes me is that he appeared so cartoonish but it didn't take long to realize he was formidable. I don't know what skills he would have outside of the Armenian community but it looks like his leadership skills are applicable to almost any situation. First impression. He's our man."

She started to laugh. "Notice how I said ours? Every time I'm with you two and your friends I have," she paused for a second, "I have had quite an experience. If I was loose lipped or a storyteller I would have enough for a great movie script. He could fit into a lot of movies. Yeah, I like the guy!"

Bi Ba shook her head and chimed in. "I'm right there with Alice. There's something about him I really like. I can't put my finger on it but I really appreciate the way he got things done. With me there is always a, but, I like him, but. We shouldn't underestimate him. I sense a real dark side to him. It doesn't mean he is a threat to us or our organization. I think if he is pushed," she fumbled for words, "like Alice said he could be formidable. That goes two ways. He wants to call all the shots. So, if he goes off halfcocked we could really be in trouble. But he is really good at what he does. There is something else but I could be wrong. I think it's a real asset. The way he dresses and the way he carries himself is interesting to me. I even look at his strange body type and somehow, he makes all of that an advantage. He just powers through his enemies. For some reason, I think physically he could be dangerous. I don't know why but it wouldn't surprise me if he is into the Israeli Kav Maga. I like him. It would be all the better if he was on our side."

Bi Ba continued, "You said Frederic would be getting a full briefing later tonight or tomorrow. Let's speak about this after we talked to him. Let's see how things work out with the Armenians and what if anything has happened with Malgan. Now I have a question for you," she said looking directly into Matt's eyes. "What do you think of our Armenian friend with the 'ian' spelling?"

Papaz reflected for a moment. "If the truth be told we have only brought one person into the Papaz Group. That is you Alice. Bringing in a second person is a big deal. I like the guy. If we decide to engage him it has to be a unanimous decision. If you want me talk to Avazian myself that is okay but since we are in this together I think we should all interview him together. The only reservation I have is that he may only be Armenian centric."

Bi Ba said, "I have no problem with that because he can help us with Al Bactar. For sure we can have him work on the Four Seasons project with Sully. If we bring him in I think we should do it incrementally. Kind of like a test drive."

Papaz interrupted her, "You're right. He might even surprise us and can do stuff outside Glendale. We are in Los Angeles a lot. He might be a good resource. I really like the guy. When we see Frederic and Gisele I'm sure they'll have something to add. The important thing to me is a unanimous decision about our friend."

As the three finished their conversation, Alice's active mind was on overload and she said "I wanted to quiet down by going for a walk. Do you want to walk over to the Santa Monica pier and across the street to Ivy at the Shore Restaurant for a drink?"

When she was younger, she and many of her Hollywood friends drank at the upscale bar/restaurant because of the paparazzi. They wanted to be seen.

Alice had always said, "In my business, any recognition by the press can and will be spun. It is especially good when you're portrayed as a little wild or even a little naughty."

It was interesting to her that the Ivy even to this day was popular with the Hollywood crowd.

Bi Ba spoke for her and Papaz, "It's the weekend. It's too crowded for me. I am going to have to decline but I think you should go anyway."

Alice got up and waved over to one of the bodyguards who was standing on the other side of the room. He came to the table.

She laughed, "Honey you are my date. We are going to the Ivy and you are having a drink with me. I haven't been with a young good-looking man in quite a while. I'll be back in a second. I'm going to go to the lady's room and pretty up."

When she came back she grabbed the arm of the young man and looked at her two friends. She said, "Party animal. That's me, I am a real party animal."

Bi Ba and Papaz could hear her laughing all the way out of the restaurant through the lobby to the street.

Chapter 49

Frederic and Gisele picked up Matt, Bi Ba and Alice in front of the Loews Santa Monica hotel. They were standing curbside at the circular driveway in the beachfront hotel's entrance. Frederic pulled up in his rented Audi A8. He released the lock on the back doors and one of the valet attendants rushed over and opened the door for Alice. She got in, scooted across the back seat and Matt and Bi Ba followed.

As soon as they were seated Frederic turned around and said, "Its good seeing you. Like Gisele said yesterday, we can't believe we went through this without any pain. We didn't have to lift a finger."

Bi Ba leaned forward to address him. "We talked about that last night. What a different experience. I just hope it's a trend but we can't count on it. Let's just say we were lucky this time and Avazian was incredible."

As they pulled out of the driveway and headed south, Matt asked, "We're going to Manhattan beach?"

"Yeah," Frederick replied. "It's a perfect day. We will eat then walk around for a while. Since we're all here I have some information about last night."

Matt said, "We were wondering about Malgan. What have you heard?"

Frederic replied, "The best we can figure is that about four hours after Avazian gave up the Russian Armenians to the LAPD, Malgan was arrested by a joint operation of the San Francisco Police Department and FBI. They had warrants for all his records. A federal task force of FBI and IRS took everything out of his office. They cleaned out all of his records from his house and secured all his financials. As far as we can tell he will be held in a federal holding facility until he's arraigned. It's the weekend. He'll probably have to wait until Monday. They will try to remand him without bail. He's a flight risk. Malgan will be locked up for a long time. With guys like Malgan they try to keep him under lock and key. Usually the Marshal's office and the FBI take jurisdictional reign over local police departments on racketeering violations. There's always petty differences but not this time. Whatever Avazian did or whoever he knew, this operation was textbook. It was seamless and no one was posturing for credit. Somehow our Armenian friend got the Feds and local law enforcement to work together."

Frederic change subjects. "Our lawyers say they can get the code violations at the hotel thrown out. No court will allow a civil lawsuit to stand precipitated by a scam. They say we should throw some crumbs to the homeowners by telling them we will redo their counters and maybe repaint their places. It is easier to pay a few dollars upfront than have somebody come after us later. We will get them to sign some type of document that will indemnify us from future lawsuits. Oh, by the way, Alice I think you might find this interesting. That anti-Semitic jerk and his cousin from the hotel could be open for a civil lawsuit for coming after us. I think Matt and Bi Ba would agree that if you want to pursue it we will be happy to pay for the litigation. A criminal's suit is out of the question because the legal bar is set so much higher than a civil suit. To get a judgment on a civil suit is much easier. If you want to go after that Silicon asshole it's up to you and as a partner we will honor your decision."

Alice asked, "May I give you an answer in a few days?"

"You have a year until the statute of limitations run out. Anytime between 365 days and the filing of the suit against us is okay."

Giselle said, "Sweetie you're going to have to talk about these matters later. We'll be at the restaurant in just a couple of minutes. You should park as soon as you see an open spot."

Frederick said, "Thank you. Just one last thing," he said as he pulled up to a public parking lot on Highland Avenue. "We're going to need to talk about Alwan Al Bactar after breakfast."

They got out of the car and started walking to the restaurant two blocks from the Manhattan Beach Pier. The Kettle, local hangout in the small beach community, was a midcentury family-owned eatery maintained popularity for more than 50 years.

Frederic said, "You guys are going to love this place. Yelp has given it a four and one half star rating. The menu supposedly hasn't changed since the day it opened. The reviews say they have incredible waffles."

It was evident the restaurant hadn't been remodeled since its inception. They were seated in the back corner near the restrooms in an old red leather booth. The ambience was dark middle-American café.

After breakfast Alice said, "They aren't as good as they were cracked up to be and the coffee had a lot to be desired."

Matt shook his head and said, "What did you expect for nine bucks?"

Gisele, the French foodie, remarked, "Sometimes you go to restaurants for the ambience not the food. This time they were both poor but we're at the beach. What more can we ask. I can't think of a better place to sit and watch people. The young beach crowd look like female and male models walking down a Paris or New York fashion runway."

Fashion was very important in Manhattan Beach. All of the sixteen to twenty-five-year-old women were wearing two piece thong bathing suits, flip-flops, and carrying plastic purses. The young men all had swimmer's bodies with broad shoulders, thin six pack waists and wore bright colored baggy Hawaiian shorts. "It's great, we're at the beach, what more can you ask for," Gisele said.

They left the restaurant and walking through the small beach town's center looking at the shops on their way to the Strand. The Strand, or what some people call the bike path, was a four-mile concrete walking path along the sand going from Manhattan Beach to Hermosa Beach. As they walked south on the cement walkway, Los Angeles South Bay's world famous white sand was to the right and some of California's most expensive residential properties were on the left. Homes on the

Strand at the low end ranged from $5-$7 million and at the high end more than $20 million. Most of the homes were of Mediterranean or Tuscan design. Manhattan Beach was one of the most coveted neighborhoods for young professionals in the United States.

Frederic asked, "What do you guys think of it down here?"

Matt replied, "We already have a place in Bel Air and two condominiums in Beverly Hills. We don't need another house if that's what you're asking."

Alice said, "I love it down here but I'm too old. It's too crowded but it is certainly fun to visit. It's kind of like an upscale Venice Beach. Since you brought it up why don't you buy a place down here?"

Frederic didn't have an answer.

As they continue to walk Matt was the first to asked, "Frederic, about Alwan Al Bactar," as they approached the peer he said, "Why don't we all walk down there, pointing to the water and sit for a moment and hear what Frederic has to say about my cousin."

They all agreed. Alice took her shoes off and the others followed. They walked off the Strand by way of some stairs leading to the beach. After walking on the white sand for about 100 feet they were sitting on the water's edge looking at the crashing waves as they rushed through the pier's pylons.

Instead of looking at his surrounding Frederic was all business. "This might sound crazy but I think we can get Malgan's unseated as a beneficiary from his uncle's family trust. In the Malgan Malgan Trust he can be thrown out on grounds of moral turpitude. If we can, but I have not worked out all the details yet, we can place a phony codicil in the original draft of the trust making Alwan Al Bactar the beneficiary if anything happens to Steven Malgan. That anything will have to encompass him being terminated because of exigent circumstances. Hell, it's a natural. His position in the Middle East represents our interests. I talked to Kasogi to get his thoughts on Al Bactar. He thinks he is a freedom fighter for the Sunni cause. He as much as said he has financially backed Al Bactar in the past and would do so in the future. I didn't make any mention of the Malgan estate but it would certainly make him one of the biggest players in the Middle East."

Looking directly at Matt he continued, "I'm just throwing this out there. I want you to think about it. Before he could finish"

Alice said, "I'm Jewish. I don't know the guy! For the most part I am extremely pro-Israel. Giving money to a Sunni? I don't want to know the guy and what he does. The last thing I need to do is be brought into political matters that effect Israel. What I don't know can't hurt me. Right?"

No one knew what to say so Frederic changed the subject.

"There is one last thing. Count me in on Avazian but we need to specifically know what we want him to do. There is going to be a lot involved in getting Al Bactar into the position of being the beneficiary to the trust. I want to feel out Avazian on how far out of bounds he is willing to go. I know he did a lot of extra legal stuff for us. Not in the least, he beat the crap out of Markalyan's people before he gave them up to the police. I want to know if he's will do things like that again or if that was just personal to him. I did some checking because he was so successful. I thought he was one of those guys using all his fuel at takeoff. Everyone said he is the real thing. If we decide to help your Arabic cousin for the most part it's all electronic on our side. We just change some documents or manufacture some documents. Things we've done a million times before. We can manage the trust, that's relatively easy. It's the relationships on the ground I want Avazian to handle. He's been impressive and represented us well but getting him to work with our people in the Middle East could be complicated. I don't mean to slight the guy because I really like him but he is strange and I don't know how he will be received. We are going to need an inside person because Kasogi doesn't want to be outwardly tied to Al Bactar. Al Bactar is too hot of a commodity."

"In fact," Agnon said, "he has information that Al Bactar could be in a Syrian prison just outside Damascus. He thinks the Syrians captured a freedom fighter whose name is Adnan abu Hasna but in fact it is Al Bactar. Your cousin has many aliases and Kasogi is sure he is the man in jail. What I want to do is see if Avazian has the ability to break him out of jail. We have the money and resources. I would like to charge him with developing a plan and go from there. Obviously, we would have to sell this to Kasogi and some of our associates. We've had discussions that we might want to use Avazian here in Los Angeles, or you might use him in Istanbul helping you with your project, but I think he is better suited for developing plans to get Al Bactar out of prison. What do you think?"

He finished by saying, "We don't need a decision now but we will need one pretty soon."

They continue walking along the Strand towards the Hermosa Beach Pier. The conversation moved away from Matt Group business to more mundane social intercourse. Alice pulled out her iPhone as a tool and started taking pictures of the people passing them by on the cement walkway. The Strand was effectively a two-lane pedestrian highway for beach goers who either walked, skated or bicycled. The people parade was extraordinary. They were more homogeneous along the South Bay Beaches than at Venice Beach where eccentricity was the fare of the day. Alice could not get over how attractive the young people were. Her moviemaking instincts kicked-in. She looked at the young men and women as if they were being cast for one of her movies. Their facial structure, their physicality, their hair, their feet, anything a camera would accentuate. After more than an hour with her camera as a tool she asked Bi Ba and Gisele if she could take their pictures.

Gisele's response was interesting. "No thank you. I don't like my pictures taken. Initially it was a reaction to my work. Having a picture taken was like being outed and made public. It could call attention to me and that would have been dangerous. It is more vanity as I grow older. Now I just don't like how I look. If it is important to you for some crazy American reason, then go ahead. Please save me the embarrassment by keeping them to yourself. I don't want to see them."

Alice was now playing the old person's card. "I don't need either of you to pose. Please indulge me. I think you will like what I am going to do."

Alice had been a Hollywood executive producer and financial backer of the studios for decades. More important than her longevity were her financial successes and her access to other investor's money. She felt talent wasn't the only variable needed for an actor to have a viable career. A person's look was more compelling than their acting skills. She was convinced of that. Alice felt the purported skill level of an actor was overrated. Some great actors were never discovered or appreciated. Some were never given a chance to show their skills because of the commoditization of the art form or no access to a good script. It was no longer art. It was business. Profit not art held sway with the money people who made the final determination of what was to be produced. She knew Gisele and Bi Ba were more beautiful than any of the young women she saw at the beach. They were elegant women. Men would drool over young women wanting them as sexual possessions. But gazing upon Gisele and Bi Ba was like looking at Renaissance masterpieces. Something of beauty to prize knowing you could not obtain it. The hundreds of pictures of young women wearing skimpy outfits between the ages of sixteen and thirty paled in comparison to her two women friends. Bi Ba and Gisele had a beauty surpassing youth. They were extraordinarily beautiful like Michael Angelo or Leonardo used the finest marble quarried in Italy to sculpt the perfect female figure. Perceptual beauty had subtle flaws as was the case with the two women. There was an asymmetry in their lines. The color of their hair, their skin, and their eyes were unique but not perfect. These inconsequential physical deviations coupled with almost perfect beauty made them elegant and not replicable. Alice felt beauty was the whole not the perfect parts. Even though they wouldn't cognitively let themselves recognize it they were both pictures of pure beauty.

Alice took so many pictures, Gisele told her she was starting to be a bother and kiddingly said, "Friendship only goes so far."

Alice replied, "Okay I'll stop but you must hear me out. I am as good at what I do as anyone in Hollywood. I have been lucky to be able to see through more different lenses then any of my contemporaries. I'm going to make a proposal to the two of you. As Frederic, would say, "You don't have to give me an answer right now. How would you like to make real Hollywood movies? I don't mean the special effects. I don't mean some stupid sequels. I mean films showing your inner and outer beauty. I get scripts all the time. I know script writers. I can take you anywhere you want to go in the industry. You are both so beautiful. Coupling that with how smart you are and this is the perfect blend for leading ladies. You have all the attributes of stardom plus you are worldly beyond comparison with any of the female stars on the screen today. Beauty and intellect are like an opiate for the eyes. Maybe even more importantly, this is the last thing you would ever want to do. If your endeavor into something by chance it is always better. We can have fun with it. It would be my pleasure to work with the two of you. I have contacts. I have money. Hopefully I will have your trust. Gisele, I don't mean this in a bad way. This can get you away from all the cloak and dagger in your life. You would be a natural. As for you Bi Ba, you are certainly more than a Las Vegas personal planner executive or greeter or whatever you did. You are radiant and intelligent. I can't tell you how wonderfully that would come across on the screen. Well like I said, think about it."

Bi Ba was the first to respond. "Thanks, but no thanks. This is the last thing I need. I don't have to think it over. In my recent life, I've had to play roles that were a matter of life and death. That has been enough for me. Party planning was just fine. It was enjoyable and I didn't have to bring home any worries. What I do now with charities is just fine. It's an honor for you to ask. Truly, I appreciate what you think of me. I know it comes from love because I am not that beautiful and I sure as heck wouldn't be able to act. Maybe being out in the sun so long today without glasses has affected your eyes." She smiled, just joking. "I really do love you but this is not for me."

Gisele looked at Alice and said, "No, Madame, being a spy suits me well."

It was not a common occurrence for her to use a French word while speaking English but she was moved by Alice's assessment of her. "I am truly touched but this is not for me. Recognition would be a curse. There are too many people that this would be important to. To steal a future star's position, I know that this is a zero-sum game, by the opportunity of knowing you and not putting in any work in the craft would be bothersome to me. It would be a form of entitlement that I do not deserve. You are too gracious but I have to say no."

Alice said, "If either of you change your mind I am not going anywhere. My offer comes from my heart as well as my experience in the industry. I think you are underestimating how good the two of you can be. I was once told you can't let your past hold your future hostage. There is so much more in life for the two of you. I guess I just don't want to see you limiting yourselves. I will let this be idle but I won't let it die. Maybe you will have second thoughts."

Bi Ba said, "All that came out of nowhere. That's the last thing I would've ever expected from you Alice. That's why I love you so much."

She looked at Frederic and asked, "Can I assume we are safe from all the Armenian crap? Can we go home now? How about if we go back up to our place, our house in Bel Air not the Montague, and have a drink?"

Russell C. Arslan

Part VIII -- Lebanon

Chapter 50

A few days passed and Matt had not heard from Frederic. That was unusual. He called his friend. Frederic and Gisele were still staying at the Beverly Wilshire Hotel and if nothing else the two couples could meet for dinner later that night.

He called saying, "I haven't heard from you? Are you still working on the Avazian thing?"

"I am," Frederic said. "I told him I want him working with us. I sent him everything we have on Al Bactar. He will get back to me tomorrow. I was going to call you and ask if you wanted to be part of a meeting with me, him, and Alvarez. The three of us can see him tomorrow afternoon if you are interested. If you don't want to be part of the process or don't have enough time José and I can do it."

Matt answered, "I'd need to be here. What's a good time?" "Late in the afternoon," Frederic replied, "Is that okay with you?"

"That's fine. Sorry I haven't been in contact with you."

Frederic said, "But the Al Bactar problem is very fluid and we are getting so many conflicting updates it's hard to get a handle on it."

"I really like this guy Avazian," Frederic continued. "He's a great soldier. I mean it. He'd be great to have on our team. Before we talk to him tomorrow let's come up with some type of compensation package and make sure we can tie him up. I am all over the place with this. I have a gut feeling money doesn't mean a lot to him. Shoot, just look at the guy. Have you seen his car? I can't imagine where he lives. And the way he dresses. I don't want to insult him by either offering him too much or too little."

Matt responded, "Leave it up to me. I'll just ask him what he thinks he is worth. Let him embarrass me. Money is not an object as far as I am concerned. I think it's imperative for him to be working with us. I have an idea. Let's have a meeting at my house. That should raise the ante. Bi Ba always resents anyone who envies our money. Let's see how uncomfortable Avazian is being around us when we are not at war. I have a feeling he could care less about being rich. I have been wrong before but I think I'm right on this. I will let him determine what he's worth. If he is as good as I think he deserves anything he asks for."

"We'll set the meeting for 5:30pm tomorrow," Frederic said and ended the phone call.

Avazian was as unpretentious as he had been before. He dressed as if he spent lots of time trying to mismatch his wardrobe. His tennis shoes were new but the rest of his ensemble was almost threadbare. He wore a brown pair of corduroy pants with ribbing so worn, torn and re-sewn and the right knee was patched. The pants were noticeably dirty, un-pressed with the right leg cuff open on the inner side. His trademark plaid shirt was too tight. So much so that his hairy stomach showed through the once vertical button tab line. He tucked his shirt into his pants and with his extended belly it highlighted the convex beach ball protrusion over his birdlike legs. Avazian's outfit had a new wrinkle. He was wearing a black baseball cap with a purple Los Angeles Lakers logo embroidered on its rim.

He had to walk through the house's beautiful grotto getting to the Tuscan Villa's front doors. Looking at the Thirty-foot granite boulders and reflecting pools leading to the front of the house he felt like he was in another world. He was disheveled and out of his element because this wasn't what he had expected. When he finally got to the house entrance, it was evident the Russian Armenian sting had extracted a toll on Avazian. Up until this point he had always felt comfortable in new environments. Avazian wrote off being off tilt as just being tired.

Matt greeted him. He wanted to tease his Armenian counterpart but he thought better of it. He did not know if his perspective Damon Runyon employee had a sense of humor.

Matt could call him Dickron without laughing. "Dickron, may I call you that," he asked.

"Sure, my friends do. I hope by calling me by my first name bodes well for me."

"It certainly does," Matt said. "By the way, Frederic and Alvarez won't be here. It will be you, me and Bi Ba. I hope you don't mind."

Papaz escorted Avazian outside to sit in the backyard. They walked through the magnificent villa out to the pool area overlooking the golf course below. Bi Ba came out to say hello and offer them drinks.

She had heard their conversation when Avazian came into the house and said, "Dickron we have anything from water to the hard liquor. What's your pleasure?"

He replied, "Do you have something like a Sprite, or seven up, or even ginger ale?"

They'd all be fine. She came back from the living room bar area with three drinks, handing the Armenian his ginger ale, she and Matt drank plain tap water.

Bi Ba started talking, "It's good to see you. Matt said you were going to be on our team. I look forward to it. Let me give you a word of advice, though." Pointing to Matt she continued, "He fancies himself as a hard negotiator. I can't help but put my two cents in. I really want you to be on our team. Like I said, it would be nice to have you working with us. You were impressive with the Malgan problem. We usually delegate any type of negotiation or hiring practices to Frederic but both Matt and I wanted to do this personally. You being here means a lot to us."

Matt interrupted, "Why don't you just give away the store? He laughingly continued, "Dickron, let's get down to your working for us and get some things out of the way. Tell me exactly what you need in order to work for us."

Matt said. "We want you exclusively. I hope you don't run from this but we want you to only work for us. That's a big sacrifice, so I'm willing to let you write your own ticket. Whatever it takes I, no let me change that, we are willing to pay it. I would like to make it comfortable enough for you that working exclusively for us makes a lot of sense."

Avazian said, "I didn't expect this to be a negotiation when Frederic asked me to meet with the two of you. When he hired me to deal with Steven Malgan and the Russian Armenians he told me what I would receive. There wasn't room for negotiation. I was fine with that. It was upfront and to be truthful a lot more money than I thought I deserved. So, whatever you feel comfortable with will be reasonable. I am neither greedy nor money hungry. So, whatever you think is okay is fine."

Matt interrupted, "Dickron, we don't want to embarrass ourselves by either offering you too little or too much. So, I will embarrass us by offering you the high end. We are willing to start off by saying we will make you an offer you can't turn down. We want to get your mother a house. Any place of your choosing. We are willing to pay up to," he looked at Bi Ba, he threw a number out that he knew Bi Ba would approve. "Up to $1,500,000 dollars. We'll pay for maintenance, the taxes, anything that comes up. We will guarantee your mother an income of $10,000 a month for the rest of her life regardless of what you do for us if you stay with us for five years or more. We know you support some kid's activities in the Armenian community in Glendale. They will be put under the Papaz Group umbrella. We will set up a separate division for them that you will have control over. Not now, but later we will figure out a very handsome budget for you. As far as you are concerned, you can write your own ticket but I know you won't. So as long as you work with us you can still live in Glendale just the way you do now. No changes unless you want them. We will give you a little over $83,000 a month. That is $1,000,000 per year. If you use your newfound wealth to help other organizations or donate money to any causes, we deem worthy we will participate by matching you dollar for dollar. It is pretty obvious you don't covet money but we hope you will understand it can be a tool of your trade."

Avazian in his understated way said, "This is more than I could possibly have dreamed. I am a person of few indulgences. You have struck two of them, my mother and my community. All I really have to offer is my work ethic and my loyalty. I will not let you down. I will not embarrass you or misrepresent you. Thank you. I'm shocked because it is so much money. I don't make one tenth of that. Can we set up some arrangement to help me manage all of it? I don't even have an accountant. I wouldn't know where to begin to invest it. This may sound stupid but I really don't want it to change my life that much."

Matt replied, "It will be our pleasure. This is what we do. We will talk about it later but I promise whatever you want we can accommodate it. It is not our goal to change you. We want you on board because you have a particular set of skills that will protect us and more importantly comfort us."

Avazian wanted to change the subject, "So can we talk about your cousin Al Bactar?"

Both Matt and Bi Ba said "Sure."

"You are the guy responsible for getting him out of Syria so where are you on this," Bi Ba asked.

ISTANBUL

Avazian's demeanor changed. Instead of being deferent he became very businesslike. He became the voice of an operative to save a man's life. "As best we can determine Al Bactar whose nom de guerre is Adnanabu Hasna is in the notorious Tandor prison It is two hundred kilometers north of Damascus. It is heavily fortified and known as the black hole of Syria. Originally it was a French military barracks. It was built in 1924 as part of the French Forces Mandate as outlined by the Sykes Picot Agreement between British and the French to partition off the old Ottoman Mesopotamian Empire. The British would control Iraq, Palestine which they acquired through the Beaufort amendment in 1909, Jordan and Egypt. The French would control Syria and Lebanon. All of this was set up by the League of Nations as a way of taking over the Middle East and dividing up its treasures as part of the WWI victory over Germany. To the victors go the spoils!"

"Let me get back to Al Bactar. The prison is our main concern. When the French built it in 1924 it was a barracks for the Foreign Legion. For all intent and purposes, it was impregnable when it was constructed. That is not the case now. It is neither a barracks nor is it impregnable. It was left idle for almost 30 years after World War II. Then Assad's father changed it into a prison housing approximately 350 of Syria's most vocal political prisoners. With the advent of Arab Spring the number of inmates has increased to more than 1,000. We have confirmed that your cousin is in that prison. We even know the exact location of his cell. My team is developing a plan to breach the facility's security by a frontal attack of such great intensity that we will have the ability to extract Al Bactar and any other anti-Bashar al Assad freedom fighters. Our intelligence tells us that Syria's ability to secure their prison is weak. I have talked to Tarvan Kerkorian. He is one of the leading authorities on prisons in the United States and one of the best people I know for analyzing how to get your cousin out. He is ex-military and currently head of the Glendale Police Academy. He actually thinks Syria is ready to fall or at least concede enough soil that it's impossible to control the prison system. The Islamic State, which used to be called ISIS is moving so quickly, Assad has to consolidate all his power in Damascus. If he does, the prisons will be indefensible. The Islamic State forces want to set up a caliphate in the thirty percent of Syria and forty percent of Iraq it now controls. Once it is firmly entrenched in this area of the Middle East its goal is to dominate all Shi'a or Alawite. That will force Assad and his Baath Party supporters to concentrate their efforts and protect Damascus. Kerkorian believes Assad's dominance is a house of cards ready to fall. It shouldn't take much to free your cousin. I am confident we have the ability. All we need is the money."

"Let me talk a little bit about how Al Bactar got into this mess. My contacts in Lebanon, there is a large Armenian community in Beirut, say your cousin decided to go to Aleppo to defend the Sunnis from government forces. He and his men started working with the Islamic Front organization and together they pushed Assad's army out of the Eastern portion of the city. It was hand-to-hand combat but the Sunnis and the Christians won a hard-fought battle against the Shi'a. Just before he was going to leave and go West to the city of Hom the Islamic State forces of ex Al Qaeda Arabs mostly from Iraq and Lebanon came in and took control over Aleppo's Old City Sunni population. Here is where it gets a little muddled. The Islamic State mercenaries and religious zealots were waging war against both Assad and his enemies the Free Syrian Army and Syrian Front. Al Bactar tried to flee the city and was captured by Assad's men at a Shi'a checkpoint. We can't figure out how but they thought he was a person of high value and sent him to Tandor prison. We know he is still there. Our information tells us he is in bad shape. He has been under constant interrogation and torture. He has been there almost a month now. Like I said, we think the prison can be overrun but we have to act fast."

Matt said, "Let me ask you an important question. Is he worth saving? My cousin doesn't mean anything to me on a personal level because I don't really know him. This blood thing isn't that important to me. Hell, I have only met him once and that was for less than 15 minutes."

Bi Ba said, "Maybe less."

After relating the events in Bodrum, Matt continued, "I have no vested interest in him but I might have an interest in his future in the Middle East. One of our principles in the Papaz Group, Agnon Kasogi is a supporter of Al Bactar and to be honest, he holds my cousin's fate in his hands. If he says yes, we save him. If he says no I am of a mind to let him die. If we are going to save him we better think it over because lives could be at stake. I won't put blood or treasure on the line lightly. So, tell me why we should save him."

Avazian responded, "In truth I am a private and you are a general. You make all the calls but it will be my life that's on the line. Not yours. Let me tell you why I would give my life for your cousin."

He slowed down his speech, "Mr. Papaz he represents the little that is right in the Middle East. They are bloodletting over there to cure religious issues that should have been settled in the 600s after Mohammed died. 1,400 or 1,500 years ago no one would have cared about what all those crazies are doing. Today it is different. The world is small and if these Islamic idiots set up a caliphate or the Alawites or crazy Shi'a are allowed to be in power then they will kill my people. There are edicts now in both Syria and Iraq that if Christians don't change their faith they will be slaughtered. They are given 30 days to convert to Islam or they will be beheaded. Armenians are Christians. They are Apostolic. They will perish unless we support men like Al Bactar. He is a person of reason who might be able to temper some of the pain for my Armenian people. With the stupid senseless murderess cases of martyrdom by the Shi'a my people are in danger. He and people like him are the only hope for Christians or Jews or even atheists. These fundamentalists have no tolerance for others. I am willing to give my life to protect people like Al Bactar who are the only soldiers of reason."

Chapter 51

After reaching agreement with Papaz, Avazian went to Lebanon, put together a mercenary team that would free Al Bactar from prison. The support and command center for the operation was set in the Ba'albec Valley[6]. Avazian did not want to go into Syria. He hired the personnel, procured materials and supervised the operation from Lebanon. Only Turkish and Kurdish soldiers of fortune were used in the operation. Both fighter groups were notorious for their savagery and were the only fighters whose brutality equaled Assad's army.

Avazian's intelligence determined Al Bactar could not live more than another week in Tandor[7]. After being tortured and interrogated he was sent to Hell's hole where prisoners were isolated from the general population until they died. Hells hole was a cell approximately fifty feet by fifty feet, located in the desolate prison yard center. Half of it was above the compound's ground-level and half was underground. The underground portion of the cell was three feet deep. Two feet of which was filled with water. The water was never changed but when evaporation in the hot desert sun lowered its level additional water from the latrines was added keeping a constant depth of twenty-four inches.

The pool was a dense mix of brown and gray. Its smell was so toxic that being in its proximity made prisoners as well as guards regurgitate or in some cases pass out. The stagnant pool was filled with human excretion. Above the ground was a cage extending six feet into the air. The roof was wire mesh open to the elements of the prisons central courtyard. Prisoners thrown into the cage had to sleep standing up in the two feet of liquid housing some of the most toxic compounds and bacteria known to man. Food was passed through the bars of the cell walls once a day. Each prisoner received approximately 1,000 calories of cracked wheat or bulgur a day. Their individual water ration was less than one quart of latrine water a day provided to all prisoners in a common leather bota--bag. In the prison's history, no one ever came out of the hellhole after two weeks, unless they were granted clemency. The mortality rate was 100%. Death came in many forms. Dysentery being the most prominent. Prisoners usually died within five days. Al Bactar was placed in the hole the same day Avazian arrived in Ba'albec. As in most cases when a person's life was on the line, the clock was ticking.

    Avazian's Lebanese Armenian associates provided him with thirty-six ex-military commandos who would be flown in and out of Syria by six Apache helicopters. The raid on the prison was set for 12:00am and would commence two days after the arrival of Avazian. The night of the operation was moonless. Under normal circumstances the skies would have shone brightly under the stars. This night the desert was agitated with a high wind sweeping sand into the air with such fury the visibility was no more than 1,500 feet. Under cover of darkness and the sandstorm, the helicopters flew at 200 feet altitude, undetectable by radar. The plan was simple. Avazian purchased eight rear engine Penguin B UAV drones. The six-foot wing spanned robotic aircraft retrofitted with surface to surface missiles SSM, RPG 7 and AT-2 Swatters antitank missiles. He purchased illuminating parachute flares to be fired from artillery seven miles away. The deadly firepower coupled with the 36 commandos and five command and control personnel in Lebanon were all he needed.

At exactly 10:45pm four Apache helicopters armed with sixty-four missiles and carrying four teams of nine commandos left the Ba'albec Valley for the one hour and twenty-minutes flight to Tandor Prison. The two remaining helicopters were held in abeyance for search and destroy mission contingencies. The four attack helicopters cruised below 200 feet across the Syrian Desert with an ETA of 12:00 AM. At exactly 11:59pm illuminating flares fired from hand-held rocket launchers brightening skies above the prison to such intensity the guards were virtually blinded. At exactly the same time and in conjunction with the flares, the eight drones carrying thirty-two rocket propelled grenades flew into the prison walls. Hell's hole was exactly in the center of the prison courtyard. Blinding bright lights, massive explosions and thirty-six Turkish and Kurdish soldiers of fortune were more than enough to pull Al Bactar out of the life draining cesspool. He was whisked into one of the waiting helicopters.

Avazian's team were tasked with one order, extract Al Bactar from the prison and bring him to safety. Over 700 other Sunni fighters escaped when the prison guards abandoned their post as a response to the military incursion. Tandor Prison was eerily quiet as the sun rose at 4:26am.

The whole operation took less than two hours and forty minutes. One hour, twenty minutes to reach and extract Al Bactar from Tandor Prison and one hour, eighteen minutes to bring him back to Ba'albec Valley. Avazian's team had no casualties. The operation was deemed a complete success.

When Al Bactar reached the Lebanon base camp, he received immediate medical attention from doctors assembled by Avazian's associates. He was cleaned up, given antibiotics, and an IV to rehydrate his body. Just outside Ba'albec valley, on the small 7,000-foot runway sat a Gulfstream-4 retrofitted for medical evacuations. The plane was waiting to transfer Al Bactar to London.

He entered Great Britain with a new identity, William Ashley Atanbury, freelance writer for the London Globe. He was admitted to Hampstead Heath Hospital.

The battered and beaten reporter laid semiconscious in the emergency room for more than two hours before being placed in his private room. His passport and papers were bagged with his clothing and sitting on the only open chair left in the room. The other three chairs were being used by Matt Papaz, Bi Ba Lamanas and Dickron Avazian.

Chapter 52

Al Bactar woke up, "You saved my life. Why? You owed me nothing. Why did you save me?"

He was defiant. This was not the response that Papaz expected.

Avazian broke in and started speaking in Armenian. "We saved your life, yes? That is enough for you to express appreciation. We want nothing other than for you to hear us out."

Avazian broke back into English, "Do you know your cousin Matt Papaz? He is the one who saved your life. He has an offer for you."

Avazian return to Armenian, "You are an ungrateful pig."

Papaz could not understand a word but saw contempt in Avazian's face. "Dickron, no more, please. Alwan you owe us nothing. You are safe here in the hospital. You are under our protection until you leave London. There are three of our men outside of your room who will protect you."

Papaz offered him a phone knowing he would not take it. "It's clean. It can't be monitored. Do with it what you will. I will take your apprehension towards me as nothing more than the fog of war. You are unclear of my intentions. Why I pulled you out of Syria? I assure you if you hear me out you will want to join our alliance."

Al Bactar finally spoke. His dark brown eyes flashed with anger. He said, "Tell me of your demands as a price for saving my life."

He tried to sit up in his bed to have more of a physical posture and create some advantage in their dialogue. He did not like lying on his back like a dog who was being dominated. Al Bactar's attitude was clear. In his voice, there was an expression of rage.

"I owe you nothing. You took away my martyrdom. My name would have been echoed off the walls of the desert for generations. I owe you nothing!"

Papaz did not know if he was delusional or if he was a jihadist devoid of perspective.

Bi Ba grabbed Matt's hand and looked at Avazian. "Let him be. We need to leave. He is in no condition to speak."

She looked directly at Al Bactar and said, "I don't know if you remember me from the beach at Bodrum but we will honor your wishes and leave you alone. If you change your mind we will be in London until you are well enough to leave the hospital. Our guarantee of safety will be kept no matter how you feel about us."

Papaz interrupted, "We will give you passage to anywhere you want to go. If you need a new identity, we will furnish it. Get some rest. Hopefully we will talk. When you are well enough you should call us."

The three of them got up and started to leave. On his way to the door Avazian looked at Al Bactar and said in

Armenian, "Abush. Its simple translation it meant, stupid ingrate."

Bi Ba said, "What the heck did you say?"

Avazian replied, "In Armenia abush is something like, good luck my friend."

By the time, they were driven back to their flat on Bulgravia Road in London West End, Gisele had called.

"Matt, Frederic and I have worked out all of the details and we will be able to change the Malgan Malgan Trust. How are you guys doing on your end?"

Papaz told her how agitated Al Bactar was, "He was almost to the point of being delusional. I wrote it off as his being temporarily out of his mind. If I look at him any other way, he is not the person I believed him to be. That would suggest to me we leave the trust stand as is."

He told her of his cousin's aggressiveness and total lack of appreciation for being saved.

Gisele responded, "Give him a few days. We have nothing to lose. He is safe and he can't be identified by British authorities. He is incapable of hurting himself or anyone else. I am no psychiatrist but it is probable he is suffering from post-traumatic syndrome disorder. I think it will take time. Don't write him off yet. How many times has one of us been through hell and took time to right ourselves?"

The word hell hit a cord with Papaz. He couldn't imagine what Al Bactar had gone through in the prison. He thought it over for a few seconds and said to himself, "We should give him as much time as he needs."

He told Gisele, "We should hedge on this and if he's the wrong person let the trust stand. If he is our guy we should implement the changes in the trust."

Gisele replied, "Maybe we should get him some psychological help unless you think that could open him up to unwanted scrutiny by the English? I don't know how it works in Great Britain but I know there are patient-doctor privacy rights that might be different from the US." She continued, "I will have our people look into it. We should be able to get our doctors to talk to him. If we can't find one maybe our friend Avazian has some contacts."

Five days passed before Al Bactar submitted to any psychological examination. Avazian had an Armenian psychiatrist sent over from Boston. The Boston area had a large Armenian community. Under the pretext of being a neurosurgeon, James Emerzian, the US psychiatrist had Al Bactar take a battery of tests to analyze his cognition. Emerzian concluded that Al Bactar was suffering from a mild form of PTSD and amnesia that would change over time and environment. Emerzian suspected because of Al Bactar's secretive and paranoid nature, that actual therapy sessions would be unproductive.

He said, "It is just a matter of time for him to recover emotionally. He was beaten badly and he needs time to close his wounds. He will get back to normal. We need to determine what normal is. Dickron, there is no more that I can do for him." Emerzian returned to New England the next morning.

Al Bactar was in the hospital for another eleven days, before he was discharged. During that period, he did not communicate with anyone. The telephone laid idle at his bedside. He had no visitors except the hospital's medical staff. When told of his release, he asked one of his security team to call Papaz. He still held to not using anything electronic.

Papaz agreed to see him by himself. When he entered the room Al Bactar said, "I need to talk to you. My thinking is clearer now. I am indebted to you for saving my life."

Papaz said, "There is no need to say anything more. What are your plans?"

He did not want to push Al Bactar. He wanted to play it slow.

Papaz's Turkish cousin said, "My only plans are to get back to Turkey and fully recuperate. You wanted to talk about something important when you were here. Is that still true my cousin?"

Papaz replied, "The doctors say you are well enough to leave the hospital. I would like to get you into the fresh air and take you for something to eat. We can talk there. We will be in public hiding in plain sight. It will be good for you to leave this room. You are safe. No one knows your identity here in England."

Within the hour, Al Bactar was discharged and Papaz's car took them to the other side of London. He was taken to the Upper Crust of Belgravia restaurant three blocks from the famous Harrods department store. Papaz and Al Bactar entered the restaurant and were immediately seated.

Papaz noticed how frail his cousin looked. In Bodrum Al Bactar's brief appearance at the beach left a lasting impression of looking like a freedom fighter who would have been perfectly cast in a Hollywood version of Arabian Nights. At the West End restaurant, Al Bactar appeared to have lost twenty-five to thirty pounds, he had trouble ambulating from the car to the eatery, he was now clean-shaven making his appearance long faced and dim eyed. He was not the romantic looking freedom fighter Papaz met in Turkey. Papaz thought it was better if he talked to his cousin one on one and Bi Ba and Avazian remain at the flat. He was all business and laid out the scenario of Alwan Al Bactar being the sole beneficiary to the Malgan Malgan Trust as soon as Al Bactar was seated.

Papaz said, "Yes, because of your father you will have $400-$600 million at your disposal. He laid out how the new trust would work. It is not traceable. Obviously, there are some restrictions on how much money you can draw at one time and under what circumstances. Let's just say, you will be a very rich man. You will be able to finance your activities in such a way as to circumvent any national security agencies in the world from tracing your funding. The money will be free from any strings. It will be plentiful. You can use it as you wish."

Al Bactar asked one question. "Why? Why my cousin?"

Papaz said, it's the right thing to do. It will give sanity a greater voice in the Middle East. That is all my cousin. It is the right thing to do. Maybe sometime in the future I can call on you for help. I will never jeopardize you or your people. I will never ask anything of you that you can't say reject. There will be no strings attached to this gift from your father. He would be proud of you my cousin."

Before they finish lunch Papaz said, "I have to leave early because Bi Ba is expecting me."

Al Bactar knew his cousin didn't want to extend the conversation because it might become uncomfortable. The passing of the trust title was conversation of men's work and now that it had run its course. Papaz would simply get up and leave.

Al Bactar got up and extended his hand and said, "The winds of the desert will be our messenger."

Papaz crossed the table and hugged his Armenian cousin. Before he could say goodbye Al Bactar said, "Words are not enough my cousin. First you saved my life and now you bestow treasure upon me. May Allah be kind to you."

Papaz turned and walked away.

Russell C. Arslan

Part IX – Home Again

Chapter 53

Matt and Bi Ba were home in Bel Air for more than three weeks. Sitting in his office looking at some spreadsheets dealing with their Kenya operations, he decided to call it a day and went down stairs to sit by the pool. It was approximately 7:30am, still early morning. He sat outside relaxing with a warm cup of tea and milk looking down at the far away Pacific Ocean.

With the Armenian problem put to rest, he and Bi Ba were comfortable with Al Bactar's birthright acceptance. He thought to himself, the world is good.

As the phone rang, Matt read the caller ID saying 'Sully'. It was late night in Istanbul so his first intuition was there was a problem. It wasn't a call for help from his old friend. It was more information passing.

Sully said, "How are you? We have another name for you. I wanted to call and explain it before you receive the file. This candidate is most unusual. It's the first time but we've sent you a candidate with a negative image. His name is Faysal Soylemez. There is no reason you would know of him. If you Google his name you will see he resides in the underbelly of Istanbul. He is not as we say, a good man. In fact, he is a drug dealer and considered very violent. Our team came up with a fortune coincidence for him giving rise to his criminal career, but it was at your personal expense. Please Mr. Papaz, listen to what our team has come up with before you shut the door on this candidate."

Papaz said, in a most sarcastic way, "I'm all ears."

Sully continued, "Let me first say it was my decision to send you the file. I told the team to do the research because you will find the relationship interesting. He was not Armenian, has no Armenian association and is outside the research guidelines. Except for other criminals, he has no social standing. He is the worst of Turks. I am submitting his name because you two have crossed paths and as we say in Turkey, 'the crumbs falling from the rich man's plate can be a complete meal for the misfortunate'."

Papaz did not know what to say. Most people didn't call him rich to his face. He finally broke in and said, "Sully, okay, okay just send it to me. I'll read it even if it's not appropriate for the museum. I've always trusted your judgment. Don't worry about it."

Papaz still had not told his Turkish friend the project's product would not be displayed at the hotel. He and Bi Ba felt it would make more sense and be easier for Sully if they told him at the project's conclusion they had to scrap the museum because of cost considerations. They would make it appear as if it were a last-minute decision. In reality both he and Bi Ba looked at the research as a job program for Sully and his academic team. Bi Ba had strong feelings, even if the academic efforts weren't going to be displayed at the hotel it already paid dividends. Because of Sully's work they had created a relationship with Al Bactar that would never have existed. The Papaz

Foundation became a privileged donor to the great woman Turkan Dink's causes.

"Sully it's okay. Your work has exceeded all our expectations. So much so that Bi Ba and I want to give you a 10% bonus. I don't want to tell you what to do but if you think your team should receive a bonus we will gladly give them whatever you think is appropriate. This is up to you. We know we are comfortable expressing our appreciation to you for the work you did. It makes us feel good. But if you believe giving a bonus to your team could be a disincentive by giving them praise before they have completed the project then we'll wait until its conclusion. We can give them bonuses when they are finished. Like I said it's up to you. I want you to know it is not a zero-sum offer. Their bonuses will not have any influence, in the least, upon yours. We're putting money in your account this afternoon. Let me know what you want us to do relative to your team."

"Now that I have that out of the way, just send me the materials on Faysal, I forgot his last name. I'll read it for my own interest. Does that make you feel any better?"

Sully sounded relieved. "Mr. Papaz, I don't want you to think I or my team are padding the bill by working on a candidate you will never use at the hotel. After they passed it on to me, I agreed with them that it was most interesting. They felt it was important to be balanced even if you didn't include him in your collection of prominent people who had been at the hotel. They even told me if you were put off by their choice, you didn't have to pay them for their hours. They thought you would find it interesting to see how this man Faysal Soylemaz and you crossed paths."

Papaz said again, "Sully just send everything to me. I promise to read it. I trust your judgment. You're making a bigger deal out of whatever this is than necessary."

"It is very interesting Mr. Papaz." He paused for a second and cleared his throat. "Do you remember the first time you stayed at the Four Seasons Hotel in Sultanahmet?"

Papaz said, "Sure, why? How is this relevant to this guy, he fumbled for his name, Faysal."

"Do you remember reporting you lost your watch?"

"Of course," Papaz said. "They never found it and we just wrote it off. In fact, we did not even report it to our insurance company because we never made out a police report. In reflection, I think we thought we could have been wrong about where I left the watch and did not want to get anyone in trouble by saying maybe it was taken from our room. I think I just mentioned it to the manager and said if it turned up. It was kind of odd they didn't even have a lost and found at the front desk. I didn't want to be emphatic about it because I thought heads would roll. That would have really bothered me. You know, the ugly American."

"Sully, what does this have to do with the infamous Mr. Soylemez?"

There was a seriousness about Sully's reply. "We have determined that he stole the watch and ultimately sold it."

Papaz said, "That was 15 years ago. I'm sure as hell not going to press charges now. Just go on and finish your story."

Sully continued, "Soylemez was part of the housekeeping staff. Like I said he stole your watch. You can read about what lengths he went through to sell it. It is all in the file. The important thing is he took your property and financed a small drug operation. If not for your watch, your crumbs as it were, thousands of poor Istanbul children would not have been introduced to cheap drugs and put under Soylemey's brutal ways."

Papaz responded quickly, "You are blaming me because I had a watch stolen? This kid stole my watch and parlayed it into some kind of vast criminal organization and you're blaming me?"

He wanted to go off on his Turkish friend but figured there was something more to it. "Sully, even for you this is over the top. Why are you so emotional? What do you have invested in this?"

Sully backed off saying, "I will explain. I let my emotions get the best of me. My thoughts were clouded. I am sorry. I am too close to this. There is a degree of separation between me and Faysal Soylemez. Because of your watch there is separation between you and him also. We are all tied together my friend. I don't want this to affect our future. You know I live on the Bosporus European side. I am fortunate because of people like you. Your crumbs are not as large for me as they were for Soylemez but they made me a rich man by Turkish standards. I hope you know how much I appreciate our business relationship and our friendship over the years. I am not a large part of your life but for me you have made the difference between being an ordinary man and what many here considered to be a successful man."

"I hope you know how hard I work for you and how important it is for me to do my best. I cherish our relationship and would never do anything to harm it…"

Sully just blurted it out, "Faysal Soylemez is my sister's son. I became successful because of crumbs I earned when they fell off of your plate. He became, what you call it in America, a gangster by stealing crumbs from you. It was my nephew who stole the watch and indirectly it financed his drug empire. He is an embarrassment to me and my family. I am sorry. There is some element of separation between you and him. What makes it worse is I got him the job at the hotel. Of course, you and I did not know each other then. It was 1998. Fate is a strange fellow my friend. He is not only into drugs; but he is into smuggling, kidnapping, money laundering, and protection. My friends at the Four Seasons have told me as we speak he is trying to put a squeeze on the hotel for protection. They don't know he is my nephew. All they know is he is dangerous. I am sorry!"

Papaz said, "Our friendship is not weighed by your relatives. They are not an extension of you. We pay the hotel people handsomely to deal with problems like this. It is none of your concern. Just put it in proper context. This shows me how small the world is. You didn't create this gangster. Don't worry about it. I certainly have the resources to deal with him, Sully," Papaz started laughing, "There's a reason why you get a bonus. Boy! Am I glad I'm not you," and continued laughing.

Before he said goodbye to his friend, Matt said, "Really it's not a problem."

Chapter 54

Within the hour Papaz received the email containing the file on Faysal Soylemez. There was a simple pre-log from the authors.
Attention: Mr Papaz
Presenting a narrative about the Turkish gangster is more expressive of his ways than a historical treatise. As usual we take license but the facts are undisputed. We understand our biases' editorializing will be evident, but we have no tolerance for criminal activities. We will not romanticize Soylemez's life or his exploits.
The narrative began: In 1997 the seventeen years old Faysal Soylemez was hired to work at the Four Seasons Hotel Sultanahmet. He was a very rebellious teenager and left secondary school under a cloud of expulsion. He was permanently suspended for selling drugs specifically glue and paint thinner. His father Sargan Soylemez was abusive and exploited his children for income. Upon expulsion, he was given a choice; go into the Turkish Navy and relinquish his income to his father or choose a form of employment in Istanbul that his uncle Sulaman Suzer provided for him. Suzer or Sully recommended him for a position at the Four Seasons Hotel where he had maintenance department contacts. Sully's role in getting employment for his nephew was equivalent to

paying for the employment. The conduit, the hotel head of maintenance, received fifty percent of the young man's first year pay. Another twenty-five percent went to his father. The alternative was Faysal's four years Turkish Navy enlistment with his father receiving 100% of his pay. Young Faysal's maintenance department hiring included arriving at work at 4:30am. His only break was a thirty-minute break for lunch. He left the hotel every night at 7pm. He was trained to clean all the granite surfaces at the hotel with the exclusion of the guest rooms. A good employment record could lead to an apprenticeship with a granite and marble master. That eventuality could take more than ten years; apprenticeship, journeymen, master.

Sully had recommended Faysal for the job which came with a personal indemnification for the hotel of any damages his nephew might cause. This was standard for any recommended person. Faysal was only at the hotel for nine months when you, Mr. Papaz, stayed at the hotel in room #207. It is only conjecture but he stalked you because of his great affinity for your unusual blue watch. He told his friends who later become gang members after seeing your Ulysse Nardin blue Le Locle Susse he had to have it. He devised a plan for breaking into your room and stealing the watch when the opportunity arrived. He was not part of the housekeeping staff and did not have a key to your room but he stole a master card key from one of the supervising maids on the hotel second floor. On occasions prior to taking your watch, he broke into random suites on the first floor stealing anything of value from hotel guest feeding his sniffing habit. He minimized his theft and only stole from guests occasionally so as not to be caught. You, Mr. Papaz, were the exception. He plotted for and executed the theft of your watch. He wore the blue masterpiece socially in the drug trade for six-months before he sold it in the black market for less than ten percent of its value. He took it to a friend who sold knockoff watches at the Grand Bazaar and was told it was valued at $11,000 dollars. Faysal kept it as long as he could as an asset to be used in the future. He never took the watch off his left wrist and was given the 'street name,' *Koruma Adam*, which in Turkish meant watchmen.

Four months after stealing your watch, he quit his job at the hotel, left his father's home and lived with two high school classmates on the streets of Cihangir, a small suburb of Istanbul. He and the two of his lowlife friends, Sahin and Agit, found refuge under a bridge two blocks from the Bosporus. They had to fight for a space under the substructure of the bridge where fifty people already lived. The bridge protected them from the elements.

The dense low fog of the late evening and early morning coming off the Golden Horn portion of the Bosporus had taken many lives. Hundreds of street people were dying from consumption or pneumonia in the unprotected sea passage areas near the water every year. Enclosed encampments were essential. They lived with the fittest and most violent of the street people. Faysal and his friends thrived in this environment. They had a place to stay, a good product and sales were up to such an extent he saved almost eighty American dollars in less than two months.

Faysal used their savings to purchase more glue and paint thinner. Approximately twenty percent of the purchase was for their own consumption. The other eighty percent was for selling on the streets. Glue was purchased for one dollar per eight-ounce tube. Paint thinner was more expensive and purchased for eight dollars per one liter cans. The glue would be sniffed or huffed after being placed in a plastic bag and blowing air into it. The paint thinner was poured onto a cloth and then inhaled via the mouth or nose. Profits on the sale of glue and paint were exceedingly high but with twenty percent of the product being consumed by the three gangsters and protection money being paid to older more mature drug dealers they made little for themselves. Because of their expenses, the product selling margins were low, but within three months they were successful enough at hawking the lower level drugs they expanded adding crack to their street inventories. Faysal was well suited for the violent nature of these neighborhoods. His abusive father prepared him for pain. He was beaten by the ponderous man and knew what pain one must endure for survival. The three young drug dealers were now bringing in twenty dollars a day revenue and after expenses they were saving more than two dollars a day.

They decided to move because they were profitable, but moving and purchasing more products necessitated the sale of his watch. It took less than a year for Faysal successes in the criminal world to buy a new ULysse Nardin which he still wears to this day. Sale of the watch, steady income stream and moving to an apartment in Gulsuyu on the Asian side of Istanbul where neighborhoods of old mid-nineteenth century apartment buildings were heavily populated. The highest Western Asian population density coupled with its extreme poverty created a breeding ground for gangs.

Children lived on the street because of domestic violence, economic difficulties, broken families and problems linked to immigration. Desperation lent itself to drug consumption. Many area children lived in cave like holes in the cities' 1,600-year-old city wall. The fortunate lived in apartments or tenement houses with one bathroom per floor, infested with rats and vermin, and subject to the whims of drug lords.

Faysal, ever the thinker, wanted to find the most strategic living area to increase his drug sales. On Ahemet Street, in the eastern sector of Gulsuyu, they picked an apartment beehive building with young people as the heaviest population. Apartments lined the old narrow cobblestone streets on both sides. It was a mixed-use area. Butcher shops, markets, stores selling used electronics parts, an antique store and a Kurdish men's club were in the old bleached-out gray wooden building's bottom floors affixed to each other like chips at the end of a backgammon board.

Faysal picked the apartment with the greatest amount of young people foot traffic. He and his two friends barely had enough money to rent what was called a middle apartment. It was in the middle of a large four-story one-hundred-and-fifty-unit complex. The room had no access to the outside other than a maze of hallways. At first the boys had to fight their way to and from the unit but that changed because of Faysal's ability to defend himself.

When their business activity increased and they had enough money, they rented a new room in a more upscale neighborhood with windows and a door opening to the less violent street. By then Faysal made a name for himself because of the product quality and his savagery dealing with other gangs. Demand in the ghetto followed supply. His clients remained loyal and followed him. Drug dealing was extremely territorial and survival was for the Darwinian fittest. In less than a year he became the alpha drug dealer in his section of the city.

As a larger drug culture player, he decided to expand operations to selling other drugs and other areas of Istanbul. He left his friends Sahin and Agit with the low-end drugs money machine continuing the Gulsuyu district business. Faysal developed relationships with heroin and cocaine dealers in more upscale neighborhoods. His new clients were young professionals working primarily in the city's economic financial sector. Being the proverbial smallest fish in a large pond was at first difficult for Faysal because of his hatred for authority and his continual use of glue and paint thinner. Although, a heavy consumer of his own drugs he was a functional drug addict he could skillfully do his job. He acquired new more sophisticated skills matching his new higher end users' product. He impressively decided to stop sniffing glue and blocked himself from other narcotics usage. He was drug clean for the next two years. During that time, he became a major enforcer for the city's largest drug cartel. As any ambitious businessman, he started plotting take-over of the cocaine trade and did so in what law enforcement called the

Great Massacre of Istanbul. He and his two friends, Sahin and Agit, slaughtered the cartel's boss and eleven of his men while sitting in one of Istanbul's most popular bathhouses.

Faysal became the king of low-end and high-end narcotics in the great city. He would run the high-end trade of heroin and cocaine by himself while his two childhood friends ran the low-end trade of glue, paint thinner and smack. The explosive nature of his rise in the underworld led to greater expansion. Drug free himself he would not tolerate his inner circle using narcotics. His dealers on the street were treated differently and incentivized by being able to buy cheap drugs for their own use as part of their pay. The two-tiered system worked perfectly: clean management with a team of drug addicted sellers and enforcers.

Faysal began an expansion plan, developing his heroin trading outside Turkey. The drug and its derivatives was becoming a drug of choice for young professionals in England. He targeting London and Manchester, he took an exploratory trip with Sahin and Agit to Great Britain viewing the market and analyzing its possibilities.

The three Young Turk's ethnicity was not obvious in London since that great city had the most heterogeneous metropolitan area in the world. Known as the Third World capital, young people from all over Asia and Africa were fleeing their birthplace hardships taking advantage of prosperity and opportunity they perceived was waiting for them in London. The cities London, Los Angeles, and New York were diverse metropolitan areas where immigrants had upward mobility chances. They figured the doors to riches were open to people of color because the proximity to wealth would create opportunities. Academics called this phenomenon the trickledown theory.

Many people flooding London took the perverse attitude that nothing was expected of them other than their own home countries' poverty. They were owed a better life solely because they were historically exploited. Their pasts entitled them to a better future. They were special because they endured great hardships getting a new life.

Once these immigrants came to London where dreams were supposed to be fulfilled and were struck by the new environmental reality, not better and in some cases worse than their old life. More was expected of them because they were now living in a modern and sophisticated world. It quickly became obvious they had no skills, were marked by their skin color and their original city's ethnicity, they failed and dreams were unrealized because they were ill-prepared to compete in this new world and exploited by yet other overlords.

Faysal, Sahin, and Agit picked up on that reality on their exploratory trip to London. Faysal coldly seized upon the poor immigrants' situation and brought his low-end drugs to East London where they lived. He exploited the immigrants even more than where they originated. Faysal charged this activity to his friends, Sahin and Agit, while he tailored his high-end cocaine and heroin business to the young professional in London's West End.

Russell C. Arslan

Chapter 55

After coming back to Istanbul, Faysal was confident he could grow his business in London. He made direct connections with Colombian cocaine suppliers. He bought product directly from FARC, the Colombian guerrilla group, sidestepping his previous relationship with the Mexican Sinaloa cartel.

Until this point he purchased Mexican cartel cocaine, but realized they were only suppliers, not producers. If he bought cocaine from the new source, the actual producers, he could lower the cost of doing business. Sinaloa shipped products to Marseille France. FARC shipped directly to London. Sinaloa's cocaine was packaged in plastic balloons, intermingled with bulk coffee and shipped from Costa Rica which was not known as an operational base for cocaine sales. The cocaine filled balloons were placed in the middle of the one hundred pounds' gunnysack bags of commercial grade non-aromatic coffee used as a blend. Thirty bags per pallet and thirty pallets per standard cubic dry container. The container dimensions were 13.556 meters by 2.352 meters by 2.694 meters. Each container had a maximum weight of 61,529 pounds of which the cocaine was five percent of the total volume or 3,000 pounds' total.

The Mexican processed cocaine was already adulterated with glucose and Xylocaine. It was ready for distribution in increments of 50, 100, or 200 grams, the amount placed in each rubber balloon. Any smaller volume of the narcotic would need processing by whomever purchased the product from the cartel. The Mexican cocaine was twenty-five to twenty-seven percent pure. For lower end clientele, it would need cutting again to twelve to fourteen percent pure which doubled its gross margin.

Faysal's negotiation with the Colombian FARC's was greatly advantageous. The shipping costs were similar. The packages of cocaine were more defined and came in units of one, three, four, eight, thirty, sixty, ninety, one hundred-eighty and three hundred sixty grams in clear plastic zip locked packaging. One ounce is exactly 28.3 grams so the weight of the Colombian product was more in line with English measurements. The cocaine itself was higher quality at thirty-two to thirty-five percent purity.

What made the FARC bid more attractive was their cocaine was cut with glucose and levamisole not Xylocaine like their Mexican rival. With levamisole as the adulterating agent the drug would have greater stimulating properties. The cocaine cost depended upon political factors but it ranged between 3,500 American dollars and 5,100 American dollars per pound. The Mexican product was twelve to fifteen percent lesser quality. Another factor favoring FARC's cocaine was it shipped directly to London in containers of aromatic coffee. Aromatic coffees not only taste better but has properties of deeper and richer aromas masks cocaine smell better. Drugs packed in aromatics have a greater chance of passing through customs. Another bulk packaging option making FARC's product more attractive was one kilo bricks.

Faysal was given the option of smaller sized cocaine packaging for people wanting to speedball. If he purchased the Colombian product, he would not need a processing operation in London raised his profit margins and decreased his chances of being caught by law enforcement. The biggest advantage of the FARC proposal was they guaranteed the product shipment. Meaning if anything happened to the cocaine entering any port in Great Britain, the Colombians would incur the total loss. The Colombian cocaine was less expensive, of greater quality and lesser risk. Faysal would do business exclusively with the Colombians.

The next thing he wanted was to secure the heroin supply lines for his English operation. Turkey was no longer a major opiate producer so it was necessary to continue purchasing from his existing partners in Afghanistan, where the Helmand province clan, Anoushirvan, gave him discounts predicated upon his greater volume of his purchases. It costs the Afghans approximately six dollars per kilo to produce the raw opiate. It took ten kilograms to make one processed heroin kilogram. The street value of one kilogram of pure heroin in England was almost $5,000 and Faysal purchased it for one tenth the price. The drug's street purity ranged anywhere from fifty to sixty-four percent purity.

Cheaper and lower end quality heroin produced in Asia's Golden Triangle was purchased in Laos for one half the price of Afghan premium grade. The problem with Southeast Asian opiates were their colors. British higher income consumers favored brown Afghan opiates not yellow Laotian heroin so he continued buying product from the Afghans.

Once Faysal lined up heroin producers able to deliver twenty kilograms a week, he wanted a method to get it through British customs. Opiates produced in Afghanistan ship directly to Istanbul and Faysal created a scheme to get the product to London. He developed an elaborate plan to using the Turkish dance company Anatolia to ship one year's supply of heroin to London in one shipment. It would be a great financial risk but he felt that a single run of drugs was less risky than multiple European border crossings.

Anatolia had a truck fleet carrying its equipment, sets, costumes and animals used in its acts. The trucks' undercarriage hid the opiate as they crossed Europe and then the English Channel for its final London destination. Faysal purchased the company through a third-party. Even if it only broke even on the business side, it would be a financial success. The transportation cost of drug movement could be as expensive as seven percent of its street value. Tying the drug business into the entertainment business made financial sense.

Cocaine sent to London in coffee bags destined for one of the Soylemez Company's warehouse. Faysal created a Turkish Coffee Shop. It was a boutique coffee house in Hendon, North West London and owned by

Faysal under the pseudo-name Turkish International Companies. It was the first of eleven boutique coffee houses established as distribution centers for narcotics as well. The last of his retail properties used to sell drugs was a Camden nightclub. Located in the industrial part of the impoverished city, it targeted low-end workers. His England business, once actually started, opened two high-end London West End clubs.

Faysal's plan was simple. He had product brought to his London retail operation with multiple distribution centers and nightclubs. All he needed now to carry out the project was a team of dealers and enforcers. For this purpose, he partnered with the unsophisticated, violent Hoxton Mob in exchange for a percentage. The English gangsters had been selling poor quality drugs for over a decade in London. Faysal preferred white gangsters over colored ones because he felt they presented a more odious overlord.

On paper, everything was in place for the Turkish gangster starting his drug empire in England. The operation was almost two years in the making. Once he opened the doors his success was meteoric. By 2006 Soylemez was the largest drug dealer in London. His virtual monopoly on low-end drugs now had the seventeen coffee house distribution centers in the poorer areas of London. He owned three nightclubs. He was the largest dealer of heroin and cocaine for young professional businessmen in London's old city financial district. He knew this only took place because of his relationship with the Hoxton Mob and increased their proportion to ten percent of the operations. He developed the business, he fronted the money for the business, he ran the business, but he let his British counterparts do the dirty work. It was successful beyond any expectations. Now, he moved into new areas with his British partners. He became the money man for loan sharking and protection.

The Drug Lord life and his proximity to money and cocaine were too much for Faysal once again. He started snorting epic quantities of coke. This time his addiction overpowered his will and he became a functionless addict which led to his incarceration in 2011. Faysal Soylemez was convicted of drug possession with the intent to sell, arms violations, money-laundering and illegal banking practices. His conviction came with a five-year sentence without possibility of early parole. He was incarcerated at the Altcourse Prison just outside of Liverpool in the County Merseyside. It was a maximum-security prison for adults and young offenders. Faysal managed to hold his own against British nationals in the prison. Within one year he became the largest drug dealer in the prison. He had a couple of his "girls" from the nightclubs bring in cocaine and heroin. They placed the drugs in condoms and put them in their cunts was the way he explained it to prison authorities before he was sent off to solitary confinement for three months. While dealing product in the prison he traded drugs for phones, food, tobacco, but more importantly security. Before his sentence was fully served he was extradited to Turkey where he served out the last year and four months in Izmir Closed Prison, a maximum-security prison.

With Faysal in prison his English empire collapsed because his partners did could not manage the sophisticated narcotics trade. They were exposed as unskilled thugs. Turkey was a different story. Sahin and Agit kept the fire burning in Istanbul and upon his release from prison he went back to running the organization.

Chapter 56

In less than a week, Papaz received communication from Sully. This time instead of an email Sully called.

"I hope all is well my friend. How are you and your wonderful Bi Ba?"

Papaz said, "We are fine, thank you for asking. How are you? Does this call have anything to do with your nephew? Don't worry about it. I've read the folder. He is a bad guy but in no way shape or form is he a reflection upon you."

Sully said, "Thank you, but that is not why I am calling. Those are very kind words but I want to share something with you before you receive the next set of documents. The new materials are not conventional; much like the document on my nephew."

Papaz laughed, "I can't wait to see what you're sending me," he said sarcastically. "Sully we have not talked about your nephew but we have a phrase for people like him, he's a piece of work. He should be off the streets but that's not my problem. I'm sure you've heard this before, the further you are away from him the safer you will be."

He started laughing again, "Remind me that once we are in Istanbul, to stay as far away from him as possibly. Now, what does your team have for me?"

Sully said, "I probably shouldn't be doing this. I am speaking for me not the team. So, I might not be as clear on their goals as they would be. In one of the meetings, you remember Ismet Cul, he shared his view of the gallery at the hotel. He wanted five to six major presentations with displays, pictures, videos and any artifacts representing their candidates. It was actually very impressive. As an example, for Prime Minister Erdogan, they prepared replicas of legislation pieces of he signed, pictures with world political leaders. Famous for a speech on education, they have excerpts in Turkish and also translated to English of the Prime Minister's speech. For Malgan Malgan there will be a display with some of his inventions. People can interact with them. Again, pictures, videos, and a running commentary on all of his charitable work. As for Tarkan Dink there is television coverage and videos of her clinic work and her schools. Cul thought we should display them in an old box television with an antenna on top. Now for Soylemez the team unanimously felt he should be mentioned. People should know the dark side of our history. They want his display played down but feel it is important to be equal sided about our past. I am having them send you a simulation of what the gallery will look like."

"Now, as for their next set of documents, they are unconventional. They will send you one more file, how do you say, more bona fide candidates. Their names are Lucy and Albert Shamshoian. That will make four prominent candidates, Malgan Malgan, Erdogan, Dink, and the Shamshoians. Then there will be a lesser discussion of Soymelez and some other dark figures in our history. Finally, and this is their doing, they will send you information on ten Armenians. Six being Americans and all ten candidates have ties to the Four Seasons. They are important but less prominent guests. The team feels this is, how do you say, more interesting or entertaining to someone who is not so interested in pure history. The files will not be very detailed. They will be summaries of the guest histories and accomplishments. Most of these people will be celebrities or people in the public's eye. I hope you find this most interesting. And again, may I thank you for understanding my relationship with my nephew. I will make certain you never meet him even though he frequents some of the same places you do when you are in our wonderful city."

Papaz replied, "Sully, I am sure you will alert me about Faysal if the need ever arises. Like I said, don't worry about him. I hope you know we appreciate what your team has done. Your guidance has been terrific. I look forward to the Armenian museum wing. Tell the team we appreciate everything they have done. I like their thinking. It's not unconventional, but it is thinking outside of the box. I like the direction."

Papaz received an email within the hour. There were ten names in the file. He called Bi Ba, "Can you come over here for a second? They were sitting on opposite sides of their large media room. "I think you'll find this interesting."

She had already read the Soylemez document. She found it interesting because he was, as she called him, "A low life piece of crap."

"I haven't read this yet but Sully says these documents are much more lighthearted and we will find them interesting. Would you like to look at them?"

"Sure," she said, "just forward them to me. We can go over them together."

The names were in alphabetical order. Andre Agassi, Charles Aznavayour, Cher, Mike Connors, Edward Goorjian, Calouste Gulbenkian, Kevork Hambartsumian, Varaziad Kazanjian, Sergie Parajanov, and William Saroyan. Everyone stayed at the hotel or visited the prison.

The team could not confirm each stayed in room #207 but we do know six of them did. Only Agassi, Gulbenkian, Kazanjian, and William Saroyan did not stay in the suite. Sayoryan died in the 1970s but he visited a cousin who was in the prison when he was a young man. Gulbenkian in 1929 was given a tour of the prison. Agassi stayed with his wife Steffi Graph on the first floor on their 2011 visit and Kazanjian did medical rounds in the prison in 1928.

The Armenian portion of the document consisted of subsections dedicated to ten individuals containing historical links for each, pictures, videos and inventory of any physical objects relevant to their presentation.

André Agassi, the world's number one tennis player in 1995, won Wimbledon, the US open, the French open and an Olympic gold medal.

Charles Aznavour, French singer and actor

Cher (Cherylin Sarkissian), singer, actress, Academy award winner and half of the musical team duo, Sonny and Cher

Mike Connors, actor, star of the television series Mannix

Ed Goorjian, head of the legendary US basketball family. Son Greg a noteworthy American basketball player and sons Brian and Kevin international basketball coaches

Calouste Gulbenkian, one of the wealthiest oil barons in the Middle East, owning 5% of British Petroleum.

Kevory Hambartsumian, physicist. Developed theories and computing mass nova stars' ejection of young star clusters.

Varazaid Kazanjian, father of plastic surgery and Harvard professor.

Sergei Parajanov, Soviet Armenian surrealist painter.

William Saroyan, a Pulitzer Prize writer for his book, *Time of Your Life*.

You were kind enough to let us set our research parameters. Instead of a rigorous social science approach we were in the value judgments realm and selective or subjective fact interpretations. We thank you for allowing us to cast off the academic protocols and rigors that usually predetermine answers. Our problem is if we extrapolate our approach of who stayed at the hotel or visited the jail or any combination thereof it is not a random interpretation of Istanbul.

We would prefer displaying a more diverse experience than our model will project. That is why we have advocated recognition for Faysal Soylemez and people who displayed more antisocial behaviors, but certainly not to the same extent as our other candidates or even the American Armenians.

We know it is presumptuous of us trying to even out the field of people coming in touch with your property. You and your hotel are in the highest quartile of Turkish life but the average Turks do not share your same experiences. Our question is, should your patrons only see a five-star interpretation of our city because they are staying at your five-star hotel? Or, do they deserve a five-star history showing we live in a two-star environment? We have a saying in Turkey: the truth is not always addressed because it is easier to turn our heads.

This, Mr. Papaz, is our dilemma. I hope our thoughts are not offensive. Team leader, Ismet Cul.

After looking at the document Bi Ba said, "That was really neat. I can't believe how many of those people I've heard of. What's unbelievable is the name Ed Goorjian. They said he stayed in our suite on his way to Saudi Arabia when he coached the royal family's basketball team. Do you remember anything about the University of Nevada at Las Vegas' basketball teams under Jerry Tarkanian?"

Papaz said, "Sure, anybody who loved basketball in the late 80s early 90s knows who they were. I think they won the NCAA in 89 and lost 90. I was a young kid but everybody loved those guys. The Running Rebels, right?"

Bi Ba said, "Well, Goorjian was their defensive coach. Man, they were great on defense. It was probably ten years later but I had the pleasure of meeting him. It's amazing because when I was in Vegas they were still talking about those teams. They were legendary. They called Tarkanian and Goorjian the crazy Armenians. That little summary on Ed Goorjian doesn't even come close to defining the guy. I was really into basketball after college so when I was in Vegas I went to lots of UNLV's games at the Thomas and Mack Stadium. I followed the post Tarkanian years. They weren't so good after the Armenians left. I'm not really sure but I think Tarkanian went to Fresno State or something like that. I didn't know much about Goorjian until today. Anyway, I really followed basketball and I think it was around 1999 or 2000 there was a coach's convention at the Encore. It was in conjunction with the ten-year anniversary of their championship run. Just on a whim I went to a seminar where I met Goorjian. He was one of the speakers. He was such an inspiration. He was everything a coach was supposed to be. He was intense but funny at the same time. Great stories but more importantly he showed his team values in a way that stuck with me. Everything was about trust, discipline and sacrifice. He talked about loyalty and the meaning of something bigger than the individual. He was like a fiery John Wooden. When the seminar was over I can't believe it, but I walked up and introduce myself. He was terrific. I remembered how he shook my hand and how he looked into my eyes. We only talked for a couple of minutes. As I walked away I noticed how many people were still around him. All they wanted to do was show their appreciation and acknowledge what he had done for them. He was UNLV's defense coach but you would have thought that he was the head coach. Everyone was extremely respectful to him. That always stayed with me. I had the feeling I was better off after meeting him. His love of the game and his love for life were passed on to hundreds of his players who became successful because of what Goorgjian instilled in them. I still remember everything that happened that day. There must've been 100 people approaching him, fellow coaches, ex-players and others. I'll never forget it. Matt, it was a great day."

Papaz said, "I guess the guy really impressed you. I've heard you mention his name over the years but I really thought he was your coach. If he impressed, you that much and you carry around his vision of what it takes to be a good person then I can't imagine what an impact he had upon his players."

He continued, "I guess there are some really special people in the world that cast a very large shadow. If you feel that way about Goorjian then it's not unreasonable to think a museum dedicated to people like him is important. I'm not saying I've change my mind on the gallery but maybe the idea is not as dumb as I thought it was. There are some people who should be remembered and I'm sure he's one of them."

Chapter 57

Papaz received an email directly from the team: Mr Papaz per our previous communications we felt it would be acceptable to you to send another unconventional candidate. In this case, it is two candidates. We are sending you a partially completed version of our research with a completed version to be delivered within three weeks. Once you see the file you will understand why. The draft will identify; Ms. Lucy Shamshoian and Mr. Albert Shamshoian. They are not related. We believe they are worthy of your scrutiny.

Another matter we want to bring to your attention, please consider this as a note of warning that should promote further discussion: Turkey is a very conservative society and the Shamsonians will be viewed as Jew lovers. They saved Jews from the German concentration camps and were outspoken on Armenian repression. They put into place what Americans would call an underground railroad.

Today we are faced with the unusual circumstances of war in the Gaza Strip between Hamas and Israel. Because we are faced with possible escalation of the war to the entire Middle East anything that legitimizes Israel or Jews or sympathizes with Armenian history is unacceptable to most Turks. When the Muslim world is on fire we become irrational and old hatreds fill our eyes.

A history of the Shamshoians being Armenian and helping Jews might be intolerable to a majority of the Turkish population. Turkey has two zones of tolerance for Armenians, Istanbul and the North-Eastern territories outside Ankara. There are no Jewish zones of tolerance and hence their numbers have dwindled to less than one-half of one percent of our population over the last fifty years. Our predominantly Muslim population even under the secular laws we possess are anti-Semitic and very Christian intolerant. Turks are xenophobic and backwards. They feel their homeland should be for Muslims and Turkish speaking people.

That being said, it might not be an appropriate time to set up a gallery at your hotel. We, the team, are ardent supporters of your project and in no way, want it to be suspended. Our work is not as rigorous as the academic community would demand but we feel it is important. We think it could be deemed inappropriate at this time to inaugurate a gallery.

We ask, if your schedule permits, could you please come to Istanbul so we may discuss the matter. We also are in the process of completing a mockup of the gallery scaled to one-twelfth percent. We would like to share it with you. The Shamshoian file will be completed by the time you arrive in our great city. It was signed, team leader, Ismet Cul.

Papaz immediately shot off a reply. "Professor Cul, we will be delighted to meet with you for further discussions. We will be in Istanbul three weeks from today: December 14th. Matt Papaz."

He couldn't believe how fortunate he was. Instead of having to pre-fabricate a story why he and Bi Ba would not be opening their gallery they now had to sound disappointed in the circumstances leading up to scrapping the project.

He called Bi Ba and left a message on her cell, "I have great news. Call me as soon as possible."

He leaned back in his office chair and stretched. He sat there and reflecting. Papaz said to himself, "It certainly feels good when life is easy."

Within five minutes he received a copy of the abbreviated Shamshoian file.

On November 17, 1922, a child was dropped off in front of the Greek Orthodox Church in Cappadocia's capital Gorene. The four-year-old was draped in rags, the crate he had been placed in was small and cushioned in long dark brown smelly grass, and he was cold and dirty. There was no note. Not even a sighting of who had dropped off the young child. He was nameless. Father Gregory of the small Greek Orthodox Church on the outskirts of the village brought the sickly spindly looking child to an orphanage run by two unsavory flesh peddlers who portrayed themselves as foster parents. The Anatolian foster home was no more than a way station for children who were sold by the establishments' proprietors. Haig and Sidoun Shamshoian took in abused children and cared for them until they could be sold as indentured slaves to landholders or artisans in Cappadocia. The children were housed in a barn on their property. It was dilapidated. Its roof was smattered with holes that in the coldest and warmest of times provided no insulation and no protection from the elements. The structure's outside cedar siding was so worn, they rotted leaving a gray fascia that did little more than block the sun. The building had no ventilation and was vulnerable to earthquakes and high winds. The floor of the old structure was used for domestic animals. Horses, donkeys and cows were put into the barn in the heat of the day. The rafters decking the barn's inside divided the area into small pens functioning as three feet x four feet x six feet cages. The boxlike cells were made of cedar sticks and had front loading doors with a slip lock mechanism imprisoning the children at night. They were routinely beaten and rarely fed by the elderly Shamshoians.

The little boy was appropriated to the orphanage by the Greek Father who received a broker's fee and gladly handed over the four-year-old child. Sidoun Shamshoian accepted the undernourished sickly child but his value was lower because of his poor condition. Fifty percent of the smaller ones died before they could be sold. She named him Albert Shamshoian. The next week the fortunate Father Gregory was given custody of another small child. This time it was a young girl whose parents lived in helpless circumstances causing them to abandon their child. Gregory took her to the Shamshoian orphanage for his pittance. Sidoun named her Lucy. Because of her size and the offhand chance of her survival the little three-year-old girl was thrown into the same cage as Albert. The two of them lived together for the next three years.

The Shamshoians called them little animals, since they were no more than beasts of burden. They lived a subsistence level life. They were fed only enough food to enabling them to work and at some point, in their futures be sold into indentured slavery. The farm orphans had ages from three years to sixteen years. There was a constant turnover with numbers fluctuating from thirty-five to forty children sold depending upon the demand. The children never intermingled or cultivated friendships since they were limited by their turnover to buyers who had them live in worse conditions than at the orphanage. Life was hell in the foster home but their future prospects were worse.

When Lucy and Albert reached nine and ten years old, they were mature enough to be sold. They chose to escape. With help from two older stablemates and what other people believed was God's will, the four escaped to freedom amidst a horrible earthquake. They found refuge in the old underground Christian city of Kaymaki, Cappadocia which forms a hotel of its sandstone rock formations. The old volcanic region of central Anatolia was filled with million-year-old minaret structures created by winds, torrential rains, the temperature extremes which eroded the sandstone and pumas alluvial plains of the region. Layered sedimentary rock carved out over a million years left thousands of square miles of desolate areas looking like the dinosaur spines encircled by deep valleys. The convoluted soft rock contour provided geologic building blocks for the Anatolian people. Huge underground cities were dug below the Earth's surface to protect the Christian inhabitants from Muslims around them. The city of Kaymaki was a Christian stronghold built in 650 A.D. housing 8,000 people and giving them safety from their enemies. Underground houses, churches and storage areas were carved into hillsides and minaret structures where thousands of people lived. The four children found refuge in these abandoned cities and followed what Christians and people of minority faiths had done for more than 1400 years. They hid from their oppressors.

The two older children, Asher Rabin, fourteen and Ester Hersher thirteen, were Jewish. Abducted from the old Jewish Quarter in Ankara and sold to an artisan, ran away after three years, were captured and were again sold to the Shamshoians who were brokers in Jew trade.

The four children banded together, as street children do today and overcame their harsh environment. They lived like Romas. After three years living by their wits, in the worst conditions in the old carved out dwellings, they traveled 700 miles to Istanbul. A point of separation, they found refuge in the old abandoned Sultanhemat prison. The two girls, Lucy and Ester found employment as seamstresses in a leather shop near the Grand Bazaar. Albert and Asher were employed as day workers on the Bosporus docks near the spice market. It took almost six months to save enough Jewish Quarter, room rent money for the four young adults. Jews were not welcome in any of the Istanbul Muslim or Christian communities. By choice Lucy and Albert exclusively corroborated with Jews.

Turkey aligned itself with Germany in the beginning of the pre-World War II European conflict. Jewish discrimination became part and parcel of Turkish life. Even the liberal Istanbul was infected with the horrible Jewish persecution injustices. The Jewish community near the Galata Tower closed its ranks and became a guarded camp against the anti-Semitic demonstrations of Jew hating Turks. When World War II broke out Ester and Asher were taken from their flat and shot by a street mob of Islamic religious zealots. Lucy and Albert witnessed the execution and pledged they would do something to help the Jewish community. The natural antipathy between Muslims and Jews and the so-called Hitler solution to the Jewish problem made Istanbul's Jews marked targets. The Jewish population of the city shrank by over ninety percent and the remaining ten percent lived under siege.

    Lucy and Albert made their mission to help any way they could and sought Jews needing relocation. There was an Armenian sympathizers' network to the Jewish plight. They shared their homes, food and helped the few remaining Jews. Many found safe haven in the abandoned Sultanahmet prison or the old rat infested Basilica Cistern. The conditions in the old prison and century's old underground reservoir were horrendous, but safe in comparison to the Jewish Quarter. A network ferried Jews to Izmir and other southern coast Turkish cities. Some passed to Lebanon, Jordan and Egypt where Jews were still discriminated upon but not to the same extent as the Turkish Jews. By the end of the war, Lucy and Albert helped more than 500 Jews escape from mainland Turkey. Between 1945 in 1948 they helped create an underground railroad allowing many more

Jews to leave France and Eastern Europe. The ultimate goal was for these European or Ashkenazi Jews to proceed to Palestine with the hope of the region becoming a Jewish state.

With the independence of Israel in 1948 Lucy and Albert directed their energies to fundraising for the new nation. By 1954 they had set up the first anti-defamation league in Europe. The Turkish Anti-Defamation League was small in volume because the Jewish population had dropped to less than two percent of the Turkish population. But it symbolized the need to redress the wrong the Turkish population had done to another minority. In the early part of the century the Turks had perpetrated genocide upon the Armenians and by midcentury they had extricated the Jews from their country.

In the early 1960s Lucy and Albert again redirected their work. This time they helped Armenians suffering continuously from the 1914 genocide to the present. In a demonstration to show their support for the small Armenian community still living in Istanbul they were jailed. Two days later they were found hanged in their cells. They were not siblings, they never got married, they never had children but they lived together for more than forty years.

EDITOR'S NOTES: as stated earlier, this is a preliminary report. It constitutes a rough draft summary of Lucy and Albert Shamshoian's activities for more than four decades. A more detailed analysis is forthcoming. We hope highlighting their activities will not be viewed as contentious. We have a saying in Turkey, you are a collection of yourself. You make all your own choices. The Shamshoians chose to champion the cause of the only people they knew who were family. They chose loyalty and friendship over the hatred tide in their country. Turkish progressives thanked them for bringing us into the modern world. We hope their story will be placed in the halls of your hotel. Team leader, Ismet Cul

Chapter 58

After a late lunch, Matt asked, "Bi Ba, do you want to go down the hill and walk around Westwood?"

He was still thinking about the Shamshoians file, consumed by the details he wanted to relax.

She said, "Sure. How about going to the 3rd Street Promenade instead?"

The promenade was a retail, outdoor shopping mall next to the beach in Santa Monica. The twenty-five-minute drive was surprisingly relaxing to Matt. When they arrived at the beach he luckily found street parking and they walked three blocks towards the pedestrian outdoor mall. Matt could not completely get Turkey out of his mind.

He told Bi Ba, "We must leave for Istanbul in three weeks. I am a little apprehensive about having a meeting with the team."

"I know they understand about discarding the museum because of political uncertainties, but bringing everything to a close is a little unsettling."

Bi Ba's mind was more on shopping and comparing the 3rd Street Promenade to Bodrum. She said, "You know it's ironic that Bodrum is just as upscale as Southern California. Some of the retail areas near the marina over there were just as nice as here in Santa Monica and certainly a lot safer."

"You are right but it is not one of my favorite places after that asshole, Ozkan, beat the crap out of me," Matt said.

By now they were walking on the bluffs overlooking the ocean a block from the promenade. As they passed a filthy bare chested beggar with his hand out asking for a dollar Bi Ba said, "Sometimes this place really bothers me. I know there is no place for these people, but when they get in your face it's unpleasant. We know we can take care of ourselves but I'm sure they scare the hell out of most people."

Matt said, "Yeah, they can be pretty menacing and I'm sure the tourists don't expect it.

Santa Monica, known as the homeless capital of the United States because of its temperate climate determined by its closeness to a massive body of water and the city's progressive attitude towards indigents.

Matt said, "It's simple, the rest of the world has caught up with us, but we're still romanticizing how special we are and no one has what we have. Don't get me wrong, Santa Monica is great but it sure as heck has a lot of problems. You know, when I'm really being honest with myself, Beverly Hills is not so special anymore either."

"There must be a hundred places as nice."

"Shoot, even the Beyoglu District, you know, that place in Istanbul near the Ritz Carlton is pretty close to being as nice as Beverly Hills."

He thought for a moment and said something shocking to her.

"I always thought, the only city I wanted to live in was Los Angeles, but heck, we have houses in Toronto and New York. How about if we look into a house on the Bosporus?"

She said, "What? Are you kidding me?"

Matt replied, "We own a hotel in the city. I'm going to ask Frederic to look into the tax consequences, if we buy a house. Nothing to lose."

Bi Ba responded, "I thought we bought the hotel not only as an investment but as a place to stay, like an expensive timeshare. I don't think we would ever use a house in Istanbul."

Matt thought for a second, "Maybe we'll just buy something as an investment. Nothing is etched in stone. It's just a thought. Frederic wanted us to diversify our personal investments and be more international. He says some emerging market prices of real estate is lagging. I'm just talking out loud, if you think it's stupid we will forget it."

She changed the direction of the subject, "I've put some thought into something else dealing with the hotel."

Matt said, "Well, let me hear it."

"I don't think anyone at the hotel should be put off by us. If we're staying on the premises, I think we should introduce ourselves to the staff. When Stephen Wynn came by the hotel," he was the owner of the Encore Hotel in Las Vegas where Bi Ba had worked for six years, "He put pressure on all of us. I knew him really well and it still was uncomfortable. It was not a good experience for anybody. We can't be buddies with the staff. We don't want them to be frightened of us either. There is a delicate balance so if we are going to stay where we work some things must be worked out differently."

"Is there something else?"

"I'd like to create a Prominent Guest Program for some special guest. I would build it like the one in Vegas. I don't want to manage it but I would like to set it up. Maybe we can get Sully involved. I really want the hotel to be rated as one of the top ten hotels in the world. I love goals. I think it would be enjoyable for me. All the charitable stuff we do is fine but it's not like being on the firing line. It's more like an activity to fill up my time. There is no responsibility other than donating your money."

Matt stood there with a smile on his face because she was getting embarrassed about the remark that it was his money.

"You know what I mean."

He shook his head, laughed and said, "I'm just picking on you."

"I understand." she continued, "Every place I drop off money they cater to me and it seems disingenuous. I need something else in life. I want something entrepreneurial with measurable results."

"Like the top ten?" Matt asked, "It sounds like a really good idea. I don't know what my two cents are worth, but you might want to do a couple of things. Talk to some of your Las Vegas friends, you can enlist Sully's academic team, maybe figure a way to incentivize the staff with profit participation. I won't be involved. This is your baby. Just run with it. The only thing I ask is you pass the financials by Frederic."

So engrossed in conversation, they walked to Palisades Park continuing along the ocean to the northern Venice Beach boundary instead of going toward the Promenade. By the time, they noticed overshooting their destination. They were three quarters of a mile south of Santa Monica pier and at least twenty minutes from the Promenade. It was an exceptionally beautiful afternoon with low seventies temperature and a light breeze. They turned around to find a place for an early dinner and walking back to their car by way of the promenade. While passing the trendy LeGrange Restaurant on Main Street, they asked for a table outside overlooking the water. After sitting ordering Spanish sangria and appetizers, they continued their conversation about Turkey.

Matt approached Bi Ba, "I need your opinion on something."

She answered, "Sure"

"Tell me," he said, "Do you think I'm overreacting, being skittish about even going back to Istanbul because of that piece of crap Ozkan beating the garbage out of me. I don't know why it's so hard for me to get over it. For some reason, I have a premonition things could get ugly when we go back there. I know it sounds stupid but that little voice in my head tells me to be careful.

"We have assurances from the Prime Minister's office."

He continued, "Yeah, but guys like Deputy, Under Secretary Omat, who made our safety declaration are seldom right about someone else's safety, but they're never uncertain. Ozkan is on a short leash. It's just hard for me to get that beating out of my head."

She suggested, "You think Alvarez could help?"

"Would you think it's unreasonable to have Alvarez meet us at the hotel and provide security?"

"I completely agree with that suggestion, but not necessarily for the same reason. I don't really think Ozkan is reckless enough to make a move on you. If it makes you feel safer that Alvarez is there that's all that matters to me. I think we should make it obvious to Ozkan you are protected. I never thought I would say this but I like José. We should let him stay at the hotel as if he were traveling with us."

After their drinks and light food, they walk to the third Street Promenade and looked for gifts for Sully and his academic team. They would be in Istanbul in less than three weeks.

Part – X Istanbul

Chapter 59

On this trip, Matt and Bi Ba took different flights to Istanbul, flying on Turkish Airlines' new nonstop flight taking twelve and one-half hours. They did not stop in London. Nervously awaiting them in customs, Sully met their 12:30am arrival at Istanbul's Ataturk International Airport. The three talked the night before and Bi Ba filled him in on her Prominent Guest Program. He was enthusiastic and bought into it completely.

At the airport, he was uncharacteristically quiet and seemed edgy. On the drive to the hotel Matt suggested Sully was either tired or had lost his enthusiasm. He wasn't his usual conversational self.

Matt said, "What's the matter?" as he leaned forward from the back seat putting his arm on the console between the two front seats to look into the Turk's eyes. "You are either working too hard or something's wrong. I have never seen you like this before. What's going on?"

Sully's usual temperament was lightheartedness and exuberance. He always carried himself as understated, smart with quick humor, and charming.

"Not tonight, Mr. Papaz. "We must talk about a serious problem."

Matt responded, "Can it wait until we get to the hotel?"

Sully said, "Yes of course, but we need to talk as soon as possible."

The remainder twenty-minute drive to the hotel through Istanbul's heart was deafeningly quiet. Three attendants waiting curbside for the Papaz party, sprang into action when the town car pulled up in front of the hotel. The hotel situated in the Sultanahmet district's old part with narrow cobblestone streets, barely wide enough for two cars. There was no hotel driveway. It stood across the street from a store selling antique ceramics and Persian rugs. The short block was made up of a small corner market and a pharmacy.

Once the car made a full stop, at the hotel's entrance one attendant walked to the right front door helping Sully exit while the other two open the right and left doors assisting Matt and Bi Ba. Each got out of the vehicle almost simultaneously and started walking to the hotel's large double front doors being held by two attendants.

Before the doormen could open the large mahogany doors, a car thundered around the corner squealing its brakes and rammed into the back of the Mercedes limousine. Two swarthy looking Turks jumped out of the car. The larger of the two, sitting shotgun, ran to Papaz, grabbed him by the jacket collar and yelled in Turkish, "We told you not to come back. Istanbul is not a place for you. You didn't learn your lesson in Bodrum, did you? You are not wanted here!"

His hands released while throwing Papaz into the mahogany door. Both Matt's and Bi Ba's martial skills kicked in and a scuffle broke out. The hotel attendants and doormen tried to restrain the huge Turk but to no avail. They were not trained in combat. Matt got in one good blow as did Bi Ba but the scuffle was short-lived. Sully's reactions were so slow all he could do was stand there and watch. The designated hit man broke from the fight and yelled to the driver who was now standing in front of the car. They both ran down the side of the hotel on the dark cobblestone street towards the Hogia Sophia Mosque. It was one block down and one half block to the right from the hotel. They were immediately lost in the shadow of the great building.

Matt, not physically hurt, was noticeably disturbed and anxious about the altercation.

Looking at Sully he said, "What the fuck just happened? Did you pick up what he said?"

Before Sully could answer the hotel-manager was standing between the two men and told Matt, "The police are on their way."

Papaz leaned towards Sully and whispered, "We'll talk after the police leave here."

Within five minutes the police arrived. Four police cars flashing their red, white, and blue lights surrounded the three victims and cordoned off the crime scene. The unusual brightness in the dark moonless, Turkish night revealed a few hotel employees, passersby and gawkers from the restaurants and clubs down the street.

The inspector escorted Bi Ba, Sully, and Matt into the hotel and all four sat at a lobby table. The inspector turned to Matt first who had not taken a blow and was all right, except for a torn jacket. He was asked to recount and explain what happened to the best of his ability.

Matt started off by saying, "It was all too fast. All I can remember is after I stepped from the limo, this black car flew around the corner and bumped into the back of limo. Some big mongoloid looking guy got out screaming and grabbed me. He was sloppy and probably six feet four inches tall, at least two-hundred- fifty pounds. He was distinctive looking because he virtually had no forehead. His short black hair ran down from the top of his head to his thick black eyebrows. I think he had what we call a lazy eye. My instincts were to go after him. I just remember throwing a punch. He was screaming something but heck I have no idea what he said. It was in Turkish. He smelled like he'd been drinking. I'm sure he was drunk and just letting off some steam. He probably just had too much to drink and I was the closest thing to him."

The inspector questioned the other two and recorded their similar stories. He apologized, "Mr. Papaz," as he looked at the two cars in front of the hotel, "I'm sure we can gain some evidence and find out who did this. These things don't happen in Saltanahmet. We will find out who did this, I promise you."

Matt said, "Bi Ba and Sully are fine and so am I. Just write it off as a drunk. No big thing, he ripped my jacket, that's all. If you are finished with us I think I would like to go upstairs and have a drink."

The inspector said, "All I need to do is have the manager sign off on a police report."

He thanked the two Americans and Sully for their understanding.

Matt, Bi Ba and Sully walked through the lobby, down the hallway, past the reservation desk on the way to the elevator banks that would take them to suite #207, their permanent Istanbul residence. Entering the large suite, they went into the living area where Bi Ba and Sully sat down while Matt walked over to the bar.

"I'm just going to have a ginger ale or something soft. Do either of you want a drink?"

They both said water.

"No hard liquor for me." Sully said.

Matt walked back into the living room with the drinks and sat down.

He looked at his Turkish friend, "Before all hell broke loose, you said you wanted to talk to me. Does the stuff down stairs have anything to do with your request?"

Looking at his friend Sully said, "This might be all my making. I am so sorry. It had to be my brother's son, my nephew!"

Matt and Bi Ba both uncomfortably shuffled their bodies and sat more erectly in their chairs waiting for his answer.

He continued, "I am so sorry."

Matt lifted his right hand and extended it out slowly to calm him down. "Just tell us everything you know."

Sully was so shook up, he started speaking in Turkish.

"Slowdown, slowdown," Matt said. "We can't understand a word of Turkish. You have to relate what happened in English. But before you tell us anything, what the heck did the guy in front of the hotel say to me?"

ISTANBUL

Sully said, "It was a warning, I didn't get it all but something like, 'you shouldn't have come back. This is our city.' He wasn't that clear but it was something like 'we told you never to come back'."

Matt thought for a second. He did not want to break Sully's concentration. He did not want to discuss what happened in front of the hotel any longer. He wanted to separate the two events, Sully's troubles first and then the incident in front.

"Sully, just tell me why you are so convinced you caused this.

The Turk began to fall apart.

Matt and Bi Ba had to console their friend. "It's okay. Whatever is going on we can solve it. Just tell us what you think happened?"

He started off by saying, "Right after we had our conversation last night I talked to my nephew. I thought I could convince him to back off on his protection and labor practices at the hotel. The conversation didn't go well. I called Faysal and told him I needed to talk to him about the Four Seasons. He sent one of his drivers for me and took me to his boathouse on the Bosporus. I was really scared. I know what his men do to people there. I told him I had been approached to be part of the hotel's new program for prominent guests. I told him I would help oversee the high-end people and I needed him to help me out."

Sully started to sweat profusely.

Matt told him, "It's okay, just slow down."

He continued, "Here in Istanbul we have a tradition that a worker is sponsored for employment. I get a job for someone using my name and they pay me a fee for the first year of their work. You call it a kickback. We call it a fee. I wanted my cousin out of the business at the Four Seasons Hotel. One of his money schemes is to protect employment brokers. That is what we call the ones who get jobs for people in the hotel industry. For procuring a job, they get a percentage of the new worker's salary. My nephew gets a percentage from them. I wanted him to lower the percentage. He reacted by slamming me down in the chair and putting a gun in my face. He told me whatever it took when the program starts he wants me to run the whole thing. That way he would be able to make a greater percentage. He even wanted to put some of his men in key positions at the hotel stealing information from the prominent guest. It all went backwards. Over his lifetime, I had tried to act as a father to him. My brother is poor and his wife died when Faysal was young so I tried to help. I got him out of jail he was fifteen. I got him jobs. I helped him when his father cast him off. I thought that he would do me this favor. I made everything worse. I am so sorry."

Sully was so nervous he couldn't stop talking.

"I went to ask him to pull away from the hotel because of all the things I had done for him. I tried to be his father. He was infuriated. He told me I had no choice. I had to do what he said. Then he put the gun to my temple. He said he would kill me, if I didn't follow his orders. He told me he should have killed me many years ago, Mr. Papaz, Ms. Bi Ba I am sure those were his men at the hotel. I am so sorry."

Neither Matt nor Bi Ba could get a word in edgewise. Sully was hyperventilating.

"Slow down, slow down," Bi Ba said.

Matt finally found a crack in the one-way conversation and said something.

"Sully it wasn't your fault! You said the guy at the door yelled something like, I should not have come back. There is no way your nephew would say anything like that. I have never met him, nor worked with him, or anyone that knows him except for you. So, why would the guy at the door, if he's one of your cousin's associates, tell me not to come back to Istanbul? It doesn't make any sense. This has nothing to do with you."

Bi Ba interrupted, "Sully we can't tell you everything but you have to trust us. This had nothing to do with you. There is nothing for you to be sorry about."

Both she and Matt knew it could only be the work of Ozgur Ozkan. It was his way of reintroducing himself.

She continued, looking directly into his eyes she said, "You did the right thing with your nephew. It could only have led to more problems if he found out about your job after the fact. If it's the tradition for people to work at the hotel to be involved in kickbacks and you didn't tell your cousin you would have made things much worse. Your intuition about wanting to help us just let me know that we made the right choice about you running the project. You didn't do anything wrong. You said he was dangerous. You are right. Now, here is what I'm going to ask you to do. The first thing is we never had this conversation. I want you, sooner rather than later, to tell him you are comfortable working with him. After thinking about it there are more ways to extract money from the Americans and you want a small percentage. Tell him once you get into the Prominent Guest Program you are going to figure out a way to control all the hiring practices not only in the program but throughout the hotel. Tell him the stupid Americans trust you. Say you think we are not very good business people and you will have easy access to our pocketbook. You have to make him believe you. There is something else that's important. From this point on you cannot try to protect us or the hotel. He is too dangerous. Leave everything up to us. This is not your problem. Don't personalize it either because he would have done this to anybody who ran the new program."

"Oh, and there is something else," Matt said, "One of our associates will be here at the hotel later this morning."

He looked at his watch and it was 2:30am.

"He'll be here in a few hours. Obviously, he doesn't know anything about what happened. He is the head of our security for some of our other companies. It's just a coincidence he's going to be here. We wanted him to assess the security needs for our Premium Guest Program." He continued the lie. "He worked with Bi Ba in Las Vegas. We thought we could use his services in the new program here at the hotel. His name is José Alvarez. The two of you and Bi Ba will be working together. I think you will get along with him. Like Bi Ba said, you are not responsible for any of this. I think you did the only thing you could have with your nephew. Don't worry. I even think we can use this to our advantage. It makes a lot of sense not to break with Turkish labor traditions of employment contract. Your contracts are not written but your handshakes and your customs make them just as ironclad as ours. We will let your nephew get a greater percentage of what I will call the finder's fee. It will only increase our labor cost about thirty percent. That can easily be offset. Just from the new program efficiency, we can offset that."

He looked at Sully, "I'm good with numbers just hear me out. Labor costs are maybe ten percent of doing business here at the hotel. A thirty percent increase in labor cost only means a three percent increase in operating expenses. We can make that up through efficient and increased occupancy. It's simply not a problem. Look at it as our cost of doing business here in Turkey. I only see a problem if he gets his people working at the hotel. They can steal information from our guests and that is totally unacceptable. That's not going to happen. Bi Ba is bringing in some of her friends she worked with in Las Vegas. If they could deal with anyone as ruthless or smart as the Mafia, then they can deal with your nephew. You will be kept out of all of it. Sully, you must trust us. Just let your nephew think he's in charge and everything will be fine."

Both Matt and Bi Ba knew they would deal with this problem 'the Papaz way.' At some point in time they would have to kill his nephew. All they had to do was make sure Sully would never find out. Hiding the truth was always more difficult than killing someone. They knew they had to keep the truth from their Turkish friend. He wasn't the type person who was equipped to deal with death so close and personal. The Papaz group would do what they did best, eliminate another enemy.

Chapter 60

Between the auspicious greeting when they arrived at the hotel and their jet lag, both Matt and Bi Ba were awake. Sully finally slowed down. It was nearly 4:00am and the three were still discussing events that took place earlier that morning.

Matt told Sully, "If you want to go home for a little while, that's fine. I think I'm going to wait down stairs in the lobby for our friend Alvarez. He should be here soon. When we set the trip, we tried to coordinate it so we would get here about the same time. I think he's flying in on British air."

Bi Ba had an airline arrival and departure times app on her phone. She pulled the phone out of her purse and clicked the icon. She input the flight, carrier, and number. Within a few seconds, it flashed, British Air flight #317: arriving at 4:57am. Sully decide to wait.

Alvarez would be at the hotel within an hour and one-half. Two American friends and a Turkish national who he would work closely with for the next few weeks met him. When his town car pulled to the hotel's entrance, a security officer directed it to the hotel's side driveway. The police barricades were still in place. Alvarez was escorted by a bellman, carrying his luggage into the hotel and was directed to the reception desk.

Before he reached his destination, he heard Papaz calling his name.

"José."

Turning around he saw his friend and Bi Ba sitting in a small lounge decorated in Louis XIV Baroque furniture overlooking the hotel's patio area. He went over to meet his two friends and the Turkish man sitting with them. As he approached Papaz, he extended his arms giving him a hug as well as Bi Ba, then extending his hand to their friend, introduced himself.

"I am Alvarez. You must be Matt's friend Sully."

Before he sat down he said to his friends, "What the heck is going on in front of the hotel?"

Bi Ba's face said it all.

"No, no," Alvarez said. "It's you guys! I can't believe it!"

He started laughing, "I shouldn't laugh but it happened again. Didn't it? What the hell this time?"

He couldn't contain himself saying, "You guys are just snake bite material. Trouble always has a way of finding you."

Matt said, "Yeah, it had something to do with us. It's not a big deal! Let's change the subject. Are you hungry?"

He called over one of the attendants and asked him to register his friend. The sun was coming up on the courtyard patio. The restaurant would be opened at 7:00am. Matt asked one of the staff if he could bring them some coffee and tea to hold them over until breakfast. They sat in the small sitting room off the main lobby until the restaurant opened.

Alvarez started laughing again. "Okay tell me. No, maybe I need to hear this on a full stomach."

Matt said, "It really wasn't that bad. We'll talk about it later."

Alvarez took his subtle hint and did not pursue it further. They chatted for about twenty minutes until the restaurant finally opened. They walked from the lobby through the hotel's double doors into the cold drizzling morning and into the glassed-in solarium restaurant. Sitting at a table facing the old prison wall security post, now a vista overlooking the beautiful Bosporus, Papaz made things sound normal bring up the morning incident.

"Okay José, about this morning, do you remember the jerk in Bodrum who was irritated at Bi Ba and me over not paying all of our extra fees when we rented his stupid sailboat. All that crap about him expensing out an extra crew member and gas and food he never delivered. Well, I think the little Turkish mafia ass hole had two of his goons come after us this morning. It was just a small altercation. No big thing. But the hotel had to make out a police report."

Alvarez started laughing again, looking at Bi Ba, "Did you go ninja?"

Smiling she said, "I didn't have a chance. By the time, I jumped in he was running around the corner."

Sully had never seen this side of his American friends. He did what all respectful deferent people do. He smiled, held his tongue, and intermittently politely laughed at their banter.

Papaz sensed the awkwardness of the conversation for his Turkish friend and tried to tie up their little discussion by saying, "When all is said and done, it's no big deal. None of us were hurt. The hotel manager has the police report. Maybe as a matter of security you had better look at it. Take my word, it's probably not worth your time. You're not here to deal with this minor stuff. You are here to work with Sully and Bi Ba on her new program."

Matt had changed the direction of the conversation. While looking at Bi Ba and his Turkish friend he continued, "Are you guys up to working this afternoon?"

She replied, "I have no problems if we do it relatively early so we have some leisure room this afterward."

They all agreed to meet later. After finishing breakfast Sully decided to go home and come back at 12:00pm. Alvarez was taken to his room after going to the registration desk and finishing there. Matt and Bi Ba retired to their suite to sleep for a few hours.

The four met in Matt and Bi Ba's Istanbul home, suite 207, at 12:00pm. There was no conversation regarding the morning incident and Matt stayed clear of discussing Ozgur Ozkan in front of Sully. The discussion was focused on setting up a basic structure for the Prominent Guests Program. Bi Ba had a detailed business plan but it came down to:

1) Bi Ba and her Las Vegas consultants would line-up clients with their contacts and make Istanbul an attractive destination for the very rich.
2) Sully was given responsibility of displaying the city and its environs, creating a world-class experience.

3) Alvarez would guarantee their client safety. It was clean, clear and simple.

Bi Ba threw in one more item.

4) She gave Sully responsibility for having his academic team consider the viability of legalized gambling in Turkey.

She said, "I know there is apprehension and opposition to gambling on religious and historical grounds, but I want your researchers to investigate it. Have them explore the revenue effects. How much will this mean to the government's coffers, local and national revenue? There is an employment multiplier effect in Las Vegas. We measure economic activity by rooms built. Every new room built at a hotel with a casino is worth two and one-quarter full-time long-term jobs and three part-time jobs. They are not all related to gambling. I want your team to test the correlation between gambling, employment, and higher incomes for people in the country. In Las Vegas, the average bet is $27. In Macau it is $92. Have you forecast the bet size predicated on a customer demographic set? From that we can project the positive effects of legalized gambling. I also want them to look at the negative effects of gambling. Tourism historically needs low skilled employees which causes low level wages. Is there anything we can do to offset that affect? There is a so-called crime affect relative to gambling. Is it real? If so, how do we counter it? How do we deal with the gambling addictions? I want your team to do an academic analysis. No value judgments to make the material interesting like they did for the hotel. I want the statistical truth."

Bi Ba continued, she had taken over the whole meeting. "Let me just clear things up for my own benefit. I will be responsible for the clients. She looked across the table at Sully, you will be responsible for their experience. She looked at José, you're responsible for their security. Sully, do you know exactly what I'm asking from your team?"

He nodded his head, "Yes."

"As usual there is one more thing." she looked at Matt. "We were supposed to talk to the staff today. Let's talk to the manager and reschedule. I'll do it in a couple of weeks after everything calms down. There could be rumors but we will have him deal with them. That's all I really have to say."

Papas spoke up, "Sully do you have anything else to add?"

He said, "No. In fact if you don't mind I would like to leave and go to my office and start working on some of this. I know my team will be excited and of course they will appreciate working with you again. Before I contact them, I do have one question. What can they expect for payment for their services?"

Papaz unhesitatingly said, "Tell them we have such appreciation for their work, we will give them a twenty percent salary increase."

José looked at his two friends and said, "I'm clear on everything. I just need some of your time after Sully leaves."

Sully got up and said his perfunctory goodbyes and walked out of the restaurant.

José immediately said, "What the hell happened this morning?"

Papaz told him more than he expected to hear.

"We have two problems. Let me talk about the simplest one first. The hotel employees are being forced to pay protection money and fees to a guy named Faysal Soylemez. He also has eyes on getting into the hotel's operation and is not beyond using force. Number two, is this morning, we had to deal with what happened. It was my old friend Ozgar Ozkan. He sent some of his goons to rough us up. I'm sure it's just his way of trying to intimidate."

Alvarez thought for a second and said, "Do you mind if I get a hold of Frederic and have him contact Al Bactar. He knows the lay of the land here in Turkey. I feel we should pass things by him. I also want to get Kasogi involved. We have two great assets, Al Bactar and Kosogi. They know what actions are best in the Middle East. Matt...." he paused for a second, "and you to some extent, Bi Ba..." as he looked them, "How do you guys want to play this? How involved do you want to be? When I get a hold on Ozkan and I will. Do you want to kill him? Do you want to be there when we kill him? Or do you just want to hear about it? The same goes for this guy, Soylemez!"

Chapter 61

On the fourth morning after arriving in Istanbul, Papaz was still feeling the jet lag effects. He was wide awake at 5:30am after falling asleep at 1:45am. He decided to go for a walk. He kissed Bi Ba gently on her forehead, not to wake her, opened the closet holding his clothes. He pulled out a pair of shoes, jeans, warm sweater and a long shearling jacket. He dressed for the weather outside. In the midst of winter Istanbul was cold.

He planned to walk to Sultan Ahmed Park flanked by the Blue Mosque, Hogia Sophia and the Hippodrome. It was an easy fifteen-minute walk from the hotel. He knew vendors assembled early mornings to meet the demand of the city's labor force walking or taking public transportation to the other side of the Bosporus. He wanted to get something warm. A cup of coffee even though it was not his drink of choice. He found a kiosk selling drinks and baklava pastries.

Being outside with the cold fresh air flowing off the city's great waterway was invigorating. People were starting to gather in the old city's open area. They were lining up for the trolley car going to the Asian side of Istanbul. With breakfast in hand, he walked towards the Blue Mosque and sat on a bench in front of the great edifice facing its four great minarets. He savored his

ISTANBUL

surroundings. His thoughts were engulfed by things Turkish.

Alvarez had a four-man detail following Papaz at all times. They were close by as he sat on the old wooden bleacher structure and scripted out his day. The team leader reported back to Alvarez.

"Everything is okay. The client is taking in fresh air and sitting alone facing the Blue Mosque waiting for sunrise."

The sun coming up behind the fifteenth century mosque was one of the city's greatest sights. As he sat on the bench reflecting on what he and Bi Ba might do that day he caught a glimpse of an old Kurdish man. When the figure was approaching him in the dimly lit portion of the park, he noticed the old man's striking features. He was wearing a cameleer costume. An outfit someone could have worn on the Old Silk Road in the 1,500s. His gray beard was long and thin, but it was his eyes that struck Papaz. They were of beautiful hazel green. Much like the famous photograph by Steve Curry of the Afghan Girl on the cover of National Geographic in the mid-1980s. The old man's eyes were hauntingly familiar. They were the orbs of the young man who had visited Matt and Bi Ba at the beach in Bodrum. It was Alwan Al Bactar. As the old man approached Papaz, Alvarez's sentinels started to close in. He waved them off. The old broken down camel herder stared at Papaz, who was sure it was his cousin. Slowly moving over to the isolated bench, Alwan Al Bactar spoke first.

"You have many men my cousin," alluding to the security team. "They are good. They have known of my presence from the hotel. My men are also here to protect you. May we talk?"

Papaz shook his head in the affirmative. "Please sit."

Al Bactar remained standing. "May I express my gratitude for your gift of my father's fortune? It will breathe life into my people. Now it is my turn to repay you. I have heard of your troubles. These men, Faysal Soylemez and Ozgar Ozkan are swine. They will not darken your door again. In your land this is a time of giving. This will be my present to you. They will be dealt with swiftly as with all pigs when they are slaughtered. If you want them to have a slow death and feel the pain of their blasphemy. Your wish is my command. I will ever be indebted to you for your beliefs in me."

He extended his hand as Papaz got to his feet. He clasped both of his hands around Papaz's hand and said, "May the winds blow gentle into your face."

As quickly as he arrived, he left. Alwan Al Bactar turned and walked away with the slow gait of a broken down old camel herder. He vanished into the dark cold morning.

Papaz sat back down trying to understand what just took place. He took his phone out of his pocket and placed a call to Alvarez to tell him what had happened.

He was conflicted and told his friend, "It was so God damn fast. I should be elated. I should be happy as hell that he will clear up the mess."

Matt wanted both adversaries killed but the option of doing it himself was just taken off the table. He didn't know if that's what he wanted but now it was out of his hands.

Papaz abruptly finished the call, got up slowly and for some reason his nose picked up the scent of potatoes. In reality it was chestnuts roasting on an oil drum heater at a kiosk in the distance. He turned to see where the smell was coming from and saw his cameleer dressed cousin gently putting his hand in the air to wave goodbye.

Russell C. Arslan

The End

Russell C. Arslan

The starting point for Russell Arslan's political and social progressive leanings developed growing up in southwest Los Angeles and graduating from the ethnically and racially diverse Dorsey High School. His academic achievements led to an advanced degree in international economics and a lifelong career in academia. At the early age of twenty he became a full-time member of the Long Beach Community College instructional staff and six years later was employed as a full time adjunct member at California State University Long Beach where he retired from both institutions more than five decades later.

During his academic career, he was affiliated with the ACLU, the Club of Rome, The Western Economic Association, and worked with the Jimmy Carter administration.

His economics and finance background guided his involvement in hotel and motel acquisitions, purchasing commercial and residential real estate and ownership of a financial institution. The academic and business career combination augmented by extensive international travels took him to more than one hundred-fifty countries, Mr. Arslan believes storytelling is a platform for expressing one's experiences and convictions. Events and historical facts are intertwined into story lines to entertain the reader.

Writing a book and knowingly taking poetic license is like being an oral historian with the agenda of entertaining an audience. The purpose of his novels and the protagonist Matt Papaz is to entertain the reader in a fashion of reality and current events.

ISTANBUL

End Notes

---

[1] **Degrees of Separation**." Conjectures were expanded in 1929 by Hungarian author Frigyes Karinthy, who published a volume of short stories titled *Everything is Different.* One of these pieces was titled "Chains," or "Chain-Links." The story investigated in abstract, conceptual, and fictional terms many of the problems that would captivate future generations of mathematicians, sociologists, and physicists within the field of network theory.[1][2] Due to technological advances in communications and travel, friendship networks could grow larger and span greater distances. In particular, Karinthy believed that the modern world was 'shrinking' due to this ever-increasing connectedness of human beings. He posited that despite great physical distances between the globe's individuals, the growing density of human networks made the actual social distance far smaller.

This idea both directly and indirectly influenced a great deal of early thought on social networks. Karinthy has been regarded as the originator of the notion of six degrees of separation.[2] A related theory deals with the quality of connections, rather than their existence. The theory of three degrees of influence was created by Nicholas A. Christakis and James H. Fowler.

Milgram's article made famous [7] his 1967 set of experiments to investigate de Sola Pool and Kochen's "small world problem." Mathematician Benoit Mandelbrot, born in

Warsaw, growing up in Poland then France, was aware of the Statist rule of thumb, and was also a colleague of de Sola Pool, Kochen and Milgram at the University of Paris during the early 1950s (Kochen brought Mandelbrot to work at the Institute for Advanced Study and later IBM in the U.S.). This circle of researchers was fascinated by the interconnectedness and "social capital" of human networks. Milgram's study results showed that people in the United States seemed to be connected by approximately three friendship links, on average, without speculating on global linkages; he never actually used the term "six degrees of separation." Since the *Psychology Today* article gave the experiments wide publicity, Milgram, Kochen, and Karinthy all had been incorrectly attributed as the origin of the notion of six degrees; the most likely popularizer of the term "six degrees of separation" would be John Guare, who attributed the value 'six' to Marconi.[9]

Guare, in interviews, attributed his awareness of the "six degrees" to Marconi. Although this idea had been circulating in various forms for decades, it is Guare's piece that is most responsible for popularizing the phrase "six degrees of separation." Following Guare's lead, many future television and film sources would later incorporate the notion into their stories.

Music critics have fun tracing the history and dissecting the popular song "Der Kommissar" which was first written and recorded by Austrian musician Falco with German vocals in 1981, then passed on and reworked in English by British band After The Fire in 1982, then lyrically rewritten and renamed "Deep In The Dark" by Laura Branigan in 1983 in the U.S., then retitled again to "Don't Turn Around" and rerecorded in a punk rock style by The Squids in 1996 also in the U.S., then passed on to Brazilian rap band Comunidade Nin-Jitsu in 2005 and renamed "Rap Do Trago", then finally back to the U.S. and rerecorded in its traditional style in 2007 by Dale Bozzio, who is the former lead singer of new wave band Missing Persons. In this situation, connections among six such diverse musical expressionists were generated through a song. At the beginning, the composer might never thought that the song can spread so far. However, the six degree has demonstrated that "the small world" does exist. SixDegrees.com was an early social-networking website that existed from 1997 to 2001. It allowed users to list friends, family members and acquaintances, send messages and post bulletin board items to people in their first, second, and third degrees, and see their connection to any other user on the site. At its height, it had approximately one million users. However, it was closed in 2000 because the idea was too new for its time.

[2] ***Laicism definition***, the nonclerical, or secular, control of political and social institutions in a society

[3] ***Secularism definition***, Indifference to or rejection or exclusion of religion and religious considerations.

[4] ***Siirt*** a city in southeastern Turkey and the seat of Siirt Province. From 1858 to 1915 the city was the seat of a bishop of the Chaldean Catholic Church. Most of the city's Assyrians, including their archbishop were killed during the Assyrian Genocide.

[5] ***Sepsis*** a toxic condition resulting from the spread of bacteria or their toxic products from a focus of infection especially

septicemia.

⁶ **Ba'albeck,** Lebanon's greatest Roman treasure, can be counted among the wonders of the ancient world. The largest and most noble Roman temples ever built, they are also among the best preserved.

Towering high above the Beqaa plain, their monumental proportions proclaimed the power and wealth of Imperial Rome. The gods worshipped here, the Triad of Jupiter, Venus and Mercury, were grafted onto the indigenous deities of Hadad, Atargatis and a young male god of fertility. Local influences are also seen in the planning and layout of the temples, which vary from the classic Roman design.

Gravity: $G = (M1 - M2) \times 32$

⁷ **Tandor -- Tadmor prison (**Arabic: سجن تدمر**) is located in** Tadmur **in the deserts of eastern** Syria **approximately 200 kilometers northeast of** Damascus **(***Tadmor* **or** *Tadmur* **is the** Arabic **name for Palmyra).**
The structures were originally built as military barracks by the French Mandate **forces.**
Tadmor prison was known for harsh conditions, extensive human rights **abuse,** torture **and** summary executions. **During the 1980s Tadmor prison housed thousands of Syrian prisoners, both political and criminal and it was also the scene of the June 27, 1980 Tadmor Prison massacre of prisoners by** Rifaat al-Assad, **the day after the Syrian branch of the** Islamist Muslim Brotherhood **failed in an attempt to assassinate his brother,** president Hafez al-Assad. **Members of units of the** Defence Brigades, **under the command of Rifaat al-Assad, entered Tadmor Prison and killed an estimated thousand prisoners in the cells and the**

dormitories.
Tadmor prison was closed in 2001 and all remaining detainees were transferred to other prisons in Syria. Tadmor Prison was reopened on June 15, 2011 and 350 individuals arrested for participation in anti-government demonstrations were transferred there for interrogation and detainment.

www.ingramcontent.com/pod-product-compliance
Lightning Source LLC
Chambersburg PA
CBHW070549100426
42744CB00006B/251